MODERN IRAN

A HISTORY IN DOCUMENTS

PRINCETON SERIES OF MIDDLE EASTERN
SOURCES IN TRANSLATION

General Editor, M. Şükrü Hanioğlu

MODERN IRAN

A HISTORY IN DOCUMENTS

Edited, translated, and introduced by

Negin Nabavi

 Markus Wiener Publishers
Princeton

For information, write to: Markus Wiener Publishers
231 Nassau Street, Princeton, NJ 08542
www.markuswiener.com

Library of Congress Cataloging-in-Publication Data
Modern Iran : a history in documents / edited, translated, and introduced by
Negin Nabavi.
    pages cm. — (Princeton series of Middle Eastern sources in translation)
  Includes bibliographical references.
  ISBN 978-1-55876-600-6 (hardcover : alk. paper)
  ISBN 978-1-55876-601-3 (pbk. : alk. paper)
  1. Iran—History—Sources. I. Nabavi, Negin, 1965– editor, translator.
  DS272.M58 2015
  955—dc23
                 2015018934

Markus Wiener Publishers books are printed in the United States of America
on acid-free paper and meet the guidelines for permanence and durability
of the Committee on Production Guidelines for Book Longevity of the
Council on Library Resources.

Contents

PART TWO
1911–1978
— 111 —

PART THREE
THE IRANIAN REVOLUTION: 1978–1979
— 181 —

PART FOUR
IRAN TODAY: 1979 TO THE PRESENT
—199 —

Preface

One of the many challenges of teaching the history of modern Iran at college level in the United States in the twenty-first century—a time when negative stereotypes abound, and when scholarly links between the two countries are limited at best—is to remind students that like any other society, Iranian society has been replete with complexities and contradictions. Therefore, in order to better understand this history, it is important that attention be brought to the different voices and perspectives that make up the historical narrative. History, after all, is not only about events but also about what people make of events and how they respond to them as they unfold.

This sourcebook is an attempt to facilitate such an approach. Covering the period from the early nineteenth century to the present, it brings together primary sources, in translation, that shed light on diverse aspects of the political, social, cultural, and intellectual history of modern Iran, and also provide an opportunity to see how men and women in the past understood the impact of certain events as they took place. Inasmuch as primary sources enable unfiltered access to voices in both the distant and not-so-distant past, it is hoped that these texts stimulate discussion and encourage students to question and challenge prior assumptions.

While in the past ten years, a number of published sourcebooks on the modern Middle East have also included sources on Iran, this is the first book of its kind to focus exclusively on Iran.[1] It makes use of a combination of documents (from the early 1800s to the present) that are of varying lengths, and have been taken from a variety of genres, including newspa-

---

1. See for example, Camron Amin, Benjamin Fortna, and Elizabeth Frierson, eds., *The Modern Middle East: A Sourcebook for History*. Oxford: Oxford University Press, 2006; Akram Fouad Khater, *Sources in the History of the Modern Middle East*. 2nd ed. Boston, MA: 2011; Julia Clancy-Smith and Charles D. Smith, *The Modern Middle East: A History in Documents*. Oxford: Oxford University Press, 2014. The one exception in dealing exclusively with Iran is Lloyd Ridgeon, ed., *Religion and Politics in Modern Iran: A Reader*. London: I. B. Tauris, 2005. However, this book, as indicated by its title, focuses for the most part on the expressions of religion, with particular emphasis on Sufism in the writings of a number of intellectuals and reformers in nineteenth- and twentieth-century Iran.

pers and the periodical press, diaries, memoirs, letters, speeches, and essays. In particular, it provides a window onto the momentous changes that society has experienced in the past two centuries in terms of not only political events and developments but also ideas, perceptions, and mindsets. Thus, in addition to well-known texts of major diplomatic conventions, this book also includes lesser-known passages that describe the reception and response to major developments on the part of different segments of society, both men and women. So, for example, while it includes the text of the Anglo-Russian Convention of 1907, or that of the decree issued by the Qajar king Mozaffar al-Din Shah (r. 1896-1907) granting a constitutional government in 1906, it also brings attention to the reactions to the convention of 1907, as well as to the idea and concept of constitutionalism as reflected in the Persian newspapers published in Iran at the time. In a similar vein, the book devotes four chapters to the 1979 revolution and its aftermath, comprising texts ranging from the infamous January 1978 *Ettela`at* article, which set off the first demonstrations and the series of events that ultimately led to the overthrow of monarchy, to the very first open letter addressed to Ayatollah Khomeini, also in January 1979, expressing the sense of unease that a number of secularist revolutionaries felt when they first heard the term "Islamic Republic." An effort has also been made to include the voices and perspectives of women, who were carving a space for themselves at different junctures throughout this period.

This book is intended for use in the classroom and thus aims to serve as an aid and supplement to the general narrative accounts of Iran. Therefore, it conforms by and large to the chronological periodization often found in these books. Also, each text is prefaced by a brief comment that provides important background information and offers students some suggestions as to what might be learned from the source.

My aim throughout this book has been twofold: to bring attention to the different voices that make up the historical narrative and to underscore the changing mindsets that have complemented the process of social transformations that took place in much of the long nineteenth and twentieth centuries. To this end, I hope that this collection ultimately helps to make teaching and studying modern Iranian history at the college level more accessible and nuanced.

I am grateful to the encouragement and advice of Nahid Mozaffari, Houchang Chehabi, and Rudi Matthee who did not hesitate to share their thoughts as to what sources might be useful for classroom purposes. I am also much obliged to Manuchehr Kasheff for his help in translating some of the more difficult expressions in the texts, and to Shaun Marmon for reading parts of the book and making useful suggestions for ways to improve it. Thanks are also due to Janet Stern and Shanti Hossein, whose meticulous editing of this manuscript has made the end result much more consistent and readable than it would otherwise have been. Last but not least, my thanks to my mother, Afshin, and to Jawid for their unconditional support, which took different shapes and forms throughout this project. Needless to say, all errors are my own.

A Note on Translation, Transliteration, and Dates

The translations are for the most part my own. In those cases when an already available English translation has been used, full bibliographical details are provided.

I have used a simplified form of Persian transliteration, making allowances for pronunciation and omitting all diacritical marks, with the exception of (`) for ayn and (') for hamzeh. Proper names are rendered the way they most commonly appear in sources: thus, "Turkmanchai" as opposed to "Torkmanchai." While every effort has been made to maintain consistency in transliteration, in certain instances when sections from already published texts have been reproduced, there may be some discrepancy.

With regard to dates, three different calendars are reflected in the sources: the lunar calendar in the earlier documents relating to the Qajar era; the solar calendar following 1924, for much of the Pahlavi era; and the Imperial calendar for a short period between 1976 and 1978. All original dates have been given together with their equivalents in the Gregorian calendar.

Timeline

1904–1905 ...... The Russo-Japanese War

Aug. 5, 1906 ..... Mozaffar al-Din Shah issues a royal decree, granting the establishment of a National Consultative Assembly.

Sept. 9, 1906 ..... The Electoral Law, dividing the electorate into six estates, is ratified by Mozaffar al-Din Shah.

Oct. 7, 1906 ..... The first session of Parliament is convened in Tehran

Dec. 30, 1906 .... The Fundamental Laws (consisting of 51 articles) are ratified by Mozaffar al-Din Shah.

Jan. 8, 1907 ...... Mozaffar al-Din Shah dies.

1907–1908 ...... Mohammad `Ali Shah's reign

Oct. 7, 1907 ..... The Supplementary Fundamental Laws (comprising 107 articles) are ratified by Mohammad `Ali Shah.

1907 .... The abolition of the Ministry of Publications followed by the proliferation of a range of dailies, weeklies, editorial newspapers, and satirical newspapers, as well as newspapers written in colloquial Persian

Aug. 31, 1907 .... The Anglo-Russian Convention of 1907 concerning Iran, Afghanistan, and Tibet is signed by Britain and Russia in St. Petersburg. On the same day, in Tehran, Mirza `Ali Asghar Khan Amin al-Sultan, the long-term Prime Minister of Naser al-Din and Mozaffar al-Din Shah, is assassinated in front of the Iranian *majles.*

Feb. 8, 1908 ..... The Press Laws, defining the boundaries of what can and cannot be published, are passed.

June 23, 1908 .... Bombardment of the *majles* resulting in the closure of Parliament, and the execution of a number of pro-constitution journalists and activists, marking the end of what has come to be considered the "first constitutional era"

1908–1909 ...... Civil war between pro-constitutionalist and royalist forces

July 1909 .... The victory of the pro-constitutionalist forces over the royalists, resulting in the "takeover" of Tehran and the removal of Mohammad `Ali Shah, the appointment of his son, Ahmad Shah, as the new king at the age of 12, and the announcement of a new regency

July 31, 1909 .... Shaikh Fazlollah Nuri, one of the leading and most learned *mojtaheds* in Tehran, who had taken an openly anti-constitutionalist stance, is executed publicly by the constitutionalists.

1909–1925 ...... Ahmad Shah's reign

Nov. 1909 .... The second *majles* opens.

Sept. 1910 .... *Danesh* (Knowledge), the first women's weekly addressing women's concerns, is founded by a woman, Mrs. Kahhal, the daughter of Mirza Mohammad Hakim Bashi, also known as Dr. Kahhal.

Dec. 24, 1911 .... Closure of the second *majles*, as a result of a coup by the Regent and backed by the two powers Britain and Russia, often seen as marking the end of the constitutional revolution

1913 . . . . *Shokufeh* (Blossom), the second women's newspaper, is founded by Maryam ʿAmid Mozayan al-Saltaneh.

1914 . . . . Iran declares neutrality in World War I.

July 1919 . . . . *Zaban-e Zanan* (The Tongue of Women), a biweekly by Sadiqeh Dawlatabadi, begins publication in Isfahan. It is noteworthy because it is the first time that the term *zan* (woman) is used in the title of a publication.

Aug. 9, 1919 . . . . . The 1919 Anglo-Persian Agreement between the British and Iranian governments is made public.

July 1920 . . . . *Nameh-ye Banovan* (The Ladies' Paper), a fortnightly newspaper by Shahnaz Azad, a woman journalist and activist, begins publication.

Feb. 1921 . . . . Coup d'état led by Reza Khan together with Seyyed Zia al-Din Tabataba'i

1925–1941 . . . . . . Reza Shah Pahlavi's reign

Jan. 8, 1936 . . . . . . Announcement of the "Unveiling" Policy by Reza Shah

1937 . . . . Arrest of the "group of fifty-three"

Sept. 1941 . . . . The Allied occupation of Iran, the abdication of Reza Shah, and the assumption of the throne by his son, Mohammad Reza Shah. In the same month, the Tudeh Party is established from the nucleus of the "group of fifty-three."

1941–1979 . . . . . . Mohammad Reza Pahlavi's reign

Feb. 1949 . . . . Attempt on the life of the Shah, allegedly by a member of the Tudeh. As a result, the Tudeh party is officially banned although it persists with its activities underground.

April 30, 1951 . . . . Appointment of Mohammad Mosaddeq as Prime Minister of Iran

June 1952 . . . . Mohammad Mosaddeq's speech at the Hague Tribunal in the Netherlands

Aug. 19, 1953 . . . . Mohammad Mosaddeq is removed from office as a result of covert action orchestrated by the CIA/ MI6.

1956 . . . . The first ever nationwide census taken in Iran

1962 . . . . Opposition of a number of ʿulama to a parliamentary bill that was to grant suffrage to women and replace the phrase "holy Qur'an" with "holy book" in the oath of office

1962 . . . . Publication of Jalal Al-e Ahmad's *Gharbzadegi*

Jan. 26, 1963 . . . . Referendum to approve the White Revolution

1963 . . . . Iranian women are granted the right to vote (as part of the White Revolution).

1966 . . . . The establishment of the Women's Organization of Iran (WOI)

1967 . . . . The passing of the Family Protection Law, which makes it more difficult for men to initiate divorce unilaterally, take a second wife, and have the sole right to child custody

1975 . . . . Establishment of the Rastakhiz Party

1978–1979 . . . . . . The Iranian Revolution

Jan. 16, 1979 . . . . Mohammad Reza Shah Pahlavi leaves Iran

Feb. 1, 1979 . . . . . Ayatollah Khomeini returns to Iran after fifteen years in exile

Feb. 11, 1979 . . . . Surrender of the armed forces and the victory of the revolution

Feb. 26, 1979 . . . . The Family Protection Law is abrogated.

April 1, 1979 . . . . . "The Day of the Islamic Republic," when the Islamic Republic officially comes into being by means of a referendum

Nov. 1979 . . . . Students take over the U.S. embassy, taking 52 Americans hostage for 444 days until January 1981 and marking the beginning of what comes to be known as the "Hostage Crisis."

Dec. 1979 . . . . Ratification of the 1979 Constitution by means of a referendum

1980–1988 . . . . . . The Iran-Iraq War

April 1983 . . . . *Hejab* is made mandatory by law for all women, Muslim and non-Muslim

July 20, 1988 . . . . Announcement of the decision to end the war in the course of a statement made by Ayatollah Khomeini in which he famously compares this decision to that of drinking a "cup of poison"

June 1989 . . . . Ayatollah Khomeini dies, and Seyyed 'Ali Khamene'i is appointed as Leader of the Islamic Republic; Akbar Hashemi-Rafsanjani is elected president.

July 28, 1989 . . . . Ratification of the 1989 Constitution by means of a referendum

1997–2005 . . . . . . Mohammad Khatami's tenure as two-time President of the Islamic Republic

1998 . . . . Emergence of a new but short-lived vibrant press that sees its task as furthering the project of reform

July 1999 . . . . Student unrest, initially in protest at the closure of a reformist newspaper and later exacerbated by a raid by plainclothes men on the student dormitories at Tehran University

2005–2013 . . . . . . Mahmoud Ahmadinejad's tenure as two-time President of the Islamic Republic

Aug. 2006 . . . . Establishment of the "One Million Signatures Campaign"

June 2009 . . . . A series of protests against the election results of the tenth presidential election. This series of protests came to be known as the "Green Movement."

June 2013 . . . . Election of Hasan Rouhani as the eleventh President of the Islamic Republic

July 14, 2015 . . . . Iran and six world powers reach an agreement on Iran's nuclear program—the Joint Comprehensive Plan of Action (JCPOA)—in exchange for relief from international sanctions.

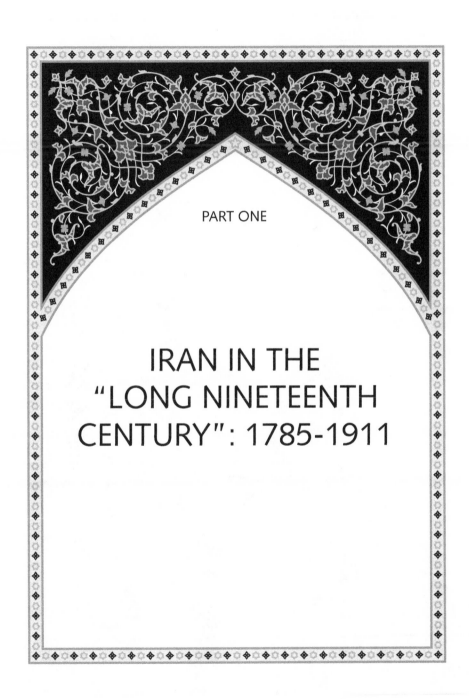

PART ONE

IRAN IN THE "LONG NINETEENTH CENTURY": 1785-1911

1

Qajar Rule, Society, and the Great Powers

Images from the Qajar Court and Courtiers, Daily Life, and Changing Times

Qajar rule extended for much of the "long nineteenth century," from 1796 to 1925, during which time there was much change at different levels of society. The passages below are selected for the most part from memoirs and diaries from this period, providing images of life among courtiers as well as ordinary people from the late nineteenth to the turn of the twentieth century.

1. The Month of Fasting (at Naser al-Din Shah's Court)

Dustali Khan Mo`ayyer al-Mamalek (1874-1966) was a grandson of Naser al-Din Shah (r. 1848-1896) through his mother. According to his own account, Naser al-Din Shah had great affection for him to the point that he had become a subject of jealousy at Court.[1] Dustali Khan was brought up in the royal palace and as a result was privy to the private life of the Shah. Below is an excerpt from his book in which he describes the ways in which Ramazan, the ninth month in the lunar calendar, also known as the month of fasting, was distinct from the other months of the year. While this excerpt,

---

1. Dustali Khan Mo`ayyer al-Mamalek, *Yaddashtha-yi az zendegani-ye khosusi-ye Naser al-Din Shah*. Tehran: Nashr-e Tarikh, 1372/ 1993, p. 11.

3

for the most part, focuses on the customs at the royal court, especially the goings-on in the women's quarter at this time, it does also shed light on aspects of life in Tehran during the month of Ramazan.

Text: *Notes from the Private Life of Naser al-Din Shah*[2]

In this month, traffic in the city [Tehran] was unrestricted at night; there was no need for passwords, nor were there the usual number of arrests at night. [Instead], there were many people who stayed up all night. At that time, seven tenths of the population of Tehran used to fast in good faith. As for Naser al-din Shah, he fasted in the early years of his rule, but as far as I remember, he had given up fasting although he observed the other customs of the month of fasting. Sometimes in the evenings, he would visit the royal gardens on horseback, and as was the custom, they would announce the shah's approach to the city-dwellers by means of the firing of a cannon. . . .

In the month of Ramazan, governmental offices were open for business at night instead of during the day. At Court, they would lay out the necessities for the breaking of the fast, after which the Shah would also see to the affairs, and give audience to the ministers.

In the women's quarter, an elaborate get-together would be organized for [both] the preaching and the prayers. In the middle of the great hall, they would draw a thin curtain. On the other side of this curtain, they would put a pulpit and a prayer niche, and Shaikh Saif al-Din, the brother of Shaikh al-Ra'is[3] who was among the princes and had become a learned man of religion, would lead the prayers. On this side of the curtain, the ladies would stand in a line, and follow the Shaikh in doing the prayers. After the prayer, the afore-mentioned Shaikh would go to the pulpit, and the ladies would ask religious questions from behind the curtain. The late Shaikh who was much better in moving his head, hands, and eyebrows than in expressing himself, would give answers that were almost incomprehensible, and so the gathering would end at around sunset.

At night, the older wives of the Shah would get together in each other's houses, and have a spectacular meeting in order to compare the Qur'an and

---

2. Ibid., pp. 68-69.
3. Abolhasan Mirza Shaikh al-Ra`is (1848-1920) was a grandson of the second Qajar king, Fath `Ali Shah.

discuss issues related to the *shari`a*. Shaikh Asadollah, a blind reciter of the Qur'an, would correct their recitation of the Qur'an and provide solutions to their problems.

The so-called middle-aged women . . . would also get together and spend the time playing dice whereas the young women would spend the time between having broken their fast and having said their prayers, and dawn, talking, joking, and laughing as was fitting for their age. . . .

Some nights, the Shah would appear in the women's rooms unannounced, and watch each of the gatherings for a short while. Since the women would stay awake until dawn and keep the lights on, I used to get excited as children do, and we would spend the time running and playing with `Aziz al-Sultan[4] and his boy-servants. On one of those nights when we were playing "hide and seek," the Shah had hid behind one of the bushes, and whistled unnecessarily. Thinking that the whistling came from one of the children, we swore at this imagined wrongdoer when suddenly the Shah jumped out of the rose-bush, and we ran away. After much laughing, the Shah called us back to him, and gave each one of us a gold coin.

Between the breaking of the fast, and dawn,[5] they would have four meals: a light snack to break the fast, consisting of seasonal fruits, all kinds of sweets like *paludeh*, *angosht-pich*, and so on;

the breaking of the fast itself, which consisted of all kinds of soups, *kufteh*, *kuku*, *shami,* rice pudding, *ferni*, jelly, and *yakh dar behesht*;[6]

a night snack which was eaten at midnight and consisted of *zulubiya*, *bamiyeh*, and *pashmak*,[7] and finally the meal at dawn which consisted of several kinds of mixed rice, white rice, and stews.

At the time of the breaking of the fast and at dawn, four cannons would be fired in succession. Each of them had been placed for this purpose in one of the four corners of the city above the moats.

---

4. `Aziz al-Sultan, also known as Malijak, was perhaps Naser al-Din's most favorite young boy at court. He had gained access to the court through his familial links with Amin Aqdas, his aunt and one of Naser al-Din Shah's favorite wives. Naser al-Din had such fondness for `Aziz al-Sultan that he not only took him on his foreign trips but also allowed him to get away with anything, often to the embarrassment of the senior courtiers and bureaucrats at court.

5. Dawn is when another day of fasting begins.

6. This list consists of a variety of meat and vegetable dishes as well as a number of desserts.

7. *Zulubiya, bamiyeh*, and *pashmak* are sweets which contain a lot of sugar and are therefore usually consumed during the month of fasting.

2. Ramazan and Gambling

One of the favorite activities of Qajar courtiers was gambling. The excerpt below is taken from the diaries of `Ayn al-Saltaneh, Qahraman Mirza Salur who was a nephew of Naser al-Din Shah. Being a member of the royal family allowed `Ayn al-Saltaneh both access to the royal court and connections to prominent figures among the Qajar elite. This excerpt is from the entry dated Ramazan 1326 q/ late September-October 1908. That Ramazan, a month generally associated with fasting, prayer, and thus self-denial, is here referred to as the "season of gambling" (an activity that was otherwise religiously prohibited) only underlines the popularity and prevalence of this pursuit among not only members of the Qajar elite but also the population in general, as this excerpt suggests.

Text: *The Diaries of `Ayn al-Saltaneh*[8]

The usual round of parties began the night before last. I held the first party. Last year, there were too many people and it was not good. This year, I have been careful, and have invited only those who would always come. Holding the round of parties in Ramazan is very prevalent. It is more than eighteen years that we have had these parties: guests come after the breaking of the fast, and leave around dawn. . . .

Ramazan is also the season of gambling. In no other month do people gamble so much. In all the cities of Iran, it is common for people to gamble on the nights of Ramazan. In our round of parties, it is only a few of us who don't gamble, and that may be because we don't have the money! This year [1908], the tendency is to gamble big sums. Fakhr al-Mamalek, the son of Fakhr al-Molk,[9] being away from his father, has gambled twenty-five tumans, and he has also already lost quite a bit. He does not know how to play at all, but insists that he does. . . .

One must fast for fourteen hours a day exactly. On the first couple of days, I got very thirsty. . . . My daughter `Ayn al-Moluk has come of age this year and is therefore fasting. She gets restless in the evenings, but it is a religious precept, and she is compelled to fast.

---

8. Qahraman Mirza Salur, *Ruznameh-ye khaterat-e `Ayn al-Saltaneh*. Tehran: Entesharat-e Asatir, 1377/ 1998. Vol. 3, pp. 2180-2181.
9. Fakhr al-Molk was one of the members of the Qajar nobility.

3. Two Instances of Bread Riots in Tehran

Contrary to conventional wisdom, there is much evidence that women had a major presence in protests in Iran from the mid-nineteenth century onwards. While these demonstrations were, for the most part, ostensibly related to the shortage of bread, they were often political in nature in that they were in protest against other underlying factors, such as the mismanagement of affairs by the authorities. The two instances mentioned below both took place in Tehran. While dating from different time periods, they show that women were present in the public sphere when times got difficult and did not shy away from expressing their anger and outrage, and from demanding accountability from figures of authority. The first instance relates to the bread riots on 29 March 1861. This was a time of famine which had also resulted in the spread of cholera. Evidence suggests that this was one of a number of demonstrations carried out by women in that year. In June 1900, the second instance described below, while the combination of the shortage, poor quality, and high cost of bread seem to be what drew the women into the streets once again, the incompetence and corrupt nature of the figures of authority also played a part in further provoking the crowd. What is of interest in both passages is not only the aggressiveness and forcefulness with which women expressed their outrage, but also the fact that women seemed to be the instigators, initiating the protests which then broadened to include men.

BREAD RIOTS OF 29 MARCH 1861

Text: *The Notes of Farhad Mirza Mo`tamed al-Dawleh*[10]

In the afternoon, a group of women assembled in protest at the shortage of bread. They went to the Shah's Mosque. They beat up Shahbaz Khan, the Master of Ceremonies, instead of Mirza Musa the Minister. . . . They also dragged Aqa Seyyed Morteza, the brother of the late Friday prayer leader, to the doors of the mosque at which point he fainted, and fell. They had wanted to take him to the Citadel so that he could talk to the Shah. From

---

10. *Yaddashtha-ye Farhad Mirza Mo`tamed al-Dawleh*, quoted in Fereydun Adamiyat, *Andisheh-ye taraqqi va hokumat-e qanun-e `asr-e Sepahsalar*. Tehran: Entesharat-e Khwarazmi, 1351/ 1972, pp. 79-80.

there, another group went to the house of the British Minister Plenipotentiary. The latter closed the door to his house. So they pelted the door with
rocks and pieces of wood. Soldiers and guards stood at the gate of the
Citadel. The uninhibited and aggressive nature of the women became more
intense. They pulled off Aqa `Ali, the servant who was going to the house,
from his horse, and beat him up . . . and plundered the bakeries.

The king had been riding at this time, and no one had informed him of
the circumstances until he returned one and a half hours to sunset. The
Chief Sentry notified him of the events.

. . . Among the group of women demonstrators, there was a negro
woman . . . and since she was holding the wooden board belonging to the
bakery, she attacked Sepahsalar's group. She was arrested, together with a
number of other women, with much difficulty. The ears of a number of the
men, too, were cut in the middle of the mosque, so as to pacify the sedition.
The other women dispersed. . . . Truly, the women did their utmost in be-
having without any restraint. Every day there was a shortage of bread. And
today, as a result of the plundering of the bakeries, there was a greater
scarcity of bread. Three kilos of bread would be bought and sold for two
riyals, and that was not even for pure wheat.

THE TEHRAN RIOTS: 1900

Text: *The Diaries of `Ayn al-Saltaneh*[11]

Wednesday 15 Safar 1318/ 4 June 1900 – Today a small riot took place because of the shortage of bread. Even though wheat has fallen in price, bread
continues to be sold at a high price. A group of women went towards the
governor's house to complain about their situation to Asef al-Dawleh. His
Excellency the Governor got angry, and ordered that the women be kicked
out of the courtyard of his house. The servants beat them up. The women,
not being able to bear it, forced their way in and attacked. Crowds of men,
too, who were in the streets and in the vicinity, set out to protect the women,
and they prevailed. They entered the building, broke all the doors and win-
dows, and plundered whatever there was in the way of furniture. Asef al-

---

11. Qahraman Mirza Salur, *Ruznameh-ye khaterat-e `Ayn al-Saltaneh*. Tehran: Entesharat-e Asatir,
1376/ 1997. Vol. 2, p. 1467.

Dawleh escaped to the roof, and from there went to Sho`a al-Saltaneh's[12] house. From there, the crowd went to the house of Mirza Ashtiyani.[13] The Hojjat al-Islam [Ashtiyani] did not come out, despite the fact that the day before, he had promised to support the people, and had expressed his readiness to fight such acts of injustice. The women entered the outside and interior courtyards of the Aqa [Ashtiyani]'s house, and no matter how much they pleaded and begged, the Aqa did not answer, and did not come out. The women lost their patience, and began to throw stones and pieces of wood, breaking whatever there was to break. . . . Then the Sepahsalar came and with much effort, dispersed the women.

The shops closed, and troops from the army came to protect the city.... Two to three women and several men were wounded. It was said that two women were also killed. In any case, this was a riot and God help us! This Asef al-Dawleh has pocketed half a million, and people from all walks of life have complaints about him.

4. Schooling and the Role of *Akhunds* in Everyday Life

Modern or "New" schools were increasingly established in Iran from the turn of the twentieth century onwards. That is, with the exception of the state-sponsored Dar al-Fonun, generally hailed as the first modern school in Iran and founded in 1851, the other "New" European-style schools that came about did so, for the most part, through the efforts of private individuals as well as private organizations in Tehran, Tabriz, and other cities from 1898 onwards. However, maktabs *or "traditional" schools continued to exist as providers of elementary education, on the whole, until the introduction of universal secular education under Reza Shah in the 1920s and 1930s. The passage below is from the memoirs of Sa`id Nafisi (1896-1966), a historian and literary scholar. What is interesting about this passage is that while, on the one hand, it describes what a "traditional" education at the* maktab *consisted of in the days and years that preceded the emergence of "New" schools, it also depicts the indispensable role that local low-level clerics or* akhunds *used to play in the everyday life of the people in the neighborhoods of Iranian cities.*

12. Sho`a al-Saltaneh (1880-1922) was the second son of Mozaffar al-Din Shah, and a Qajar prince.
13. Mirza Hasan Ashtiyani (d. 1319 q/ 1901-1902) was one of the celebrated religious scholars of the time who played an instrumental role in bringing about the annulment of the tobacco concession. (See "The Concession for the Tobacco Monopoly and Its Aftermath" in this same volume.)

Text: *In the Words of Sa`id Nafisi: Political, Literary, and Memoirs of Youth*[14]

At age six, I began my education. . . . It had been two years since the so called "modern" and European-style schools had opened. Prior to that, children used to go to *maktab*s or *maktab-khaneh*s. The *maktab*s consisted of a storefront or sometimes an upper-chamber which an older cleric would rent, and would accept young children to teach for two or three years.

The fathers would give a nominal monthly fee to that teacher who used to be called "*akhund-e maktabi.*" The children would spend the day from dawn to dusk in the *maktab.* At the front of the *maktab*, the *akhund* would place a mattress or a piece of sheepskin, where he himself would sit, and the children would sit on the left and right of the *akhund* according to age, so that the youngest would end up sitting at the back of the group.

The best and oldest pupil would act as the assistant to the *akhund*, and was called "*khalifeh.*" When the *akhund* got tired or had something else to do, he would entrust the teaching of beginner-level students to the *khalifeh*, for the *akhund* also took care of tasks other than, and in addition to teaching. For example, when people who did not know how to read or write received a letter, they would give it to the *akhund* to read, or ask him to write letters to this or that person.

Sometimes, the *akhund* would prescribe medication; other times, he would practice divination by means of a rosary or the Qur'an. At other times, he would write a document, a lease or an invoice for people, or on occasion he would complete the formalities of marriage, marry and divorce women. In short, the local *akhund* was the problem-solver of the neighborhood, and people would consult him and ask for assistance for anything.

On the occasions when the *akhund* was busy with other things, the *khalifeh* would fill in for him, and he was even allowed to punish lazy and disobedient pupils. The *maktab* tended to last no more than three years. It is clear that the children would start first with the alphabet. . . . After learning the alphabet in almost six months, they would immediately take on reading a pamphlet that was called "*`amma juz`*" as it consisted of the last section of the Qur'an, from the chapter of *naba*[15] until the end. Because the first

---

14. Sa`id Nafisi, *Beh ravayat-e Sa`id Nafisi: khaterat-e siyasi, adabi, javani.* Edited by `Alireza E`tesam. Tehran: Nashr-e Markaz, 1381/ 2002, pp. 645-648.

15. The chapter of *Naba'* (The Tidings) is chapter 78 of the Qur'an.

verse of this chapter starts with "*'Amma yatas'aluna*,"[16] it was called
"*'Amma juz'*." Now imagine the kind of big problems that a child who had
not yet learnt to read Persian and knew not one word of Arabic would have
had with this. Learning this section of the Qur'an would take the child
about six months. In the second year, the child would be taught all of
Sa'di's *Golestan*.[17]

In the third year, he would first read *Tarassol* followed by *Tarikh-i
Mu'jam*. "*Tarassol*" is a literary expression which is used to denote the skill
of letter-writing, and in this context, it consisted of a book which contained
samples of different sorts of writing, ranging from regular letters, leases,
deeds of sale, marriage contracts, deeds of donation, testaments and wills,
to invoices and bills of exchange and such kind of documents that were
needed by the general public. Students had to learn the format of these letters by heart, and when necessary, they had to write them exactly, word for
word. . . . In addition, as part of "*Tarassol*," beginners would learn seven
kinds of handwriting that were prevalent in Persian. . . .

Tarikh-i mu'jam was a book that was written in a very obscure style, for
it was full of difficult Arabic words, many of which were not used in Persian. . . . After a very abstruse introduction, this book consisted of twenty-
eight sections made up of historical stories of pre-Islamic Iran, and of kings
such as Kiyumars, Hushang Tahmures, Lohraseb, Goshtasp, Bahman, Dara,
Eskandar, Ardeshir Babakan. . . .

The last stage that the pupils had to go through at the *maktab* was to
learn by heart the poems of *Nisab al-Sibyan*, which was a composition in
verse of the prevalent Arabic words with their equivalents in Persian. This
book has been written by Abu Nasr Farahi, who was among the literary
men of 6th century hijra/12th century C.E., and who has written each of the
different poems in one of the meters and rhymes of prosody. Learning this
book by heart had two very important advantages: one was that people always remembered the meaning of Arabic words, and the other was that
since they learnt by heart the names of the meters and rhymes, they could
scan any poem and find out its rhyme scheme. I imagine that there still

16. Literally, this first verse has been translated as "Concerning what are they disputing?" (See *The
Holy Qur'an: Text, Translation and Commentary* by A. Yusuf Ali. Leicester, U.K.: The Islamic Foundation, 1975.)
17. *Golestan*, translated as "Rose Garden," was written by the renowned thirteenth-century Persian
poet Sa'di of Shiraz and is considered to be one of the most celebrated works of medieval Persian
literature.

exist a large number of learned people in Iran, from the age of thirty-five and over, who learnt the *Nisab al-Sibyan* by heart in the *maktab*s and that perhaps they still remember it completely.

Usually, boys would finish the *maktabkhaneh* at age ten or eleven. Some of them would stay an extra two years with the same *akhund-e maktabi*, and cover higher levels. However, most of the learned people, after finishing this course of time at the *maktab* would go to one of the seminaries which existed in large numbers in Iran at that time . . .

5. Coffeehouses in Tehran

Coffeehouses—urban spaces that served as gathering places primarily for men—are thought to have been in existence in Iran since the turn of the seventeenth century in the Safavid era. In their early days, coffeehouses tended to be grand and attractive institutions, located in the central parts of the Safavid capital, Isfahan, and frequented by the elite, which included artists, poets, high officials, and sometimes even Shah Abbas I (r. 1587-1629) himself, who accompanied foreign visitors. By the late Qajar period, however, they seem to have become places that catered for the most part to a less privileged clientele. The passage below, taken again from the memoirs of Sa`id Nafisi, concerns coffeehouses, probably in the early years of the twentieth century in Tehran. It is interesting because, while it is nostalgic in tone and paints a happy picture of the coffeehouse culture of that era, it does reinforce the idea that coffeehouses accommodated primarily the working-classes and the guilds at this time. What it is at odds with, however, is the general viewpoint put forth by the opponents of coffeehouses, namely, women as well as some Iranian modernists who, from the 1880s onwards, tended to associate coffeehouses with idleness, gambling, opium smoking, and thus immorality.

Text: *In the Words of Sa`id Nafisi: Political, Literary, and Memoirs of Youth*[18]

During our childhood and youth . . . the most important places for purposes of entertainment were several very big coffeehouses. A number of them

---

18. Sa`id Nafisi, *Beh ravayat-e Sa`id Nafisi: khaterat-e siyasi, adabi, javani.* Edited by `Alireza E`tesam. Tehran: Nashr-e Markaz, 1381, pp. 636-638.

had very large gardens and open spaces. The working-classes used to gather there in the early evenings after having finished a day's work, and sit with each other for an hour or two. They would even arrange to meet each other there. . . .

Most of these coffeehouses were specific to a particular guild. For example, construction-workers would gather in one coffeehouse, and carpenters in another. Even apprentice construction-workers . . . would go to their own particular coffeehouses. Many of these coffeehouses were pleasant places with their own running water and trees. People would sit next to each other on large carpeted benches that were there, either on their heels, or crossed-legged, smoking pipes, drinking tea, while the older men would smoke water-pipes.

Each coffeehouse had several young twelve or thirteen year-old boy-apprentices who were constantly on the go, seeing to every customer that entered, calling out his[19] order to the person standing next to the samovar, announcing in a singing voice: "three cups of tea with sugar-cubes on the side for the second bench," or "two cups of tea with sugar-cubes on the side for the fifth bench." The coffeehouse keeper would pour out the tea immediately and give it to the apprentice, and the latter would serve the customer with a speed that one could never imagine in the coffee-shops or restaurants nowadays. Two or three young boys were also in charge of "bringing the fire"-that is, a chained metal container which was full of burning fire. Anyone who wanted to prepare a pipe would call out to him, and he would place a glowing piece of charcoal on the pipe with a set of tongs, and once the pipe lit up, he would remove it and leave. .

Every coffeehouse had its own number of story-tellers. These story-tellers ranged in age, although often they were older. . . . They would stand in between the benches in the coffeehouse and recount long tales and stories off by heart smoothly and in a pleasant and manly tone. They paid much more attention to the epic stories of those days—like "Hosayn-e Kord," "The Secrets of Hamzeh," and "Shiruyeh and Shahriyar"[20]—relating them with a particular kind of affectation and bombast, changing their tone in the sensitive parts of the story . . . even acting out some of the violent

19. Since coffeehouses were primarily frequented by men, I have used here the masculine third person singular possessive adjective "his."
20. While "Hosayn-e Kord" and "The Secrets of Hamzeh" were popular folk tales often told orally, "Shiruyeh and Shahriyar" is a story originally from Ferdawsi's *Shahnameh*.

scenes. People had much interest in listening to the heroism and fearlessness of the champions of ancient Iranian history. . . .

In the early hours of the night, they would tell stories from the *Shahnameh*, and a man who knew all the poetry of the *Shahnameh* by heart, would recite the stories of Rostam and other heroes with amazing fluency and eloquence. . . . The people did not have to give anything to the storytellers or *Shahnameh*-reciters but when the latter's story would reach a sensitive point, the audience would get so excited that without thinking, they would get up one by one and give some money to him according to their ability. They used to call this payment *cheraqollah* [literally "the lamp of God"]. The story-tellers and *Shahnameh*-reciters were much respected among such trusting and gallant people. . . .

Of course, itinerant dervishes, too, also frequented coffeehouses, praising the Imams. They would take a stem of mint or another aromatic plant . . . to anyone there, and get something in return.

6. Roads, Railways, and Changing Times

The late nineteenth century was a time when ideas of reform and social change were increasingly articulated. The passage below is from Ketab-e Ahmad *or* The Book of Ahmad, *written in two volumes by `Abdol-Rahim Talebof (1834-1911), an intellectual and reformer, in 1893-1894. It is considered to have been one of the more influential treatises of the late nineteenth century. Inspired by Jean-Jacques Rousseau's* Emile, *it is written in the form of a conversation between the author and his fictional seven-year-old son, Ahmad, whose curiosity and constant questions provided his father with the opportunity to talk about a wide range of subjects. What is of particular interest in this passage is the way it brings attention to how railways, roads, and the growing global interconnectedness not only changed realities on the ground but also led to a new mindset reflecting fresh ideas and aspirations.*

Text: *The Book of Ahmad*[21]

Ahmad said, "Sir, there is no harm in learning the language of the Ottoman Turks, and the Russians who are our neighbors, but why is the learning of

---

21. `Abdol-Rahim Talebof, *Ketab-e Ahmad*. Tehran: Gam, 1356/ 1977, pp. 94-95.

English, German, and French necessary for the children of Iran, and how are these countries relevant to Iranians since they are more than two thousand *farsakhs*[22] from our borders?" . . .

I said, "It is such ignorance and misapprehension that has led us to the indescribable state of decay that we find ourselves in. . . . Fifty years ago, it would take four months to go from Tehran to Paris by carriage. Today if we were to have a railway from Tehran to Rasht, we would be able to arrive in St. Petersburg, London, Vienna, Berlin and Paris in six days. If the road to Anatolia or Asia Minor were to be completed, it would take three days to get to Damascus from Tehran. In such a case, which stupid person would be able to deny that France and Britain are not in our neighborhood, or not know or understand that because of the bad roads sometimes it takes about twelve days to go from Ardabil to Tabriz?[23] It has happened many a time that in winter, people have been delayed by one month between Tehran, Qazvin and Tabriz. However, from Tehran or Tabriz, in all the seasons of the year, the maximum waiting period to get to the capitals of the great powers has been between six and seven days. Furthermore, in order to have material wealth, we need to know foreign languages. . . . In order to sell our fruits, we need buyers and markets. It is clear that these markets and buyers are not found in the sky, but in these very same neighboring countries. In such a case, is learning their languages that would enable us to communicate with them without intermediary necessary or not? Should Iranians have links with them or not?"

An Attempt at Diplomacy and Reconciliation in the Context of the Russo-Persian War of 1826-1828

The two Russo-Persian wars, which resulted in the treaties of Golestan (1813) and Turkmanchai (1828), respectively, were of great consequence for Iran. In addition to much financial and territorial loss, setting the Aras River as the new border between Iran and Russia, these treaties also allowed Russia to gain many advantages and the upper hand in both the commercial and political sectors in Iran. In subsequent years, these treaties

---

22. Unit of measurement of distance. Each *farsakh* (or *farsang*) is approximately 6 kilometers (3.7 miles).

23. The distance between Ardabil and Tabriz is 134 miles (216 kms).

came to be ranked among the most humiliating treaties ever signed by Iran.
The excerpt below is taken from the memoirs of Mirza Saleh Shirazi, an
envoy who was sent by the Crown Prince `Abbas Mirza in the midst of the
second Russo-Persian war to explore the possibilities of negotiating an end
to the war. While Mirza Saleh Shirazi is remembered first and foremost as
the founder of both the printing press in Tabriz and the first newspaper in
Tehran, he also served as translator and secretary to `Abbas Mirza. It was
in the latter capacity, and as a trusted envoy, that he was sent to the Russian
Court in response to an inclination expressed by the Russian General, Ivan
Paskievich, towards reconciliation with Iran. This excerpt is therefore of
interest on two levels: on the one hand, it shows the different Russian and
Iranian perspectives regarding the question of which party had first vio-
lated the terms of the Golestan Treaty, as well as their distinct assessments
of the situation in 1827 in general; on the other, it draws attention to the
"behind-the-scenes" talks that took place in order to establish the grounds
for the eventual end to the second war.

Text: *The Collected Travel Accounts of Mirza Saleh Shirazi*[24]

1 Muharram 1243/ 27 July 1827- . . . on this day, all the Russian commanders and generals that I knew came to see me and each one said something
separately. The summation of all this talk was that we have come now to
redress the behavior that you had towards our provinces last year. Try to
end the dispute; otherwise, in view of our preparation, and these many
troops, we can attack any one of your provinces, and will defeat your army.
I responded to each one in a manner that was necessary, saying: in the first
place, last year, the act of transgression was on the part of your former border-guards, and their behavior was such that no one could tolerate it. As a
result, the agents of the Iranian government had no choice but to push back
this injustice.

At dinner-time . . . I went to the Russian Commander and after drinking
tea and exchanging the regular courtesies, we began the discussions.

First, the Russian Commander said, "In his letter, the Crown Prince has
not written anything that is of any use. The British Envoy has written that
you are in search of peace, but we don't see anything here that we like."

24. Gholam Hosayn Mirza Saleh, ed., *Majmu`eh safarnamehha-ye Mirza Saleh Shirazi*. Tehran:
Nashr-e Tarikh-e Iran, 1364/ 1985, pp. 422-426.

I said, "You had said, or rather you had asked Mohammad Amin Khan[25] that a reliable person be sent to you. They have sent me to come to you and to ask what request can be made of you, so that I can convey the terms of the discussions and your request to the Iranian agents. If what you say is benevolent and is in the interest of both governments, a plenipotentiary will be sent from the other side to lay the grounds for peace, but if what is said, is not close to the interests of either party, then things will remain the way they have been."

He said, "For now, tell me, what are the aims of the Crown Prince regarding this matter?"

I said, "First, we want to know what your aims are."

He said, "I won't say first; you say whatever you have to say."

These discussions did not last long. Finally I said, "What we ask of you is that if your agents and border guards treat us better than they have in the past, the treaty which was signed at Golestan, and which failed because of the unfairness and ill-treatment of your border-guards, can be agreed upon in the same way."

He answered, "You were the ones who broke that agreement. Even though on the passing of our former Emperor [Tsar Alexander I], it was incumbent upon you to send one of your princes or noblemen, in the same way that other European leaders sent envoys to express their condolences to the current emperor, you fell short. In fact, the Emperor, himself, sent General Alexandre Menschikov with gifts and presents and a kind letter, and gave him orders that he make all the dignitaries of state understand that the aim of the Russian government is that its friendship and agreement with the Iranian government get stronger by the day. In fact, in case of any misunderstandings, the aforementioned envoy was commissioned either to remove the problem himself, or to inform his government of the problem so that it could be completely resolved, paving the way for greater agreement between the two governments. However, after the said Envoy came to Iran, and reached Soltaniyeh, you did not respect him that much, and whatever he said in the way of benevolence, was of no use, as it was ignored. Instead, without allowing him to reach his aims, you sent him to Tabriz and from there to Yerevan. Secretly, and contrary to the rules of diplomacy, you put him under arrest and treated him very badly. Without

---

25. Mohammad Amin Khan was the husband of `Abbas Mirza's sister.

giving a warning to our border-guards or agents, you entered our territory with an army, and wherever our sentinels were posted, you either killed or arrested them, and took them prisoner. Whatever territory you passed through, you ravaged its crops, and destroyed the said province, and made the subjects there despondent and distraught, and caused us much loss. The Emperor heard about this at his coronation, when all the delegates and grandees of Europe were present to congratulate him. . . . The Emperor got angry at this behavior, and found it humiliating that the Iranian government should have thought him so helpless, inept, and weak. And from that day, according to the [Declaration of War on Iran by Russia published in] the St. Petersburg newspaper which you have of course seen,[26] he broke the Golestan Treaty and decided that in order to remove the humiliation and lack of respect that you had expressed towards the Russian government, he should give you a fitting punishment so that you and others understand that whoever is unfaithful to their promise to Russia, and considers that government weak, will have to bear the consequences. . . . ”

Even though I responded to every allegation made by the Russian Commander and refuted them, which in turn led to new differences, his argument can be summarized in the following way: “In order to remove the dishonor, disgrace, and the injury that you have caused us, I have been commissioned to come to your territory, and first punish those who have been the cause of this dispute, avenge their past actions, and finally, claim reparation in compensation for the loss that you have caused us, and also to draw borders that are in the interest of Russia. Now I am to implement the order of the Emperor which calls for the regions of Yerevan and Nakhchivan to be made part of Russia, and the Aras River to be the new border between the two countries, that damages be paid for the expenses of mustering troops and the losses that we have incurred. If you do other than what I have said, I will immediately take over the Abbasiyeh Castle which is the key to Azarbaijan. I will leave part of my army there, and I, myself, together with a large army, will cross the river, and go either to Khoy, or to Tabriz or to Tehran. Wherever I end up, I will not cause trouble for anyone; for our aim is not to harass Iranian subjects, rather it is to punish those who destroyed our territory last year, and humiliated us unjustly. . . .

---

26. The reference here is to the Russian declaration of war on Iran, which was published in Persian in Moscow on 26 Rabi` I 1242/ 28 October 1826 and was entitled "Statement on the dissolution of the Peace between the governments of Iran and Russia."

If you have no care, and are ready for war, let's get on with it. . . . However, if you want peace, give us the provinces of Nakhchivan and Yerevan, and set the Aras River as the border, pay the cost of war and all the preparations that we have made. If you do other than this . . . I will set off from here, and do what is my duty. But know this much that if I set off from here, I will no longer be content with what I have requested this time, for my demands then will be different and will change according to the needs that will come about in the future."

I said, "Even though I don't have the permission or the authority to tell you the grounds or the conditions, I know this much that the Imperial Government of Iran will not give you one extra span of any province except for that which has been mentioned in the Golestan Treaty. They might give you some money in compensation for your losses this year . . . since a group of ungrateful and cowardly individuals have acted treacherously and have ceded the Abbasiyeh Castle to you. But the King of Iran has assigned 12000 Turkmen cavalry with six cannons with the duty of guarding the regions of Nakhchivan from the beginning of fall until next spring, to evacuate the subjects of Nakhchivan, and to force out those who do not obey, to destroy all of Nachchivan, not leaving one person behind, and to make the surroundings of Abbasiyeh castle into an uninhabitable desert, and to put an end to all coming and going to the Castle. Also wherever you go, they will destroy and reduce your surroundings to a desert, and will attack you from every side, until we see which side will tire first. Neither we nor anyone fears your coming; rather they will be pleased if you come somewhere which you have no familiarity with, for then it will be proven to you that conquering our provinces is not going to be so straightforward, and moreover it will cause you enormous loss."

The discussion on both sides took long, and there is no point repeating it all here. In the end, it was agreed that I should convey to the Crown Prince whatever I had said to the Russian Commander, as a first step to a compromise, and let him know the answer in four days. Therefore, I chose two men to take the letter that I wrote to His Highness, the Crown Prince, saying that the summary of the words of the Russian Commander is that, if you want peace, first the borders should be drawn at the Aras River, and the regions of Yerevan and Nakhchivan should be handed to Russia, reparations should be paid by the Iranian government for the expenses of the movement of the Russian troops, and the losses that they have incurred.

After a wait of four days, in the evening of the fourth day, the answer came, saying that the elders of the Iranian government will not accept these terms. . . . After receiving the reply, I had dinner with the Russian Commander at night, and told him that if he wants there to be a compromise between the two states and for the problem to be resolved, then Russia and Iran have to come together, and try very hard; otherwise friendship and unity will not be accomplished. I also said that if he [the Russian Commander] is in search of peace and benevolence, then he should send an envoy to the camp of His Highness, the Crown Prince, so that he can convey in person what is on your mind to the elders of the Iranian government, hear an answer, and then lay the foundations for a compromise. In the end, after much insistence, he accepted to send Monsieur Alexander Griboyedov[27] who was the premier writer and among the close appointees and advisors of the Commander, and whose rank was that of a colonel, [to come] with me to the camp of His Highness the Crown Prince. From there he went to the Royal Camp so that peace talks could take place by means of the dignitaries of state and the British Ambassador.

The Russo-Japanese War of 1904-1905 and Its Reception in Iran

The Russo-Japanese War, a confrontation between Russia and Japan over their rival imperial ambitions regarding Manchuria and Korea in 1904-1905, had a profound impact on Iranians. That Japan, a non-European nation, had been able to not only challenge but also defeat Russia, one of the two major European powers in Iran, impressed Iranian observers and reinforced their growing admiration for Japan. In the words of Yahya Dawlatabadi, a constitutionalist and educational activist, "One must admit the truth that when knowledge and education are combined, they produce Japan, and when pride and arrogance are conjoined, they result in

---

27. Alexander Griboyedov (1795-1829) arrived in Tehran as Minister-Plenipotentiary in 1828, with the task of putting into effect the terms of the Treaty of Turkmanchai, much of which he, himself, had drafted. However, once the Russian mission was seen as violating Persian norms—by taking sides and actively playing a part in removing two Georgian women from the harem of a Qajar notable, because they allegedly had wanted to be repatriated to Georgia—large crowds were provoked and gathered outside the Russian Legation. This led to an attack on the Russian Legation, resulting in the loss of life of Griboyedov alongside forty other Russians, and some eighty Persians.

Russia. "[28] *The two excerpts below further underscore this widely held sentiment among Iranian reformers at the time. The first is from the memoirs of Mohammad `Ali Tehrani, a reformer and constitutionalist, written in retrospect, and the second is from* Tarbiyat, *a privately owned Tehran weekly newspaper, which in 1904-1905 gained a reputation for its detailed reporting of the war. What is also of interest is that while the first passage shows a direct link between the Japanese victory over Russia and the growth of a spirit of dissent in Iran with regard to Qajar rule, the second uses this war as a pretext for bringing attention to the increasingly prevalent talk of parliamentarianism and reform as the solution to problems when all else has failed.*

1. Iranian Feelings towards Russia and the Russo-Japanese War in the Words of a Reformist and Constitutionalist

Text: *Social and Political Observations and Analysis of the History of the Constitutional Revolution of Iran*[29]

Ever since the treaties of Golestan and Turkmanchai, and the loss of Georgia and the Caucasus, the Iranian nation looked to the policies of the Russian Tsarist government with anger. This rage grew more intense by the day, especially after the treaty that Naser al-Din signed with the Russians in order to set up a brigade called the Cossacks in Iran in 1879.

Gradually, this anger and rage grew even more intense at the time of the 1900 loan, but out of fear, no one could say anything. Finally, as a result of the actions of the Russian Loan and Discount Bank, people's hostility and resentment towards the Russians increased, and they were looking for an opportunity. Such an occasion presented itself in the beginning of 1904, when war was declared between the Royal Courts in Tokyo and St. Petersburg.

At the beginning, people were awaiting events with composure and equanimity until such time that the continuous victories of the Japanese became clear. The Reuters reporter, too, would report detailed news every

---

28. Quoted in Hamid Naficy, *A Social History of Iranian Cinema*. Durham and London: Duke University Press, 2011. Vol. 1, p. 58.

29. Mohammad `Ali Tehrani (Katouzian), *Moshahehdat va tahlil-e ejtema`i va siyasi az tarikh-e enqelab-e mashrutiyat-e Iran*. Tehran: Sherkat-e Sahami-ye Enteshar, 1379/ 2000, pp. 126-127.

day, and it would get published in *Tarbiyat* newspaper, run under the supervision of the late Zoka' al-Molk. Upon publication, perhaps more than
thirty people would gather around each copy of the newspaper, which
would then get read in the alleyways and the bazaar, and upon hearing the
news, people did not know what to do with themselves out of sheer happiness. In this way, people lost some of their fear from the Iranian Royal
Court and government. In particular, the Russian Revolution as well as the
continuous defeat of the Tsarist government led to a great awakening. In
short, whoever had some common sense and intelligence became critical
of the Qajar policies.

I remember that we used to get together in *Ketabkhaneh-ye Khorshid*
[Khorshid Bookstore] whose founder was the late *Akkasbashi*. One day,
we were busy reading *Tarbiyat* newspaper about the Japanese victories.
Everyone present was giddy with delight at the Russian defeat and the
Japanese victory. Among them was an officer who was around fifty-five
years old. I have forgotten his name, but he began crying and shedding
tears like a woman who had lost a child. The group present got angry, and
reproached him, saying "Are you a Russophile that you cry in this way?"
He raised his head, dried his eyes, and began talking. While he was holding
back tears, he said, "Compatriots, I cry for the misfortune of my homeland
and country as well as my own bad luck. I and the victorious Japanese general both studied at the same [military] school in Paris, and at the time of
the examinations, I scored higher than he did. We, each, returned to our
own countries in the same year: I came to Iran, and he went to Japan. In
this country, I turned out in the way that you see. I used to be a sharp sword,
but today have rusted away, whereas he became a shining sword whose
brilliance has [now] lit Asia and Europe, and has served his country in such
a great way. His government appreciated his worth, and as a result, he
reached this position. As for me, because of my government's lack of concern, even you, my compatriots, do not know me, and you have the right."
The words of this man had such an effect on the people present, that everyone cursed the Qajar monarchy and rule, and expressed their contempt
towards the policies of the government.

2. The Russo-Japanese War as Reported in *Tarbiyat* Newspaper

Text: *Tarbiyat*[30]

. . . The informed people should know that the world has not seen anything like the events of these last seventeen to eighteen months, and the people interested in listening have not heard such stories. In short, it is appropriate that we, too, learn a lesson, get prepared, and resolve some of our own thorny concerns.

The events of the Russo-Japanese war, whether on land or at sea, are all remarkable and cause for amazement. The battles such as those of Laioyang, Shaho, and Mukden, as well as the siege and conquest of Port Arthur are events that take place rarely in the world. By God, may no such thing happen in the future, although this is a prayer that will most probably not be heard! But the most amazing of all were the events of the most recent naval battle. It is as if the Japanese knew magic and witchcraft. . . . Otherwise, how was it possible for them to destroy the Russian naval forces at one stroke? The Russian naval force consisted of eight big armored ships and nine armored and non-armored inspecting ships as well as several other legitimate naval vessels . . . which all in all, counting both the large and the small . . . added up to more than forty. The Russians sent all those ships to the Far East in order to destroy and obliterate the Japanese naval force or at least to stop it, make the Port of Vladivostok into its center of operations, reserve the China and Japan Seas for its own exclusive use, and to disrupt and postpone the dispatch of Japanese troops to Manchuria. The Russian naval commander, with much trouble and expense and at the cost of considerable hardship and injury which cannot be described, succeeded to get the ships to reach their destination safe and sound, and it was almost certain that the Russian government had accomplished part if not all of its aims. However, suddenly, news came that within a few hours, the Japanese navy had destroyed twenty-two of the finest ships among them—that is, it had drowned seventeen, and confiscated five ships. The remainder were either destroyed or lost, and the commanders of those ships were taken prisoner. In short, nothing was left of the Russian navy, meaning that today, the ports on the Baltic Sea, which are at the heart of the Russian

---

30. *Tarbiyat*, no. 367, 25 Rabi` II 1323/ 29 June 1905, pp. 1846-1848.

government, have no guards or protectors other than the Almighty. Can there be anything more strange than this development?

Much is said and many analyses are made about the reasons for the Japanese victory and the Russian defeat. Perhaps they are all correct. However, when we turn from the details to the big picture, we see that this is all because of two or three reasons: First, the good character of the people of Japan and their superiority in this regard over the people of Russia; secondly, the advantages of the Japanese in terms of their learning and knowledge, since they have not fallen short in their education; and the third point-being a consequence of the first two reasons-is the lack of good order in the Russian government. The recent developments and troubles[31] are further proof of our claim. . . .

Following the recent naval battle, one of the Russian newspapers has written an influential article which we should read with all our heart. It says, "O you tricksters of the state and the nation, it is enough! Another lightning-bolt flashed and set fire to our harvest! We trusted Kurapatkin[32] but it came to nothing. We put our faith in Port Arthur; it fell into the hands of the Japanese! We had hope in the ships in the Baltic; they were destroyed! We ask for answers from religion, and are told that we should be content with divine fate and not be obstinate; we look for a solution in national zeal and patriotism and are told that the cure for all troubles is in the word, 'enough'! So you shameless people, you closed our eyes for two hundred years-that was enough-now is the time to remove the veil from our eyes and to cry out that enough is enough! The people of Russia have been quiet and patient until today, but now is their turn to talk. [As for] those who are responsible for these blunders and mistakes, and have brought disgrace and shame on the Russian nation, we no longer accept that this group act as middle-men between us and His Excellency the Emperor. The affairs must be run by a Parliament, which is more essential to us than the air necessary for our breathing."

Other Russian newspapers, too, write some such things, and the learned of the whole world say that the interest of Russia is in making peace immediately, and in setting about reforming the internal affairs, bringing about

---

31. This is a reference to the protests that had been taking place in Russia since January 1905.

32. Alexei Kurapatkin was the Russian Minister of War between 1898 and 1904, when he was removed from office because he was held responsible for the major defeats in the Russo-Japanese War, including the battles of Mukden and Laioyang.

the welfare of the subjects, and introducing good order in the country. Now it must be seen if such goodwill will make headway or not?

The Anglo-Russian Convention of 1907 and the Reaction to It in Iran

The Anglo-Russian Convention of 1907, which, in addition to Iran, also concerned Afghanistan and Tibet, was signed by Britain and Russia in St. Petersburg on August 31, 1907. Russia and Britain both feared the rise of Germany in Europe as well as the Middle East; thus, the two former rivals decided to put aside their differences and, instead, to bolster their common interests in Iran, Afghanistan, and Tibet, without consulting or informing the governments or peoples affected. The two excerpts below consist, respectively, of the segments of the text of the agreement between Britain and Russia that concerned Iran and the outrage expressed in the columns of the Tehran daily Habl al-Matin *once the agreement was made public after the fact. As the second excerpt shows, what was particularly offensive to the Iranian public was not only the fact that this Convention had been signed without their knowledge but also the timing of it, as if there had been no constitutional revolution, no parliament, and no talk of rights of the nation. As `Ayn al-Saltaneh, an observer living at the time, put it, "Until now, our security had been assured as a result of the rivalry and competitiveness of those two powers. Now that we have been divided between them, God help us!"*[33]

1. The Text of the Anglo-Russian Convention of 1907[34]

"1. Agreement concerning Persia
The Governments of Great Britain and Russia having mutually engaged to respect the integrity and independence of Persia, and sincerely desiring the preservation of order throughout that country and its peaceful development,

---

33. Qahraman Mirza Salur, *Ruznameh-ye khaterat-e `Ayn al-Saltaneh*. Tehran: Entesharat-e Asatir, 1377/ 1998. Vol. 3, pp. 1809-1810.
34. J. C. Hurewitz, *The Middle East and North Africa in World Politics: A Documentary Record*. New Haven: Yale University Press, 1975, pp. 539-541.

as well as the permanent establishment of equal advantages for the trade and industry of all other nations;

Considering that each of them has, for geographical and economic reasons, a special interest in the maintenance of peace and order in certain provinces of Persia adjoining, or in the neighbourhood of, the Russian frontier on the one hand, and the frontiers of Afghanistan and Baluchistan on the other hand; and being desirous of avoiding all cause of conflict between their respective interests in the above-mentioned provinces of Persia:

Have agreed on the following terms:—

I. Great Britain engages not to seek for herself, and not to support in favour of British subjects, or in favour of the subjects of third Powers, any Concessions of a political or commercial nature—such as Concessions for railways, banks, telegraphs, roads, transport, insurance & c.—beyond a line starting from Kasr-i Shirin, passing through Isfahan, Yezd, Kakhk, and ending at a point on the Persian frontier at the intersection of the Russian and Afghan frontiers, and not to oppose, directly or indirectly, demands for similar Concessions in this region which are supported by the Russian Government. It is understood that the above-mentioned places are included in the region in which Great Britain engages not to seek the Concessions referred to.

II. Russia, on her part, engages not to seek for herself and not to support, in favour of Russian subjects, or in favour of the subjects of third Powers, any Concessions of a political or commercial nature—such as Concessions for railways, banks, telegraphs, roads, transport, insurance, & c.—beyond a line going from the Afghan frontier by way of Gazik, Birjand, Kerman, and ending at Bunder Abbas [sic], and not to oppose, directly or indirectly, demands for similar Concessions in this region which are supported by the British Government. It is understood that the above-mentioned places are included in the region in which Russia engages not to seek the Concessions referred to.

III. Russia, on her part, engages not to oppose, without previous arrangement with Great Britain, the grant of any Concessions whatever to British subjects in the regions of Persia situated between the lines mentioned in Articles I and II.

Great Britain undertakes a similar engagement as regards the grant of Concessions to Russian subjects in the same regions of Persia.

All Concessions existing at present in the regions indicated in Articles I and II are maintained.

IV. It is understood that the revenues of all the Persian customs, with the exception of those of Farsistan and of the Persian Gulf, revenues guaranteeing the amortization and the interest of the loans concluded by the Government of the Shah with the 'Banque d'Escompte et des Prêts de Perse' up to the date of the signature of the present Agreement, shall be devoted to the same purposes as in the past.

It is equally understood that the revenues of the Persian customs of Farsistan and the Persian Gulf, as well as those of the fisheries on the Persian shore of the Caspian Sea and those of the Posts and Telegraphs, shall be devoted, as in the past to the service of the loans concluded by the Government of the Shah with the Imperial Bank of Persia up to the date of the signature of the present Agreement.

V. In the event of irregularities occurring in the amortization or the payment of the interest of the Persian loans concluded with the 'Banque d'Escompte et des Prêts de Perse' and with the Imperial Bank of Persia up to the date of the signature of the present Agreement, and in the event of the necessity arising for Russia to establish control over the sources of revenue guaranteeing the regular service of the loans concluded with the first-named bank, and situated in the region mentioned in Article II of the present Agreement, or for Great Britain to establish control over the sources of revenue guaranteeing the regular service of the loans concluded with the second-named bank, and situated in the region mentioned in Article I of the present Agreement, the British and Russian Governments undertake to enter beforehand into a friendly exchange of ideas with a view to determine, in agreement with each other, the measures of control in question and to avoid all interference which would not be in conformity with the principles [of] government [in] the present Agreement."

2. The Reaction to the 1907 Anglo-Russian Convention According to the Tehran *Habl al-Matin*

Text: *Habl al-Matin*[35]

. . . Well, the contents of the first two Articles of the Convention are totally

---

35. *Habl al-Matin*, vol. 1, no. 114, 2 Sha`ban 1325/ 11 September 1907, pp. 2-3. An older translation can be found in E. G. Browne, *The Persian Revolution of 1905-1909*. New edition. Washington, D.C.: Mage Publishers, 1995, pp. 183-187.

inconsistent with Article three, since the inclusion of Isfahan and Kerman-shah within the Russian political sphere of influence is clear proof of partition, and is incompatible with the independence of Persia—even if today's telegrams assert otherwise, saying that the influence of the two Powers extends to the whole of Iran, and that they have placed all of Iran as their joint sphere of influence, and have abandoned the idea of it being divided. However, in our opinion, the first reports were the more accurate. Furthermore, until now, whenever they would make any mention of their influence, they would limit it to commercial influence, but now the veil has been removed, and suddenly they say something else, as they have begun to talk of political influence. We don't know what political influence means, and what they mean by it. If it merely means dictating and interfering by force, this is not legal and cannot be considered as part of the "rights" of a nation. Hajji Malek [al-tojjar] embezzled other people's property, and then took refuge in the Russian Embassy. The Russian ambassador, contrary to all international law, gave him protection. This has nothing to do with the matter at hand, but it is outright lawlessness and bullying and has no connection to the Agreement. However, if they mean something else, then it would be advised that they explain.

Today's telegrams are worthy of attention and should be read carefully by those in authority, so that they can understand the essence of the matter, and take precautionary measures. We give an account of a number of them by way of example. . . .

The English newspapers have expressed their happiness and satisfaction with the conclusion of the Anglo-Russian Agreement, and congratulate the signing of this treaty, since this Agreement will be another means for the preservation and consolidation of peace in the world. The reporter of the [London] Standard newspaper writes from St. Petersburg that on the basis of the new Agreement, the issue of the political domination and influence of each of the two Powers in a specific part of Iran has been rendered obsolete and that they will both, equally, have the right to influence and trade, since the Russian government has agreed that the doors of the northern provinces of Iran should be open to trade and concessions granted to British subjects, and from another side, the British government approves Russian influence and trade in the southern provinces.

The beauty of the matter at hand is the fact that the Russian government authorizes the British government to open the doors of influence and trade in the northern provinces, and the British kindly give the same permission to Russia in the south! What business has Russia in Iran to give or deny permission? From the north to the south, this land belongs to us. We are neither minors to want guardians, nor are we lacking in faculties to need caretakers. Even if Mokhber al-Dawleh says in Parliament that the "Iranian nation is in need of a nanny," this is complete nonsense. Iranians have reached maturity and do not need nannies. If they did, they would not have a Parliament since having a Parliament means transferring the rights and powers to the people themselves so that they manage their own affairs, elect deputies from among themselves to act for them. Had they not reached maturity, they would not have had the right to elect deputies. It is true; we do not understand why these two Powers give each other permission to enter someone else's territory, and why they spend money from the guest's purse.

Today, the Iranian Foreign Minister must clearly inform the two Powers that any agreement that has been concluded regarding Iran, without her knowledge, is void and illegitimate. Any government that wants to enter into relations with Iran must address itself directly to the Iranian people. No one has the right to take possession of anything. Just as Iran would address Britain directly in any matter regarding the affairs of that country, so too must Britain act in this same way.

2

Reforms, Economic Concessions, and Expressions of Dissent

The Concession for the Tobacco Monopoly and Its Aftermath

On March 8, 1890, an agreement was signed, granting a monopoly to Major G. F. Talbot, a British subject, for the production, collection, distribution, and export of tobacco, which was then "the second-largest cash crop produced in Iran."[1] This turned out to be not only a mistake in the short term but also consequential in the long run. It led to a storm of protest, as well as a tobacco boycott, which ultimately forced the Iranian government to annul the monopoly less than two years later, on January 5, 1892, and to borrow £500,000 in order to pay damages to Talbot. Historians, too, have underlined the long-term significance of the Tobacco Concession, with some regarding it as a "dress rehearsal" for the constitutional movement that took place in the early twentieth century, and others, as part of a chain of events that ultimately led to the assassination of Naser al-Din Shah in 1896. Below are three documents that shed light from different angles on this important episode in nineteenth-century Iran: the actual text of the Concession for the Tobacco Monopoly; the asking of Legal Advice

---

1. Abbas Amanat, "Qajar Iran: An Overview," in Layla S. Diba and Maryam Ekhtiar, eds., *Royal Persian Paintings: The Qajar Epoch, 1785-1925.* New York: I. B. Tauris, 1998, p. 27.

from Mirza Mohammad Hasan Shirazi (also known as Mirza-ye Shirazi), the Grand Ayatollah and Marja` resident in Samarra, whose fatwa had led to the tobacco boycott; and finally Naser al-Din Shah's letter confirming the annulment of the Concession.

1. The Text of the Concession for the Tobacco Monopoly, March 8, 1890[2]

"The monopoly of buying, selling, and manufacturing of all the tootoon and tobacco in the interior or exterior of the Kingdom of Persia is granted to Major Talbot by us for fifty years from the date of the signing of this Concession, in accordance with the following stipulation:

1. The concessionnaires will have to pay 15,000*l.* per annum to the exalted Imperial Treasury whether they benefit or lose by this business, and this money shall be paid every year, five months after the beginning of the year.

2. In order merely to ascertain the quantities of tootoon and tobacco produced in the protected provinces (of Persia) the concessionaries will keep a register of the cultivators who wish to work under the conditions of this Concession, and the Persian Government will issue strict orders to the local Governors to compel the cultivators of tobacco and tootoon to furnish such a registration.

   Permission for sale, &c., of tootoon, tobacco, cigars, cigarettes, snuff, &c., is the absolute right of the concessionaires, and no one but the proprietors of this Concession shall have the right to issue the above-mentioned permits.

   The Guilds of the sellers of tobacco and tootoon who are engaged in this trade will remain permanent in their local trade and transactions, on condition of possessing permits which will be given to them by the concessionaires.

3. After deducting all the expenses appertaining to this business and paying a dividend of 5 percent, on their own capital to the proprietors of this Concession, one quarter of the remaining profit will yearly be paid to the exalted Imperial Treasury, and the Persian Government will have

---

2. J. C. Hurewitz, *The Middle East and North Africa in World Politics: A Documentary Record.* New Haven: Yale University Press, 1975, pp. 462-463.

the right to inspect their (the concessionnaires') yearly books.

4. All the materials necessary for this work which the proprietors of this Concession import into the protected provinces (Persia) will be free of all customs duties, taxes, &c.

5. Removal and transfer of tootoon and tobacco in the protected provinces (of Persia) without the permission of the proprietors of the Concession is prohibited, except as such quantities [as] travellers may have with them for their own daily use.

6. The proprietors of this Concession must purchase all the tootoon and tobacco that are produced in the protected provinces and pay cash for it. They must purchase all the tobacco, &c., fit for use that is now in hand, and the price that is to be given to the owner or the producer will be settled in a friendly manner between the producer or the owner and the proprietors of this Concession, but in case of disagreement between the parties the case will be referred to an Arbitrator accepted by both sides, and the decision of the Arbitrator will be final and will be carried out.

7. The Persian Government engages not to increase the revenues, taxes, and customs that are now levied on tootoon, tobacco, cigars, cigarettes, and snuff for fifty years from the date of the signing of the Concession, and the proprietors also undertake that all the customs that the Persian Government now obtain from tobacco shall be continued as they are.

8. Any person or persons who shall attempt to evade (the rules) of these Articles will be severely punished by the Government, and any person or persons found to be secretly in possession of tobacco, tootoon, &c., for sale or trade, will also be fined [and] severely punished by the Government. The Government will give its utmost help and support in all the business of the proprietors of this Concession, and the proprietors of this concession undertake in no way to go beyond their own rights consistent with these Articles.

9. The proprietors of this Concession are permitted, should they wish, to transfer all their right, Concessions, undertakings, &c., to any person, or person, but prior to this, they must inform the Persian Government.

10. The producer or owner of tootoon and tobacco, whenever his crop of tobacco and tootoon is gathered, shall at once inform the nearest agent of the proprietors of this Concession of the quantity, in order that the proprietors of this concession may be able to carry out the engagement

in above-mentioned Article 6, and to purchase it quickly.

11. The proprietors of this Concession have no right to purchase lands, except to the necessary extent, for store-houses and abodes, and what may be necessary to carry out this Concession.

12. The cultivators, in accordance with certain conditions which will be made in conjunction with the Government, are entitled to be given an advance to a limit for their crop.

13. If, from the date of the signing of this Concession until one year, a Company to carry it out is not formed, and the work does not begin, this Concession will be null and void, except that war or such like may prevent the formation of a Company.

14. In case of misunderstanding arising between the Persian Government and the proprietors of this Concession, that misunderstanding shall be referred to an Arbitrator accepted by both sides, and in case of the impossibility of consent to the appointment of an Arbitrator, the matter will be referred to the arbitration of one of the Representatives, resident at Tehran, of the Government of the United States, Germany, or Austria, to appoint an Arbitrator, whose decision shall be final.

15. This Concession is exchanged in duplicate with the signature of His Imperial Majesty, registered in the Foreign Ministry, between Major Talbot and the Persian Government, and the Persian text of it is to be recognized."

2. Asking Legal Advice from His Excellency, Ayatollah Mirza-ye Shirazi, Regarding the Smoking of Water-Pipes

Text: *The History of the Awakening of Iranians*[3]

Your Holiness . . . A question and answer, as detailed below, and attributed to Your Excellency, has gained currency. If it is correct, it is requested that you write it in your handwriting clearly, and in case it proves genuine, will this decree be binding once this Monopoly has been removed?

The text of the question asked from the Hojjat al-Islam, may God make your lofty shadow last: In view of the situation that has occurred in the land of Islam regarding the Tobacco Concession, what are the conditions of

---

3. For original text, see Nazem al-Eslam Kermani, *Tarikh-e bidari-ye Iraniyan*. Vol. 1. Edited by `Ali Akbar Sirjani. Tehran: Entesharat-e Agah, 1362/ 1983, p. 30.

smoking water-pipes from an Islamic legal point of view for now? What are Muslims to do? It is requested that you clarify the duty of Muslims.

Answer: In the name of God, the Compassionate, the Merciful. Today, the use of tobacco for water pipes (*tanbaku*) and tobacco for pipes (*tootoon*), in whatever shape or form, is tantamount to waging war against the Twelfth Imam, may God accelerate His coming.

Answer to the first question: In the name of God, the Compassionate, the Merciful. Yes, it is correct, and regarding the question whether this decree would remain in force should the Monopoly be removed, the answer is that in case of removal, there will be no ban. God is All-Knowing. Written by the humble [servant], Mohammad Hasan al-Hosayni.

3. The Text of Naser al-Din Shah's Letter Confirming the Annulment of the Tobacco Concession

Text: *The History of the Awakening of Iranians*[4]

Instructions on the envelope: For the attention of His Excellencies, the Amin al-Sultan and the Nayeb al-Saltaneh,[5] and to be put into effect immediately. It is essential that His Excellency, the Amin al-Sultan, and the other honorable governmental ministers consider our note, and read it for the merchants of good-standing, especially the reputable merchants of tobacco, and so on.

A decree that is issued by the king and the government will inevitably be considered as peremptory by the government. Whatever decree he [the king] issues will not be out of deceit or by mistake, regardless of whether it relates to matters inside or outside the country. At one time, it was appropriate to give the Tobacco Concession to the British Company, and this was done. A little later, it became appropriate to take that Concession away from the British Company, and so this was done. A governmental announcement was written and circulated everywhere, saying that this Monopoly has been taken away from the company. In addition, the British

---

4. Ibid., pp. 30-31.
5. Amin al-Sultan, Mirza `Ali Asghar Khan was Naser al-Din Shah's Chief Minister between 1887 and 1896; Nayeb al-Saltaneh (or Vice Regent) was the title given to Naser al-Din's third son, Kamran Mirza, who held the office of both Minister of War and Governor of Tehran at different times during his father's long rule.

company, itself, also published an announcement saying that the Iranian government had taken away this privilege from us, and we have been evicted. Whoever in Tehran or the provinces has sold us tobacco, should come, pay the money, and take his tobacco back. This announcement was posted everywhere so that all people could become aware and informed that this Concession had been annulled.

In spite of all these explanations, documents, and decrees that have been issued, confirming the annulment and cancellation of the tobacco agreements with the company, I am very surprised to hear that this erroneous impression still persists among the people, merchants, and others, that the Tobacco Concession has not been annulled and that even if it has, it is only temporary.

It is clear that these baseless rumors have been spread by seditious and despicable individuals that do not want the good of government and nation. Of course, no wise well-wisher should pay attention to these false and meaningless words. In fact, it is incumbent on all people, high and low, as well as all honest, loyal, and well-wishing subjects, that from now on, whenever they hear such words from any seditious and malicious persons, or see them write an announcement and post it, they should put them in chains, and surrender them to the state, so that they be given a just punishment. Since such groundless and harmful rumors will cause the insecurity of merchants, tradesmen, and all subjects . . . and will result in the destruction of business and trade, in order to bring back order to the affairs of the people, the government will have no choice but to introduce extraordinary, harsh measures.

Of course, following the disbanding of the Tobacco Company, the actual person heading it can no longer be involved in matters to do with tobacco. The reason why the head of the Tobacco Company has remained in Tehran for the time being is to clear the accounts that he has with people, and to settle the claims of expenses that he has made with the government. Once he has finished, he will leave, but this will take one or two months.

From another side, the head of the Tobacco Company has recalled, disbanded and dismissed all the active agents and employees in all the cities and provinces of Iran, both foreign and Iranian. As a result, there remains no one such person in the government or country of Iran. If anyone is aware of the presence of such a person, they should speak out so that he can be expelled. We repeat again that this Concession has been annulled, and disbanded for good. This is by no means a temporary measure, and from now on, the government will not give this Concession to any merchant, either foreign or Iranian. Everyone should rest assured and be at peace. [Royal signature and seal.]

This entire text that has been written here is by our order. A copy of these statements has been made by Malek al-Tojjar,[6] in order to be circulated everywhere. [1309 q/ 1892]

Seyyed Jamal al-Din Asadabadi in Iran

Seyyed Jamal al-Din Asadabadi (1838-1897), known also as Afghani, was among the most prominent men in Iran and the Muslim world in the late nineteenth century. Although born in Asadabad in northwestern Iran, he claimed to be of Afghan birth, most probably in order to be able to exert influence in the Sunni world. As E. G. Browne wrote, "[Afghani] was at once philosopher, writer, orator and journalist but above all politician and was regarded by his admirers as a great patriot and by his antagonists as a dangerous agitator."[7] Seyyed Jamal al-Din travelled extensively in the Muslim world as well as Europe, and adopted different political positions at different times. In some cases, he acted as advisor to kings and rulers, and in others, he engaged in oppositional activities against them. In Iran, however, even though he had been invited to Tehran by Naser al-Din Shah on two occasions in the 1880s, after offending and arousing the suspicion of the shah, he was forcibly made to leave Iran both times. In retrospect, Afghani has come to be remembered as first and foremost a dissident and the person who inspired Mirza Reza Kermani to assassinate Naser al-Din Shah in 1896, the first time that an Iranian king had been assassinated by a "commoner."[8] The three passages below come from different sources and point to the many ways in which Seyyed Jamal al-Din left an impression

---

6. Malek al-Tojjar was the title given to the chief of the merchants of Tehran.

7 E. G. Browne, *The Persian Revolution of 1905-1909.* New edition. Washington, D.C.: Mage Publishers, 1995, p. 3.

8. Prior to Naser al-Din Shah's assassination in 1896, if the king were assassinated, it tended to be usually either by members of his own family or those who wanted power or the throne. This time, clearly, there was no such intention, since Mirza Reza Kermani, the assassin, says in the course of his interrogation that his aim in taking such action was to "cut down the tree whose only fruit were base rogues and rascals," and thus to get rid of the source of corruption. See "Excerpts from Mirza Reza Kermani's Cross-Examination" below.

on people. The first is through the eyes of a constitutionalist reformer who paints a positive portrait of Seyyed Jamal al-Din, while also conveying all the negative propaganda that was spread about him at the time. The second is the account of the deportation of Seyyed Jamal al-Din from Iran on the orders of the Shah in 1891—an act that outraged many people who heard about it, including Mirza Reza Kermani, Naser al-Din's eventual assassin. This point is also underlined in the third passage, consisting of excerpts from the text of the interrogation of Mirza Reza Kermani after the latter's capture. It is illuminating because, in addition to showing Mirza Reza Kermani's admiration for Seyyed Jamal al-Din, it also portrays the degree of injustice that was prevalent under Naser al-Din's rule, and that drove Mirza Reza Kermani to take action.

1. Seyyed Jamal al-Din through the Eyes of a Reformist and Constitutionalist

Text: *Social and Political Observations and Analysis of the History of the Constitutional Revolution of Iran*[9]

One of the men who deserves to be considered among the greatest political men of the world and the revivers of Iran, is the late Seyyed Jamal al-Din Asadabadi Hamadani, also known as Afghani. In 1306 A.H./ [1889], he entered the house of the late Haj Mohammad Hasan Amin al-Zarb in Tehran.[10] Since, in addition to knowing several languages (Persian, Turkish, Arabic, French, and English), he was also well informed about politics as well as philosophy and religion, anyone who had any cause for distress on his mind, would gather around him, and he would talk to each group about the disadvantages of autocracy in their respective languages with great eloquence. In this way, a number of Muslims gathered around the Seyyed. In addition to urging the people to have a democratic government, he gradually began to correspond with the necessary places and gathered a number of devotees to carry out his aims. In view of the speed with which the Seyyed made progress, some hope was found in the people that perhaps

---

9. Mohammad `Ali Tehrani (Katouzian), *Moshahedat va tahlil-e ejtema`i va siyasi az tarikh-e enqelab-e mashrutiyat-e Iran*. Tehran: Sherkat-e Sahami-ye Enteshar, 1379/2000, pp. 42-44.

10. Afghani came back to Iran in 1889 at the invitation of Naser al-Din Shah, and he stayed at the house of Amin al-Zarb, a supporter and admirer and one of the most influential merchants in Iran.

with the efforts of this upright man and his followers, soon, the despotic rule would be overthrown, and replaced with a democratic government. However, Naser al-din Shah was aware and vigilant, and so with utmost speed, he prevented the Seyyed from reaching his aims. They made it seem to people that the Seyyed was a republican, and that republicanism was one of the new religions which was much more dangerous and detrimental to society than Babism, and that the aim of the Seyyed was to uproot religion and tradition and to stir up the basis of the religion of Islam.

The late Asadabadi's house was close to this author's house. At that time, I was a child and as was the habit of children, during vacations, I used to play with the children in our street. I remember it very well: when the children would see the Seyyed from a distance, they would all run away. I was the exception. My father knew the Seyyed and used to come and go with him. I would repeatedly ask my play-mates, "Why do you run away?" They would all give this answer: "The Babis make people Babis by giving them sweets and candies. But this Seyyed is a republican, and republicanism is a new religion. When the Seyyed moves, he poisons the air around him. By breathing the air, we become poisoned and therefore republican. For this reason, our parents have banned us from standing next to the Seyyed, and they have told us to run away instead, and not to return until such time that the Seyyed has moved away. . . ."

In short, they circulated such propaganda against the Seyyed that people came to despise him. Since the Seyyed no longer had confidence in being able to stay in Tehran, and the late Haj Amin al-Zarb, too, became subject to Naser al-Din Shah's anger and displeasure, the Seyyed left Tehran for Shah `Abd al-`Azim, a town which was one and a half *farsang*[11] . . . from Tehran. He decided to stay in the house of E`temad al-Tawliyeh which was considered part of the compound of the shrine, so that he could remain free of the evils of the state. However, his taking refuge in the shrine of `Abd al-`Azim did not prove effective, for at night, they arrested the Seyyed as he lay sick and asleep, and exiled him to the Ottoman empire, naked and in a very undignified way. A number of the followers of the Seyyed like the late Haj Sayyah and Mirza `Abdollah Tabib were also arrested and detained, and sent to jail in Ardabil. This action on the part of Naser al-Din

11. *Farsang* is a unit of measurement for calculating distance. Each *farsang* is equivalent to 6 kilometers or 3.7 miles.

Shah regarding the Seyyed and his followers caused people to become gradually aware of the aims of the Seyyed and sympathize with him and his followers whom they considered innocent.

2. The Expulsion of Seyyed Jamal al-Din Asadabadi from Iran

Text: *The Diary of Haj Sayyah or the Era of Fear and Terror*[12]

In short, it seemed that the presence of Aqa Seyyed Jamal Asadabadi, instead of being of use, proved to be a heavy burden for the government. It did not occur to the Shah even once why he had invited Aqa Jamal or to consult with him regarding a matter. Seyyed Jamal, too, discussed philosophical and rational topics and the virtues of liberty, with his eloquence and boundless learning, in such a way that if every day he added one person to his followers, he also provoked a hundred enemies. Troublemakers would exaggerate his every word and sometimes call him republican, sometimes, anti-religious . . . .

Around that same time, an announcement had been glued on the doors of mosques, caravanserais, public passageways and embassies saying "Why have these narrow alleyways which all Muslims, even dogs and sheep have the right to pass through, been given away to Europeans so that tomorrow Muslim children get crushed under the wheels of the carriages of foreigners?" Even worse than that was the question, "Why has the buying and selling of tobacco which belongs to Iranians, who are both buyers and consumers, become the monopoly of foreigners?" In this way, other criticisms were made regarding the actions of the government.

After learning about these announcements, I saw Hajji Amin al-Zarb[13] and said, "May God preserve His Excellency [Seyyed Jamal]! He said, "How is this any of his business?" I said, "Has there been an investigation? Is this not a means for the corrupt and the malicious to get their way?" He said, "Yes, it could be, but what can be done?"

The following day . . . an order arrives from Amin al-Sultan addressed to Mokhtar Khan, who had been appointed the governor of Hazrat-e `Abd al-`Azim, saying "Mokhtar Khan! Kick Seyyed Jamal al-Din out of the

---

12. Haj Sayyah, *Khaterat-e Haj Sayyah ya dawreh-ye khawf va vahshat.* Edited by Hamid Sayyah. Tehran: Ibn Sina, 1346/ 1967, pp. 322-330.
13. See chapter 2, footnote 10.

sanctuary, and hand him over to these horsemen." Mokhtar Khan, in turn, kisses the order, and instructs a few attendants to kick out the Seyyed, adding that if he refuses, then they should take him out by force, even if he be in the shrine.

The attendants first go to close the door of the courtyard of the shrine, then they tell Aqa Seyyed Jamal, "Come! You must leave!" Seyyed Jamal pays no attention. So they pounce on him, take him by the collar, grab his hands and feet, and drag him out into the snow, mud and sludge, as he continues to kick, with no head covering or shoes. The cord of his underwear comes undone, but they still drag him, naked, in the snow.

Aqa Seyyed Jamal faints from distress. Despite that, they drag him to the garden of Mahd-e Olya.[14] There, he gains consciousness. Mokhtar Khan orders that tea be brought. Seyyed Jamal does not drink it, and says, "Am I forced to drink?" They answer, "No, you are not." Then they take his turban, and bring a pack-horse to put him on it. From the beginning of his arrest to the end, he does not say one word in supplication or plea. After they put him on the pack- horse, they tie his feet under the belly of the horse. He tells the attendants: ". . . Of course, you will tell the Shah that we sent off the Seyyed!" They say, "Yes. If you also have something to say, say it." He replies, "Give him a message from me. Tell him, you and I have both repeated the past actions of our ancestors. You will pay for this."

3. Excerpts from Mirza Reza Kermani's Cross-Examination Regarding Injustice, Seyyed Jamal al-Din, and the Assassination of Naser al-Din Shah

Text: *The History of the Awakening of Iranians*[15]

Q: So how did you come to think of murdering the martyred Shah?[16]

A: The "how" is not so hard. It was because of the stocks and chains that I had suffered unjustly, and the beatings that I took, that I ripped open

---

14. The garden of Mahd-e Olya (named after Naser al-Din Shah's mother) was within the compound of Shah `Abd al-`Azim.

15. Nazem al-Eslam Kermani, *Tarikh-e bidari-ye Iraniyan*. Tehran: Entesharat-e Agah, 1362/ 1983. Vol. 1, pp. 101-106. An older translation of the complete text of this cross-examination can be found in E. G. Browne, *The Persian Revolution of 1905-1909*. New edition. Washington, D.C.: Mage Publishers, 1995, pp. 63-85.

16. Naser al-Din Shah came to be referred to as the "martyred king" [*shah-e shahid*] in view of the fact that he had been assassinated.

my belly. It was because of the pains that I endured in the house of Nayeb al-Saltaneh[17] in Amiriyyeh, and in Qazvin, and in jail, again and again. For four years and four months, I was in chains and in stocks, all the while when in my mind, I wanted the good of the state and the nation and wanted to serve them well. Before the Tobacco Riots[18] took place, not that I had been indiscreet, but I gave information only after they summoned me.

Q: No one would have had any personal spite and ill-grudge towards you if, as you say, you had been of service, and no signs of sedition or mischief-making had been detected in you. There was no reason for them to have inflicted such pain on you in return for your service. Therefore, it is clear that even at that time, they had detected signs of sedition and immorality.

A: Even now, after all this time, I am ready for the opposing side to send a neutral person to investigate whether I made my honest statements out of love of country, the nation, and the state whereas the people with personal motives made statements to the contrary in order to establish a claim for services rendered, and to obtain posts, distinctions, salary, decorations, and badges. . . .

Q: Who are these "people with personal motives"?

A: A low-minded, dishonest, ignoble, and unworthy person, undeserving of any of these distinctions, Aqa Bala Khan Vakil al-Dawleh[19] for whom the Nayeb al-Saltanaeh had much affection.

Q: Vakil al-Dawleh says that even at that time, he arrested you on the grounds of the seditious documents and letters that have become known to all, and that had he not arrested you then, based on the interrogation that was conducted then, you already entertained the thought of assassinating the shah, and would perhaps have carried it out.

A: So it will become clear in the presence of Vakil al-Dawleh.

Q: If as you claim, Vakil al-Dawleh and Nayeb al-Saltaneh have inflicted all this suffering on you because the former had hoped to gain distinction, and the latter went along because of his affection for Vakil al-Dawleh, what did it have to do with the martyred shah? . . . You should have taken

---

17. Nayeb al-saltaneh was the title given to Naser al-Din's third son, Kamran Mirza, who held the office of both Minister of War and governor of Tehran.

18. See "The Concession for the Tobacco Monopoly and Its Aftermath," above.

19. Aqa Bala Khan Vakil al-Dawleh was a close associate of Nayeb al-Saltaneh. He had gained notoriety for having given the orders to the troops to fire on the crowds who had gathered in Tehran to protest the granting of the Tobacco Concession, leading to injuries and much loss of life.

revenge . . . on them who had caused your hardship, rather than orphan a nation.

A: A king, who after having ruled for fifty years, can still be misled in matters, and not investigate anything; a tree that after many years, has as its only fruit individuals like Vakil al-Dawleh, `Aziz al-Sultan, Amin Khaqan, and such base rogues and rascals who are calamities on the life of all Muslims, must be cut down, so that it no longer bears such fruits. The fish begins to stink at the head, not at the tail.[20] If a wrong is committed, it is from the top.

Q: Even if it is as you say, in your specific case, it is the Vakil al-Dawleh and Nayeb al-Saltaneh who are most to blame. The martyred Shah was not perfect [in the way of the Twelve Imams] nor did he have knowledge of the unknown. When a person like Nayeb al-Saltaneh, who is both the Shah's son and the chief servant of the state, presents a matter to the Shah, especially with the documents that he had obtained from you, the Shah would be left with no room for doubt. Those who were the cause should have been subject to your revenge. The reason that you have mentioned is not sound. You are a rational and philosophical man; you should give your answers based on evidence.

A: No evidence was obtained against me, except when in Vakil al-Dawleh's house, they extracted it from me by force and violence, under threat of using the tripod and branding-iron, in the presence of two other people, one of whom was the Governor, and the other, a seyyed who in order to object to the Chief-Minister, had removed his turban and who was there at the time of breaking the fast, and witnessed what happened. I had also been taken to the Nayeb al-Saltaneh the previous night.

Q: You are a sensible man and you knew that you should not give them such evidence. On what grounds did they get evidence from you, and what did they say?

A: The grounds on which they got the evidence was this: After I told them that there was much talk and tumult among all classes of people, and that they would rebel on account of the Tobacco question, and that they ought to find a solution before it got out of hand, I also told the Nayeb al-Saltaneh, "You are compassionate towards the king, you are the son of the king, you are the heir to the throne, the ship of state will hit a rock, and this

20. This translation is borrowed from E. G. Browne, who in turn borrows it from the Masnavi of Jalal al-Din Rumi. (See E. G. Browne, *The Persian Revolution*, p. 67 n. 1.)

roof will fall on your head. It is not long before danger strikes the many-thousand-year-old Iranian monarchy, and then suddenly this Muslim nation will perish." Then he swore that he had no ill intentions, and that all he wanted were reforms. So he told me to write a letter to this effect:

"O believers and Muslims! The Tobacco Concession has been granted! The Bank and the Tramway, despite the opposition of the Muslims, will start running. The Concession for the road to Ahvaz has been given, as have those for the mines, sugar, match factories and wine-making. We, Muslims, will fall into the hands of foreigners. Little by little religion will disappear. Now that our king is not concerned about us, you should take matters into your hands and show some zeal! Unite and take action towards defending yourselves!"

This was the approximate content of the letter. He gave me instructions and told me to write such things, and added that they would show it to the Shah and tell him that they had found it on the floor in the Masjed-e Shah, so that they could begin to introduce some reforms. Nayeb al-Saltaneh swore that there was no danger for me in writing this letter. Rather the government would be under an obligation to give me an allowance and do me favors. Then when we left Nayeb al-Saltaneh for Vakil al-Dawleh's house, I wrote the letter by means of force, violence and threats.

They took away the pen-case, and brought the tools for branding and torture. They prepared the soldier's tripod, and prepared to strip me, and tie me to the tripod, asking for the names of friends and accomplices, and questions like "Where did you meet? Who are your associates?" No matter how many times I said, "What meeting-place? What accomplice? I have relations with all people, and have heard rumors from everyone. Which Muslims should I betray now? They forced me [to make a confession.] I realized that now was the time to take my life, and to sacrifice my life for the honor, dignity, and life of fellow Muslims. A knife and a pair of scissors . . . which they had forgotten to put back in the pen case, lay in the middle of the room. I looked at the knife. Rajab `Ali Khan noticed, and took the knife. The scissors still lay by the fire-place. The Governor who was sitting in the direction of the *qibla*,[21] was praying. I said, "For the sake of this *qibla* and this prayer which you are invoking, what do you want from me?" In the meantime, a letter had arrived from Nayeb al-Saltaneh. They read

21. *Qibla* is the direction that Muslims face when they pray.

the letter and laid it face down. The Governor said, "It is written in this letter that it is the order of the Shah that you disclose your meeting-place and
the names of your associates, or else, the tools for branding and torture are
ready, as is the whip." Since I saw the scissors by the fire-place, in an attempt to reach the scissors, I said, "Please sit on the cushion so that I tell
all in detail. There is no need for the branding iron or tools for torture." I
took the hand of the Governor, and pulled him towards the fireplace, and
got myself to the scissors and tore my belly open. Blood poured down, and
as it did so, I began swearing. They, then, got anxious, and began to treat
me. They stitched the wound. It was after this ordeal that for four and a
half years, I who was unfortunate and innocent, and who in my mind, had
done nothing but to serve my government, was put in chains and moved
from one prison to another, from Tehran to Qazvin, and from Qazvin to a
common jail. In the course of these two [*sic*] and a half years, I was released
three times, but all in all, I was not free for more than forty days. I had
become Nawruz `Ali Khan Qal`eh Mahmudi, or the Sabz `Ali Khan
Maydan-Qal`eh-i of the Nayeb al-Saltaneh and Aqa Bala Khan.

Q: Who was Nawruz `Ali Khan Maydan-Qal`eh-i?

A: In order to run up a bill of expense and to increase his salary and
rank, Mohammad Esmail Khan Vakil al-Molk, the governor of Kerman,
would deceive the government and every day, concoct a rebel and pretender
to the throne. For a long time, he preoccupied the government with a so-
called Nawruz Khan Qal`eh-Mahmudi. Similarly, whenever the Nayeb al-
Saltaneh failed in getting a high position, he would arrest me. Or whenever
Vakil al-Dawleh wanted additional salary or a higher rank, he would arrest
me. My wife divorced me; my eight year-old son became a house-servant,
my unweaned child was left an orphan. The first time, after two years of
imprisonment, when they returned us from Qazvin, they released ten people
from among our ranks. Two were Babis, one Haj Molla `Ali Akbar Shem-
rzadi, and the other Haj Amin. It was arranged that they be taken to jail.
Since one of those Babis was wealthy, he offered some money to His Royal
Highness [the Nayeb al-Saltaneh]. As a result, he was released, and I was
sent to jail, instead of him. It is easy to see how a man gets sick of life.
Having given up on life, he will do whatever he wants. When I went to Istanbul, and told my story to people in a gathering of learned men, they reproached me, saying why was it that in spite of all this oppression and
injustice, I had not washed my hands of life and had not delivered the world
from the evil of tyrants.

Q: All these details which you mention only strengthen my first question. In all fairness, had you been in the shoes of the Shah, and the Nayeb al-Saltaneh and Vakil al-Dawleh had brought you a document in the way that you describe, adding these details, would you have had a choice to believe it or not? In such a case, the culprits were these two individuals, and they were the ones who should have been killed. Why is it that you did not decide to kill them, and instead, decided to carry out this grave act?

A: The duty of the Shah, had he been impartial, would have been to send a third independent investigator to find out the truth of the matter between me and them. Since he did not do this, he was at fault. It has been years that the flood of injustice has been pouring on all his subjects. What had Seyyed Jamal al-Din, this noble descendent of the Prophet, done to be dragged in that disgraceful way from the shrine of Shah `Abdol al-`Azim? They tore his under-clothes to pieces; they inflicted all that indignity on him. What had he said other than the truth? . . . Does God tolerate such deeds? Are they not oppression? Are they not injustice? If there is a discerning eye, it will realize that the bullet hit the Shah in the very same spot where they dragged the Seyyed. Are these poor people and this handful of Iranian people not a trust from God? Just step out a little from the Land of Iran, and you will see how in Iraq, the Caucasus, Ashkabad, and the borders of Russia, thousands of poor Iranian subjects have fled their dear homeland, because of injustice and oppression, and have had no choice but to take on the most miserable of jobs and ways to earn a living. Whatever porter, sweeper, donkey-man, and laborer that you see in these regions, are all Iranian. At the end of the day, these flocks of your sheep need pastures to graze so that their milk can increase, allowing them to both feed their young and enable your milking - not that you should milk relentlessly as long as they have milk to give, and once they don't, to tear the flesh off their bodies. All your flock left; they dispersed. What you see is the result of oppression. . . . They get a hundred thousand tumans from some ruthless man, and in return give him the ownership over the property, lives, honor and security of a city or a province. Under the burden of this oppression, they force the poor, captive, helpless people to divorce their own irreplaceable wives so that they [the Lords], themselves, can take hundreds of wives. They spend the half a million tumans that they have earned in this bloodthirsty and ruthless way from the people, on `Aziz al-Sultan who has no use, either for the state, or the nation, or even the personal gratification of anyone. . . .[22]

These are matters that all the people of this city know, but they don't dare voice them aloud. Now that this important act has been carried out by my hands, as decreed by fate, a heavy burden has been lifted from the hearts of all. People are relieved and are all waiting to see what the new king, the [recent] Crown Prince, will do. Will he heal men's broken hearts by justice, clemency, and uprightness or not? If, as people expect, he grants a degree of peace and tranquility, and brings about the well-being of his subjects, and bases his rule on justice and equity, then all the people will be ready to die for him, his rule will be strengthened, and his good name will fill the pages of history, causing him a long life and good health. On the other hand, if he pursues the same path and method [as his father], then the perverted path will never get anywhere. Now is the time that upon arrival [in Tehran],[23] he announce and state, "O people! In this period, you have truly had a rough time. Those days are over, and now it is the turn of justice. Our rule is based on fairness. . . ."

Expressions of Reform, Social Criticism, and Dissent

In the second half of the nineteenth century, with the growth of reformist ideas in Iran, works and expressions of social criticism appeared and gained ground. They were in a variety of genres; treatises and essays, novels, travelogues as well as newspapers. The passages below are excerpts from three influential works by three celebrated thinkers and reformers of the nineteenth century, namely, Ketabcheh-ye ghaibi, *also known as* Daftar-e tanzimat (The Book of Reforms) *by Mirza Malkum Khan (1833-1908);* Ketab-e Ahmad (The Book of Ahmad) *by `Abdol-Rahim Talebof (1834-1911); and* Siyahatnameh-ye Ebrahim Beg (The Travel Diary of Ebrahim Beg) *by Zayn al-`Abedin Maragheh'i (1840-1910). While the latter two were published in the 1890s when their authors lived outside of Iran, in Tblisi and Istanbul, respectively, the first is thought to have been written in 1858-1859 in Iran.* Ketabcheh-ye ghaibi, *a treatise that has been*

---

22. See chapter 1, footnote 4.

23. Mozaffar al-Din, Naser al-Din Shah's son and the Crown Prince, had been Governor in Tabriz. Upon the assassination of his father, in order to take the throne, he had to make the journey from Tabriz to Tehran.

described as "one of the first systematic proposals for reform written in Iran,"[24] *was addressed to the shah and the members of the Court.* Ketab-e Ahmad, *thought to have been inspired by Jean-Jacques Rousseau's* Emile, *is written in the form of a conversation between the author and his fictional seven-year-old son, Ahmad, whose curiosity and constant questions provide his father with the opportunity to talk about a wide range of subjects.* The Travel Diary of Ebrahim Beg, *considered the very "first modern Persian novel,"*[25] *is a fictional travelogue that tells the story of the protagonist, Ebrahim, who while born and brought up in Egypt, was of Persian parentage, and having heard Iran praised by his father as "paradise on earth," is not only patriotic but also keen to see Iran for himself. However, the country that he finds, upon visiting Iran, could not be more different from that of his imagination, in that it is replete with poverty, hypocrisy, corruption, and injustice.* The Travel Diary of Ebrahim Beg *is therefore "first and foremost a work of social criticism,"*[26] *and perhaps it was for this reason that it (together with* Ketab-e Ahmad*) gained popularity among Iranian reformists and was read extensively in secret societies that preceded the Constitutional Revolution.*

1. *The Book of Reforms*

Text: "Iran Cannot Be Reformed!"[27]

No! This is not so! God does not want chaos, and Iran can [certainly] be reformed. It is straightforward; the means that are there for the progress of Iran have not been possible for any other nation. There have always been many obstacles in the way of reforming the government; sometimes, the ignorance of the nation was against the wisdom of the king; sometimes, the king's negligence has been the obstacle to the progress of the nation. When Sultan Mahmud[28] was thinking of reforming the Ottoman govern-

---

24. Ervand Abrahamian, *Iran between Two Revolutions.* Princeton: Princeton University Press, 1982, p. 66.

25. M. R. Ghanoonparvar, "Foreword," in Zayn ol-`Abedin Maragheh'i, *The Travel Diary of Ebrahim Beg.* Translated from the Persian by James D. Clark. Costa Mesa, CA: Mazda Publishers, 2006, p. ix.

26. James D. Clark, "Introduction," in Maragheh'i, *The Travel Diary of Ebrahim Beg,* p. xx.

27. "Iran nazm bar nemidarad!" *Majmu`eh asar-e Mirza Malkum Khan.* Tehran: Danesh, 1327/1948, pp. 4-8.

28. Sultan Mahmud II (r. 1808-1839) is known primarily for the military, administrative, and fiscal reforms that he introduced, laying the grounds for the *Tanzimat* or Reorganization Era in the Ottoman Empire.

ment, the Janissaries wanted to arrest and detain him. There was a time when in order to suppress the new reforms in France, all European states attacked the French for twenty years. Similarly, today, a hundred kinds of obstacles appear in the way of any of the European states wanting to establish [new] laws . . .

In view of all the natural gifts that God has blessed Iran with, when someone compares the situation in Iran with that of Europe, he becomes amazed at what planning the guardians of this government must have had in order to bring such a country to such disgrace! Surely the former ministers of Iran either did not realize this at all, or they could not have had any understanding, or they were traitors to religion and state. Otherwise, how is it possible that they continued to be ministers amidst all these failings, and did not attempt to remedy any of them?

In Iran, there is a governmental pestilence which has enveloped the entire country. It sets fire to the yields, turns the foundations of all that the government has built, upside down, destroys cities and uproots prosperity everywhere. This frightening calamity which in other states is called the worst and most vile kind of theft is called profit in Iran. It is years that this country has been drowning in the sea of misery, and as yet no minister has considered relieving this national calamity to be worthy of his attention.

Which of the disasters in Iran should I talk about? What is the point of stating the distraction and desperation of the army? What can be worse than failing to fulfill a promise? Or the hunger of subordinates, the transgression of rulers, the misery of subjects, the chaos of government offices, the disgrace and dangers in the domain of foreign affairs; all these problems are clearer than the sun, but the factor that has made relieving these problems and saving Iran impossible in people's minds, is the neglect and recklessness of the guardians of this government. They have been sitting with such ease and confidence as if in this way they will block the road to all agitation and disturbance for another thousand years! They think that the independence of the government and the blessings of independence are their eternal rights, whereas this is not the case! The chaos in India will not last forever; the injuries and blows to Russia at the hands of Europe will not distract Russia for good; the method of national politics will not change for the sake of anyone; Azarbaijan, Fars, Mazandaran, Arabestan,[29] these Asian

---

29. Arabestan is the old name for Khuzestan in southwest Iran.

gardens have a thousand claimants. If you only knew what sensitive points the silence of these plaintiffs had reached, then surely you would not be sitting in such a carefree manner. May God bring that day to the king of Islam when five of his ministers realize where the ship of government has reached and where it is going from here. But alas, our confidence about the past has meant that we have become completely inattentive to the present.

The general mistake of Mirza Aqa Khan's premiership[30] was that he considered the age of the *khaqan-e maqfur*[31] to be the standard for ruling the country years later. He would constantly refer to the actions of those days as support, and would point to the problems of that age as evidence of progress in his own. He really thought that the age of *khaqan-e maqfur* had taken place thirty years before, but little did he know that five hundred years had passed since then. Put a map of Asia in front of yourself; consider the history of this last hundred years, and explore properly these two surging torrents which have started from Calcutta and St. Petersburg towards Iran, and see how these two torrents, which were hardly palpable to begin with, have strengthened in such a short time, the cities they have destroyed, and the governments that they have drowned! Once you have carried out this investigation, and whenever you can rise above the views of the common people . . . determine the speed with which these two torrents have reached Tabriz and Astarabad from one side, and Herat and Sistan, from the other, and then tell me how many more minutes are left of the life of this government.

The ministers of Iran consider the oldness of Iranian history as the protection against all calamities. However much you cry out that the torrent is here, they will say, it has been this way for three thousand years, and we will continue in this way into the future, too!

Mr. Minister! In the days when you used to rule at will in Asia, a person could not cover two-hundred *farsakhs* in ten hours. . . . Those days have passed for some time now. Today, they build an iron castle at a distance of 3000 *farsakhs* from Iran, and then they come and destroy Mohammareh in two hours. Today, in the face of the power of neighboring states, neither will Arabic words, nor our ancestors' bones be of much use. What we need today is learning and insight. You may know a thousand *qasida*s (panegyric

---

30. Mirza Aqa Khan Nuri was Prime Minister between 1851 and 1858.
31. *Khaqan-e maqfur* was the title given to Fath 'Ali Shah, the second Qajar king (r. 1798-1834).

poems) off by heart, and you may express a thousand decrees about honor, but you will still not understand that the government of Sardinia which is smaller in size than Azarbaijan, had only six million in taxes ten years ago, whereas today, it is in possession of fifteen million in taxation

2. *The Book of Ahmad*[32]

. . . If we don't approve of the lighting of lamp posts in alleyways, the sweeping of public squares, the paving of passage-ways and cleanliness of the water in public baths, we will stay in the dark, amidst the mud and infection. If we don't have schools, our children will remain illiterate. If we don't found companies, we will not bring about the progress and spread of industry, if we don't wear textile made in our own country, then we will become needy of the foreigners in everything, from matches to paper; we will have to order new things to their factories every day, and we will be encouraging foreign-made goods which are not appropriate for the needs of our lives. It will mean that we will be giving our wealth, which is the soul of our own country, to foreigners for free while remaining needy ourselves. If we don't have the ability to preserve our country and the shrines of our ancestors, the foreign "masters" will dig out the bones of our ancestors before our very eyes . . . and in their place they will build a playhouse. . . . This house is ours; it does not belong to someone else. So we must keep our eyes [full of passion] and our ears [concerned with honor] open to the voice of the wise well-wishers of the country, and not listen to the idle talk of seditious mischief-makers. We should encourage all the beneficial measures taken by the government and manage our own house on the basis of documented laws. These include the implementation of the noble *shari`a* as well as all the details of civilization, the recognition of common and individual rights which constitute a barrier to the transgression of the strong against the weak, and the oppressor against the oppressed. . . . Otherwise, I swear by the Glorious God that our ignorance, lack of knowledge, absence of laws in the country, and unawareness of the rights of the country will result in our descendants becoming house-servants, subordinates and shepherds for foreign nations, with their circumstances and dignity becoming dependent on whatever takes the fancy of the foreign "masters." Thus if

32. `Abd al-Rahim Talebof, *Ketab-e Ahmad*. Tehran: Gam, 2536/ 1977, pp. 98-100.

the sound of the prayers and the dawn call to prayer broadcast from the mosque minarets interferes with the sweet sleep of their wives, it will be banned; and instead the sound of [church] bells will eliminate that call of the *muezzin*; at every passage-way, wine shops will be opened, and our veiled women will be forced to walk around with their faces unveiled, and following the saying that "Power belongs to the victors," our untainted *shari`a* will disappear at once. Then it would be too late for any sense of remorse on the part of those who always invoke the name of God in order to rule in this fleeting world and seize people's property. Whenever there is any talk of law or education in the country, without reading or knowing or understanding that these laws are only there to preserve the honor of the nation, and to strengthen the *shari`a* and respect the holy Qur'an, and not to imitate the foreigners, or God forbid, to implement traditions that are in opposition to the pure religion of Islam, they blow it out of all proportion. They consider the *shari`a* in danger, and with much skill, extinguish the light of the sun of justice which aims to illuminate the horizon . . . and to cut off the hands of oppressors . . . and instead they praise their own lack-luster tales amidst the sky of ignorance. . . . If we continue this negligence much longer . . . foreigners will set laws for us, and will force us to obey them even if they are not based on the pure *shari`a* of Islam. Then our descendants will lose religion for good just as the regions surrounding our country have already done. . . .

3. *The Travel Diary of Ebrahim Beg*[33]

. . . I have come from far away and am a stranger in this country. My religion is Shi'ism, and I am of Persian parentage. My first point to you, honorable minister, is that you hear my petitions to the end, and only then order whatever you think right, whether out of kindness or anger.

He said, "Go ahead!"

I said, "I had heard about it abroad, but now I see with my own eyes that relative to the other countries in the world, Iran is in ruins. Your Excellency who are in possession of the lofty title of Minister of the Interior, must on

---

33. *Siyahatnameh-ye Ebrahim Beg* was published in three volumes between 1895 and 1902. The excerpt here is from the first volume, which has been translated by James D. Clark. However, the passage above is my own translation from the original, *Siyahatnameh-ye Ebrahim Beg: matn-e kamel-e seh jeldi*. Edited by M. A. Sepanlu. Tehran: Entesharat-e Asfar, 1364/ 1985, pp. 54-56.

the basis of duty and the exigencies of that high position, be aware of all
the important aspects of the internal affairs of the country, and spend day
and night working towards the prosperity of the country and bringing about
the means to enhance the dignity of the country and the comfort of its inhabitants. Now please tell me, in which of the cities of this vast country,
have you built a hospital? Or a shelter for the disabled or an orphanage, or
a vocational school for educating the abandoned children of the nation?
And in which village from among the villages of the country have you
paved roads to facilitate transportation and provided the means to assist
and bring about the progress of agriculture which constitutes the essence
of the life of the country and the nation? What serious measures have you
taken in the domain of the progress of the commerce of the country. . . ?
Do you know at all what amount of Iranian-produced goods is transported
abroad, and how much merchandise enters this country from abroad? Has
it ever occurred to you that you take a measure so that the amount of domestic goods and products that are exported surpass that which enters the
country from abroad, thus allowing the income of the homeland to exceed
its expenditure and as a result, enable the subjects to gain some [purchas-
ing] power and the government treasury to be replenished? Why must Iranian subjects be dependent on the outside world for their basic living
necessities? . . . Doesn't the soil of the provinces of Iran have the readiness
to grow turnips or sugar canes? . . . Or is all this Iranian cotton which they
take abroad by the millions not sufficient to clothe its inhabitants? Mr. Minister, are you at all informed of the number of the people living in Iran? Or
of the rate of reproduction which constitutes the basis for the persistence
and strength of our nationality? Have you ever investigated the reasons for
the emigration of so many Iranians who have dispersed in Russia, India,
and the Ottoman lands, and have you taken a measure to stop it? Why don't
you take steps to alleviate the needs of the people by at least building small
factories in your own honorable name in some suitable provinces? You will
say that building factories is not the duty and responsibility of a minister.
Fine, but the decision to establish factories, to encourage the nation and
guarantee to preserve the rights of the subjects, is the task of a competent,
wise, and just minister. I swear to God that in foreign countries, these points
that I have here listed one by one are the responsibility of the Minister of
Interior. He must entrust the subjects with a series of such good fortune
wherever he has found it. If he does not, he is blamed and held accountable.

Why don't you enquire about the reasons for the dispersal and displacement of the nation, asking why it is that several thousand Iranian subjects leave their homeland and pour into Russia, India, and the Ottoman lands every year, spending their days in foreign lands, with friends and strangers in that abject and distressed condition? . . . In which country in the world has it been seen that they rent out the office of the superintendent of the police of the city, and that to the most depraved and lowliest of people? After all, there must be some fairness. In civilized countries, this esteemed taskforce is called the Department of Police. Is it right that the police be scoundrels and illiterate men, and on top of all their incompetence, that they accuse the respected sons of merchants of a variety of plots and inappropriate actions, and to trample on their reputation and credibility for a mere five tumans? And that they fine a modest and honest young man who has committed no wrong forty or fifty tumans because of the burden of the shame from his father and brother? And don't you know about the despicable condition of the customhouses without tariffs that are the cause of a thousand reproaches of friend and foe, because for a single kind of domestic or foreign good, they charge one person two tumans, another, one tuman, and from yet another whose father is a soldier or his brother, a gunner, five *qerans*?[34] Reforming this does not require money or a person with divine planning. Until when will there be nothing like a book of teachings and instructions in the hands of the oppressive governors regarding their behavior towards subjects and the taking of taxes? Until when will you not respect the well-being of these valuable trusts of God called subjects? Having left them to the whims of inhumane governors, you will have no choice but to follow the ignoble will of these vile people. Is the three thousand year-old state of Iran not capable of setting up a health department in each of its big cities, and appointing three or four physicians in those places to save the people there from the impending death which is the result of the ignorance of physicians? Why isn't there a hospital to treat leprosy which is easily treated in its early stages so that a traveler, upon entering a city, is not assailed by a group of these unfortunate people whose lips and noses have fallen off, and their eyes and mouths have become distorted as a result of this filthy illness? They extend a begging hand to people [both] familiar and foreign, and live like wild animals in the desert, are deprived of a home,

---

34. There are ten *qerans* in one tuman.

and hated in the eyes of their families. I swear to God that for a patriotic man of honor, death is easier and preferable to seeing the condition of those unfortunate people. I saw them once, and my heart is still racing . . . are these not the sons of your homeland and your brothers in religion? What troubles others undergo and what money they spend to protect the life of one of the sons of the homeland . . . ! Reforming such things which in the eyes of outsiders are cause for shame for the government and the nation and the reason for a thousand kinds of reprimands from both people familiar and foreign, does not require huge amounts of money that the state and nation would be unable to provide. I swear on the oneness of God that it is possible to get the funds [needed] for reforming such deficiencies. . . . How is it that it is possible to extract bribes and fines from poor subjects on the basis of which the descendants and relatives of a jurist who himself, with the mediation of several people within the government, only received sixty tumans a year in return for preaching, now owns two and a half million in wealth, twenty or thirty years later? But it is not possible to have recourse to public assistance in order to remove the flaws of the homeland, and to advance the sacred cause? All that is needed in this matter is good will, planning, honesty, and lack of greed. In the case where the nation considers itself at one with the state, and the state, at one with the nation, and realizes that these two are inseparable and are only two in words, but in reality are one, then all the hard tasks can be taken care of. . . . All difficulties can be overcome with the assistance of justice and equality. In the course of this trip where I have seen a small part of the domains of Iran, my heart bled. Everywhere, the country is in distress; the people are distressed; commerce is in distress; the minds are distressed; ideas are distressed; the city is distressed and the king is distressed. Dear God, what distress is this! I am amazed that with all this distress, what need there is for this number of ministers! In fact, what I wanted to ask you is, what is the cause of all this distress?"

3

Constitution and Constitutionalism: Debates and Developments

The Decree Granting a Constitutional Government in 1906

In August 1906, Mozaffar al-Din Shah Qajar issued a royal decree granting permission for the establishment of a National Consultative Assembly or Majles. *This came in response to more than a year of protests and strikes by a broad coalition of individuals and groups, who were calling for, among other things, an end to arbitrary rule and injustice and the establishment of the rule of law. The passage below is an excerpt from Ahmad Kasravi's classic study,* The History of the Iranian Constitution. *What makes it of particular interest is that while it includes the actual text of the Shah's decree granting a Constitutional Government in 1906, it also points to a fact that is often overlooked, namely, that the decree had to be revised by the Shah because of objections that the original version had made little or no mention of the people or nation* (mellat), *and that some sentences were not clear enough.*

Text: *The History of the Iranian Constitution*[1]

"To His Honorable Excellency, the Prime Minister,

Since God Almighty, Exalted be His power, has entrusted the progress and prosperity of the Guarded Domains of Iran[2] to our competent hands, and has placed our royal person as the protector of the rights of all the inhabitants of Iran and our loyal subjects, at this time, for the sake of the prosperity and security of all the inhabitants of Iran, and the strengthening and support of the foundations of state, our royal will has become intent on the gradual implementation of the necessary reforms in the national and governmental sectors. We have decided that a National Consultative Assembly be established. It is to be composed of representatives from among princes, `ulama, Qajars, dignitaries (a`yan), nobility (ashraf), landowners (mallakin), merchants, and guilds (asnaf), through elections by the afore-mentioned estates in Tehran, in order to carry out the necessary consultation and care, and give the required assistance and help to our loyal Council of Ministers in the reforms that are to take place for the prosperity and happiness of Iran. It shall also state its views regarding the good of the state and people of Iran, and the general interest and the needs of the entire population in complete confidence and security through the Prime Minister so that they can be endorsed by royal approval and be put into effect.

It is clear that as a result of this blessed decree, the regulations together with the arrangements and requirements for the establishment of this Assembly will be ready from this date in accordance with the ratification and signature of the delegates, also approved by the king. Thus, with the help of God Almighty, the afore-mentioned National Assembly, the guardian of our justice, is inaugurated and will begin the necessary reforms of the affairs of the country and implement the blessed laws of *Shari`a*. We hereby instruct that you proclaim and publish a draft of this blessed decree so that all the inhabitants become informed of our good intentions which are entirely about the progress of the state and the nation, and continue to pray for the persistence of this state and this everlasting blessing, with peace of mind.

In Sahebqaraniyeh Palace, dated 14 Jumada II 1324/ [5 August 1906], in the eleventh year of our reign"

1. Ahmad Kasravi, *Tarikh-e mashruteh-ye Iran*. Tehran: Amir Kabir, 1340/ 1961, pp. 119-120. A translation by Evan Siegel of the decree granting the constitution is available. However, the passage above is my own translation from the original.

2. *Mamalek-e mahruseh-ye Iran* or the "Guarded Domains of Iran" was the way Iran had been referred to since the Safavid times (1501-1722).

The fourteenth of Jumada II 1324/ [5 August 1906], when this decree was issued, was the birthday of the Shah. In the name of their love and support for the shah, those taking sanctuary in the embassy[3] took part in the celebration, decorating the gate of the embassy with many "Lion and Sun" flags and splendid lights. Women, too, participated in these celebrations. However, when the decree of the Constitution was printed and posted on the walls, the activists did not like it for they did not see it as compatible with their demands. They sent people to tear down the printed flyers from the walls. This was because there had been no mention of the people [*mellat*] and also, the sentences used were not clear.

In this way, nothing came of the decree. It was therefore decided that on the night of the sixteenth of Mordad (17 Jumada II)/ [8 August 1906], a meeting be held by the leaders of the activists in Moshir al-Dawleh's[4] house in Qolhak in order for discussions to take place. It was as a result of that meeting that the shah once again issued the following decree:

> "To His Honorable Excellency, the Prime Minister
>
> In completing our previous decree dated fourteenth Jumada II 1324/ [5 August 1906] where we had clearly announced the establishment of an Assembly of the deputies of the people [*mellat*], and in order to make the general public and members of the nation [*mellat*] aware of our complete royal attention, we hereby command and confirm that the afore-mentioned Assembly will be established as described clearly in the previous decree. After electing the members of the Assembly, the articles and conditions for the regulation of the Islamic Consultative Assembly should be arranged according to the ratification and the signature of the elected deputies in a way that is deserving of the people [*mellat*], the country, and the holy laws of *Shari`a* so that it can be presented and receive our royal signature, and thus this sacred aim be put into effect according to the afore-mentioned by-laws."

The people accepted this and began to celebrate.

---

3. This is a reference to the British legation in Tehran, where within three weeks more than 14,000 people had gathered and taken sanctuary in an attempt to put pressure on the Shah to grant their demands.

4. Mirza Nasrollah Khan Moshir al-Dawleh had been appointed Prime Minister on August 1, 1906. He thus became the first Prime Minister of Iran in the constitutional era, an office that he held until March 17, 1907.

The 1906 Constitution (Fundamental Laws) and Its Supplement

The Iranian constitution consisted of two documents: the Fundamental Laws, which comprised 51 articles and were ratified by Mozaffar al-Din Shah on December 30, 1906, five days before his passing; and the Supplementary Fundamental Laws, which consisted of 107 articles, ratified by Mohammad `Ali Shah a few days before his passing, on October 7, 1907. The passages below include the full text of the Fundamental Laws and sections from the Supplementary Fundamental Laws. As the passages make clear, what distinguished one from the other was that the Fundamental Laws served the purpose of laying the groundwork and rules of procedure of a parliamentary system, and the Supplementary Fundamental Laws consisted of the actual laws. The latter included innovative and controversial components, such as defining the rights of the people and the separation of the three powers: the Executive, the Judiciary, and the Legislative.

1. The Fundamental Laws of December 30, 1906[5]

In the Name of God, the Compassionate, the Merciful

Whereas according to the Imperial decree, dated fourteenth Jumada II 1324 [August 5, 1906], we gave the order to establish a National Assembly, in the interest of the progress and prosperity of the kingdom and the nation, the strengthening of the foundation of the government, and the implementation of the laws of His Holiness the Prophet,

Whereas according to the fundamental principle that each one of the people of this realm is entitled to partake in the approval and supervision of the affairs of all, we have conferred the selection and appointment of the members of the *Majles* to the people,

Now that the National Assembly has been inaugurated according to our sacred wishes, the principles and articles of the fundamental laws regulating the National Assembly which consist of the duties and responsibilities of

---

5. The original text of the Fundamental Laws was published in *Tarbiyat* newspaper, and the translation here is based on this version: *Tarbiyat*, no. 427, 25 Zi al-Qa`dah 1324/ 10 January 1907, pp. 2330-2334. The only complete English translation available is that of E. G. Browne, which appeared in the appendices of *The Persian Revolution, 1905-1909*, originally published in 1910. I have tried to translate the text into more contemporary English.

the afore-mentioned *Majles*, and the limits and confines of its relations vis-à-vis the offices of the government are mentioned below:

On the Establishment of the Assembly

Art. 1. The National Consultative Assembly is founded and established according to the decree, founded on justice, dated fourteenth Jumada II 1324/ [August 5, 1906].

Art. 2. The National Consultative Assembly is the representative of all the people of Iran who participate in the economic and political affairs of their country.

Art. 3. The National Consultative Assembly is composed of members, elected in Tehran and the provinces, and is convened in Tehran.

Art. 4. The number of the elected members for Tehran and the provinces, has, for the time being, been determined at one hundred and sixty-two, according to the Electoral Law which has been drawn separately. However, were there to be the need, the number could be increased to two hundred.

Art. 5. The Members will be elected for two full years. This period shall begin on the day that all the representatives of the provinces would have arrived in Tehran. At the end of the two years, the representatives must be elected again, and the people have the option to re-elect any of the former representatives that they are happy with.

Art. 6. The representatives of Tehran have the right to convene the Assembly and begin their discussions and deliberations as soon as they meet. During the absence of the representatives of the provinces,[6] their decisions can be validated and put into effect based on the majority obtained.

Art. 7. At the opening of the discussions, a quorum of at least two thirds of the members of the assembly must be present, and at the time of voting, at least three quarters of the members must be present. A majority can be obtained when more than half of the members present in the Assembly record their votes.

Art. 8. According to the internal regulations of the Assembly, the periods of the session and recess of the National Consultative Assembly will be determined by the Assembly itself. Following the summer recess, the

---

6. What is meant here is that, before the arrival of the representatives of the provinces to Tehran, the representatives of Tehran have the right not only to convene the Assembly but also to vote.

Assembly must be open and in session from fourteenth of *Mizan*[7] [October 7], which corresponds to the anniversary of the opening of the First Assembly.

Art. 9. The National Consultative Assembly can be convened exceptionally during public holidays.

Art. 10. On the opening of the Assembly, an address will be made to His Majesty. It will have the honor of receiving an answer from His Royal Highness.

Art. 11. The Members of the Assembly, upon taking their seats, must take the following oath and sign it:

> The Statement of Oath:
> "We, the undersigned, take God to witness and swear on the Qur'an that as long as the rights of the Assembly and its members are preserved and observed, according to this Constitution, we will carry out the duties that have been confided to us, so far as is possible, with utmost truth and honesty, diligence and hard work; that we will be truthful and faithful towards our just and honored king, commit no treason with regard to the foundations of the Monarchy and the rights of the people, that we will have no aim other than what is to the advantage and interest of the government and people of Iran."

Art. 12. In no way, shape or form can anyone, without the knowledge and approval of the National Consultative Assembly, harass its members. In the event of a member committing a crime or misconduct openly, and being arrested in the act of committing the crime, the punishment applied must be with the knowledge of the Assembly.

Art. 13. The discussions of the National Consultative Assembly, in order for their results to be put into effect promptly, should be public. According to the Internal Regulations of the Assembly, journalists and spectators have the right to be present and listen without being able to speak. The newspapers can publish all the deliberations of the Assembly, without distorting or changing the meaning so that the general people can become informed of the subjects of discussion and the details of the reports. Anyone, out of good will, can write in the public press so that no matter remains shrouded

---

7. In late Qajar Iran, the names of the signs of the zodiac were often used to refer to the months of the solar calendar. *Mizan* or Libra was thus a reference to the seventh month of the solar calendar, which was later replaced by *Mehr*.

and hidden. To this end, all newspapers, as long as their contents do not transgress any of the fundamental principles of the government or nation, are authorized and free to print and publish all matters that are useful and advantageous to the public such as the deliberations of the Assembly and the views of the people regarding these deliberations. If anyone publishes anything in the newspapers and the press out of personal motives, contrary to what has been said, or slanders and makes accusations, he will be subject to interrogation, prosecution, and punishment according to the law.

Art. 14. The National Assembly will organize its own affairs in matters such as the election of a President, Vice-Presidents, secretaries and other officers as well as the arrangement of the deliberations and divisions, according to the a separate set of Regulations called "The Internal Regulations."

On the Duties of the Assembly, Its Limitations and Rights

Art. 15. The National Consultative Assembly has the right to advise the government through the person of the Prime Minister on what it considers to be in the interest of the country and the nation, after deliberations and careful consideration have been made in all truthfulness and honesty, and with the backing of a majority vote, and with utmost security and confidence, having had it ratified by the Senate, so that it can be signed by His Majesty and put into effect promptly.

Art. 16. All laws that are necessary for regulating the affairs of the government and the country, as well as the strengthening of the foundations of the government and monarchy and the establishment of the ministries, are subject to the approval of the National Consultative Assembly.

Art. 17. The National Consultative Assembly, when necessary, shall put forth the measures needed for the creation, modification, completion or abrogation of any laws, and subject to the approval of the Senate, will submit it for Royal endorsement, and put it into effect promptly.

Art. 18. The regulation of financial matters, the adjustment of the budget, modification in the imposition of taxes, and the acceptance and rejection of charges and minor expenditure such as new auditing, carried out by the government, is subject to the approval of the Assembly.

Art. 19. The Assembly reserves the right, following the approval of the Senate, to ask the Ministers of State that they put into effect the measures that have been ratified with regard to the reform of fiscal matters, and the facilitation of relations between the different departments of the government in dividing the provinces and departments, and defining the limits of their governments.

Art. 20. The budget for each of the ministries must be determined in the second half of each year for the following year, and shall be ready fifteen days before the celebration of Nawruz.

Art. 21. Whenever a new law, or the modification or abrogation of a law becomes necessary in the fundamental laws regulating a ministry, such changes will be made with the approval of the Assembly, regardless of whether the need for such action has been stated by the Assembly or the responsible ministers.

Art. 22. Instances such as the transfer or the sale of a portion of the revenues or the resources of the country, or the need to introduce any change in the borders and frontiers of the country, will be subject to the approval of the Assembly.

Art. 23. Without the approval of the National Assembly, no concession will be granted by the State for the foundation of a public company, of any kind or under any pretext.

Art. 24. The conclusion of treaties and covenants as well as the granting of commercial, industrial, agricultural and other concessions, whether they be to someone within the country or to a foreign subject, must be subject to the approval of the National Consultative Assembly. Exceptions are made for treaties which in the interest of the state and the people are kept secret.

Art. 25. State loans, under whatever pretext, whether internal or external, will be contracted with the knowledge and approval of the National Consultative Assembly.

Art. 26. The construction of railroads or roadways, whether at the cost of the state or a private company, from within the country or a foreign country, will have to be subject to the approval of the National Consultative Assembly.

Art. 27. Wherever the Assembly detects any breach in the laws, or any negligence in their implementation, it will summon the minister responsible in that department, and the said-minister will have to give the necessary explanations.

Art. 28. Whenever a Minister, erroneously, issues written or verbal orders on behalf of His Royal Highness that are contrary to the laws which have been enacted and have received the Royal endorsement, and acknowledges his lack of attention and care as reason, according to the law, he will be personally accountable to His Imperial Majesty.

Art. 29. Should a Minister fail to give an adequate account of a matter according to the laws that have received the Royal endorsement, and should it become clear that he has violated the law and committed a transgression, the Assembly will request his dismissal from His Royal Presence, and once his treason has become clearly established in the Court of Justice, he will never again be appointed to government service.

Art. 30. The National Consultative Assembly has the right, whenever it deems necessary, to present a petition to His Imperial Majesty by means of a Committee consisting of the President and six of its members elected by the Six Estates. The time for an audience [with the king] must be arranged through the Minister of Court, and with the permission of the Royal Presence.

Art. 31. Ministers have the right to be present at the sessions of the National Consultative Assembly, to sit in the places assigned to them and to listen to the deliberations. Should they consider it necessary, they can ask the President of the Assembly for permission to speak, and may give explanations that are necessary for purposes of discussion and consideration.

On Making Statements to the National Consultative Assembly

Art. 32. Anyone from among the people can submit a statement in writing of his personal circumstances or criticisms or grievances to the office of Petitions at the Assembly. If the matter concerns the Assembly itself, it will give him a satisfactory answer. If the matter regards one of the ministries, it will refer the petition to that ministry so that the matter can be attended to and a satisfactory response made.

Art. 33. New laws which are needed shall be drafted and revised in the Ministries, and will then be presented to the National Assembly either by the Minister responsible or by the Prime Minister. After receiving approval by the Assembly, it will be ratified by the Royal signature and put into effect promptly.

Art. 34. The President of the Assembly can, in case of necessity, either in person or at the request of ten members of the Assembly, hold a private meeting with a minister, without the presence of journalists and spectators, or he can convene a private committee made up of a selected number of members of the Assembly, to which the remaining members of the Assembly won't have the right to be present. The result of the deliberations of the private meeting can be disclosed only when the matter has been discussed in the Assembly in the presence of three quarters of the members, and carried by a majority vote. Should the matter in question not be accepted in the private meeting, it will not be discussed in the Assembly and shall be passed over in silence.

Art. 35. If the private meeting has been at the request of the President of the Assembly, he has the authority to make public however much of the deliberations he deems appropriate. However, in the event of the private meeting having been convened at the request of a Minister, the disclosure of the deliberations depends on the permission of that Minister.

Art. 36. Any Minister can withdraw any matter which he has proposed to the Assembly at any point in the discussion unless his statement has been made at the request of the Assembly. In this case, withdrawing the matter depends on the consent of the Assembly.

Art. 37. Whenever a bill introduced by a Minister has not been accepted by the Assembly, it will be returned with an addendum containing the observations of the Assembly. The responsible Minister, after accepting or rejecting the objections of the Assembly, can propose the said bill for a second time to the Assembly.

Art. 38. Members of the National Consultative Assembly have to state their rejection or acceptance of measures clearly and distinctly, and no one has the right to pressure or threaten them in giving their votes. The statement of the rejection or acceptance of the Members of the Assembly has to be in such a way that journalists and spectators, too, will be able to see, in that their statement should be made with outward signs such as blue and white voting-papers or the like.

Proposing Measures on the Part of the Assembly

Art. 39. Whenever a measure is proposed by one of the members of the Assembly, it can only be discussed when at least fifteen members of the Assembly have approved the discussion of that measure. In such a case, the proposal in question will be submitted in writing to the President of the

Assembly, who has the right to have it discussed first in a Committee of Investigation.

Art. 40. On the occasion of the discussion and consideration of the bill mentioned in Art. 39, whether in the Assembly or in the Committee of Investigation, if the bill concerns one of the Ministers, the Assembly should inform the relevant Minister and ask that he or his deputy be present in the Assembly at the time of the discussions. With the exception of matters that require urgent action, the draft of the bill with its additions must be sent in advance, from ten days to a month before, to the relevant Minister. Furthermore, the day when the matter is to be discussed should be made clear in advance. After the consideration of the matter in the presence of the responsible Minister, in the event of the Assembly approving it by a majority vote, the bill will be given to the responsible minister in writing, so that he may take the necessary measures.

Art. 41. Should a minister not agree with a measure proposed by the Assembly, he must explain his reasons and persuade the Assembly.

Art. 42. Should the National Consultative Assembly want explanations on any matter from the responsible Minister, the Minister in question must give answers, and this answer must not be delayed unnecessarily or without reason, except with regard to secret matters, where confidentiality for a certain amount of time may be in the interest of the state and the people. However, after the end of specific period of time, the responsible Minister is required to make a statement regarding the matter in the Assembly.

On the Conditions for the Establishment of the Senate

Art. 43. Another Assembly called the Senate, made up of sixty members, will be established and its sessions will complement the sessions of the National Consultative Assembly.

Art. 44. The regulations of the Senate must be approved by the National Consultative Assembly.

Art. 45. The members of this Assembly will be chosen from amongst the well-informed, discerning, pious, and respected people of this country. Thirty members will be appointed by His Imperial Majesty (fifteen from Tehran, and fifteen from the provinces), and thirty members by the people (fifteen elected by the residents of Tehran, and fifteen by the residents of the provinces).

Art. 46. After the convening of the Senate, all matters must be approved by both Assemblies. If the proposals have been put forth by the Senate or by the cabinet, first, it must be examined and amended in the Senate, and accepted by a majority vote, and then it must be approved by the National Consultative Assembly. However, the matters that have been put forth by the National Consultative Assembly will have to take an opposite course, and go from this Assembly to the Senate. The exception is for financial matters which are exclusive to the National Consultative Assembly. The standpoint of the Assembly in regard to the above-mentioned proposals will be communicated to the Senate so that it may in turn convey its observations to the National Consultative Assembly. However, the National Assembly is free to accept or reject the observations of the Senate, after necessary discussions.

Art. 47. So long as the Senate has not been convened, measures will be put into effect only after they have been approved by the National Consultative Assembly, and have received the Royal endorsement and signature.

Art. 48. If a matter, after having been examined and amended in the Senate, is referred to the National Consultative Assembly by a Minister, and is not accepted, in the event of it being important, a third Assembly made up of the members of the Senate and the National Consultative Assembly, elected in equal numbers by members of the two Assemblies will convene to address the disputed matter. The result of the vote of this [third] Assembly will be read in the National Consultative Assembly. If it is then accepted, all well and good; if not, an account of the matter will be given to the His Royal Highness, and if the king supports the view of the National Consultative Assembly, then it will be put into effect. If not, orders will be issued for fresh discussion and consideration. If once again, no consensus is reached, and the Senate votes by a majority of two thirds, to approve the dissolution of the National Consultative Assembly, and the cabinet of Ministers, too, support the dissolution of the National Consultative Assembly separately, the Royal decree will be issued for the dissolution of the National Consultative Assembly, and at the same time, His Imperial Majesty will order the holding of fresh elections, and the people will have the right to re-elect the former representatives.

Art. 49. The new representatives of Tehran must present themselves within one month, and the representatives of the provinces within three months. Once the representatives of the capital arrive, the Assembly will

open and begin to work. However, they will not deliberate disputed proposals until the representatives of the provinces have arrived. If after the
arrival of all its members, the [new] Assembly reaches the same decision
with majority vote, His Imperial Majesty will approve the decision of the
National Consultative Assembly and will order it to be put into effect.

Art. 50. In each electoral period which consists of two years, orders for
the renewal of representatives will not be given more than once.

Art. 51. It is agreed that our successors and future kings should consider
the preservation of these laws and principles that we have established and
put into effect in order to strengthen the foundations of the state, consolidate
the bedrocks of the throne, and supervise the machinery of justice, and the
tranquility of the Nation, as the duty of their own rule. (Zi al-Qa`da 1324/
December 30, 1906)

At the bottom of this constitution, in the handwriting of His Imperial
Majesty, may his rule last long, the following words have been written:

These Fundamental Laws of the National Consultative Assembly and
the Senate, containing fifty-one Articles are correct.

On the back of this page are the seals of the Crown Prince and the Prime
Minister.

2. The Supplementary Fundamental Laws of October 7, 1907[8]

General Points

Art. 1. The official religion of Iran is Islam of the Twelver Ja`fari school,
which the king of Iran must profess and promote.

Art. 2. At no time must any laws passed by the Sacred National Consultative Assembly which has been founded as a result of the attention and
approval of the Imam of the Age (may God hasten his Advent!), and the
favor of His Majesty the king of kings of Iran (may God immortalize his
rule!), and the care of the hojjaj al-islam[9] (may God multiply the likes of
them!) be incompatible with the holy principles of Islam and the laws established by His Holiness the Best of Mankind. It is clear that determining
[whether such laws as are proposed] are in opposition to the laws of Islam

8. The original Persian text is available on fis-iran/org/fa/resources/legaldoc/iranconstitution.

9. Hojjat al-islam (pl. hojjaj al-islam) (literally Proof of Islam) is a rank among the Shi'i clerical
hierarchy, usually a step below that of *Ayatollah*.

has always been the task of the distinguished *ulama*, may God prolong the blessing of their existence! It is, therefore, ruled that in each era, a Committee [be elected] consisting of no fewer than five people, from among the pious scholars and jurisprudents, who are also aware of the needs of their time in this way. The *ulama* and the hojjaj al-islam . . . shall present to the National Consultative Assembly the names of twenty *ulama* who satisfy the afore-mentioned qualities. The members of the National Consultative Assembly shall then choose five or more of them, either by unanimous decision, or by means of a vote, according to the needs of the age, and recognize them as members [of the Committee], so that they can consider and investigate in depth the matters that are discussed in both Assemblies, and reject whichever proposal that may be in conflict with the sacred laws of Islam, such that it does not take the title of legality. The opinion of this Committee of *ulama* in such matters will be followed. This article shall remain in place and unchanged until the appearance of His Holiness the Proof of the Age (may God hasten his advent!)

Art. 3. The borders of Iran, its provinces, departments and districts cannot be changed except in accordance with the Law.

Art. 4. The capital of Iran is Tehran.

Art. 5. The official colors of the Persian flag are green, white and red, with the emblem of the Lion and the Sun.

Art. 6. The lives and property of foreign subjects resident in Iran are guaranteed and protected except in cases when the laws of the land make exemptions.

Art. 7. The principles of the Constitution cannot be suspended, either as a whole or in part.

Rights of the Iranian Nation

Art. 8. The people of Iran are to enjoy equal rights before the Law.

Art. 9. All individuals are protected and secure from every kind of aggression with respect to their lives, property, homes and honor, and none can harass them except in such cases and in such ways that the laws of the land shall determine.

Art. 10. No one can be summarily arrested except in the act of committing a misdemeanor and crime and in cases of major offenses save on the written authority of the President of the Tribunal of Justice and according to the law. In such cases, the accused must, immediately or at the latest, in the course of the next twenty-four hours, be informed of the nature of his offence.

Art. 11. No one can be removed from one tribunal which is to give judgment on his case and forcibly sent to another tribunal.

Art. 12. No punishment can be decreed or implemented except in accordance with the Law.

Art. 13. Every person's house and abode is protected and safeguarded. No dwelling can be entered by force except in such cases and such ways that the Law has decreed.

Art. 14. No Iranian can be exiled from the country or prevented from residing in a [particular] location or forced to live in a specific location except in cases where the Law stipulates clearly.

Art. 15. No property can be removed from the possession of its owner except by legal sanction, and [in such a case, only] after its value has been determined and paid in fairness.

Art. 16. The confiscation of the property or possessions of people in the name of punishment and retribution is forbidden except in conformity with the Law.

Art. 17. Depriving owners or possessors of control over their property or possessions under any pretext whatsoever, is forbidden, except in conformity with the Law.

Art. 18. The acquisition and study of the sciences, arts, and crafts is free except for that which may be forbidden by Islamic law.

Art. 19. The establishment of schools paid for by the government and the people as well as compulsory education must be regulated according to the laws of the Ministry of the Sciences and the Arts, and all schools and colleges must be under the ultimate management and supervision of the Ministry of the Sciences and the Arts.

Art. 20. All publications, except for heretical books and matters harmful to the true religion [of Islam] are free, and are exempt from censorship. However, if anything contrary to the Press Laws[10] is perceived in them, the publisher or the author will be liable to punishment according to the Press Laws. If the writer is known and resident in Iran, the publisher, printer and distributor will be exempt from prosecution.

10. The Press Laws were passed on February 8, 1908, for the purpose of defining the boundaries of what could and could not be published.

Art. 21. Societies and Associations that do not lead to religious or worldly mischief, and are not injurious to good order, are free throughout the country. However, members of such associations should not carry arms, and they should follow the regulations determined by the law on this matter. Gatherings in public streets and open spaces must similarly follow police regulations.

Art. 22. All postal correspondence is safeguarded and exempt from seizure or inspection except in cases excluded by the law.

Art. 23. It is forbidden to divulge or to confiscate telegraphic communication without the permission of the owner except in cases determined by the law.

Art. 24. Foreign nationals may become naturalized as Iranian nationals. Their acceptance and continuance, or their surrender of the nationality is in accordance with a separate law.

Art. 25. No authorization is needed in order to proceed against government officials in matters relating to shortcomings connected to their public functions, except in the case of ministers in which case special laws must be observed.

Powers of the Realm

Art. 26. The powers of the realm are derived from the people. The Fundamental Laws determine the way in which those powers are used.

Art. 27. The powers of the realm are divided into three branches:

First: the legislative power which is concerned with the making and the refinement of laws. This power comes from His Imperial Majesty, the National Consultative Assembly and the Senate. Each of these three sources has the right to introduce laws. However, these laws can only be established on the condition that they not be incompatible with the standards of the *Shari`a*, and that they be approved by the two Assemblies and the Royal ratification. The legislating and approval of laws regarding the revenue and expenditure of the kingdom are the specific duty of the National Consultative Assembly. The explanation and interpretation of laws are among the special duties of the National Consultative Assembly.

Second: The judicial power which consists of the distinction between laws. This power is specific to the *Shar`i* courts in matters connected to *Shari`a*, and to civil courts in matters relating to civil law.

Third: The executive power which is specific to the king. That is, laws will be implemented by the ministers and state officials in the name of His Imperial Majesty in a way that is determined by the law.

Art. 28. The three powers mentioned-above will always be distinct and separate from each other.

Newspapers, Freedom of the Press, and Censorship

The granting of the constitution in summer 1906 was followed by an atmosphere of hope and possibility, in which matters were considered public and open to debate. It was therefore no accident that in the year that followed the constitution, newspapers proliferated. There were dailies, weeklies, editorial newspapers, and satirical newspapers, as well as newspapers that were written in colloquial Persian—all because there was a belief among reformists that newspapers played an essential role in effecting political and social change. The passages below, selected from the constitutional press published in Tehran in 1907, provide different perspectives on the mood at this time. The first is a discussion of the power of the press and the role that newspapers were thought to be able to play in society; the second is an illustration of how newspapers, by explaining new political concepts in a humorous and accessible way, saw their role as involving ordinary people in the experience of constitutionalism; and finally the third represents a reminder that this optimism was short-lived, for, contrary to expectations, the censorship that constitutionalists had hoped the new era would abolish for the most part remained in place.

1. "Two or Three Sensible Words on the Responsibility of Journalists and the Press," *Neda-ye Vatan*, August 25, 1907[11]

In every country, newspapers are established in order to make people more vigilant, remove the flaws of governmental departments, refine the morals of the people of the nation, and spread civilization and education. Newspapers are the whistle-blowers and secret agents working specifically for [the good of] society. Thus whenever someone acts against the common

---

11. *Neda-ye Vatan*, vol. 1, no. 53, 14 Rajab 1325/ 25 August 1907, pp. 3-4.

interest, newspapers can humiliate them in the public forum so that others will not pursue their destructive measures which are harmful to society.

Newspapers scrutinize the flaws of every government office, and explain the way to reform so that well-wishers and reformers can become aware of how to reform the shortcomings and remove the failings.

The celebrated [George] Washington would begin by saying that newspapers have to be published free of censorship so that they can uncover the deficiencies of every government office. Bismarck used to say, "If I were to be forced to choose between closing down Parliament and newspapers, I would of course be happier to close down Parliament and would not allow the closure of newspapers." The first measure that the late Amir Kabir, the Atabak-e A`zam[12] took in Iran was to set up a newspaper called *Iran*. He wrote the first, second and third issues, himself, and appointed scholars for that important service. Today, those newspapers that were published during his tenure are extant and available in the possession of some individuals. They show a measure of the superior thinking of the late Amir Kabir. Since in the past, people had not heard the name "newspaper" and were not aware of its effects, Amir Kabir enforced newspapers on the provinces, and imposed two or three issues on the villages through the village-headman so that gradually, people would get used to reading newspapers.

The first measure that the late Amin al-Dawleh[13] took during his tenure as Prime Minster was to enable *Tarbiyat* newspaper which was published as a weekly by the Honorable Mr. Zoka' al-Molk, to become a daily . . . and gave its respected publisher utmost freedom. He also worked hard towards increasing the number of newspapers, and allowed [the Calcutta] *Habl al-Matin* into the country. In short, any minister or prince, in any country, who resolved to reform that country, would first establish and circulate newspapers, and then found schools. An independent newspaper is more effective in protecting the nation than 500,000 troops.

In a booklet on the correct methods of running a country . . . the current Minister of Culture, the honorable Mokhber al-Saltaneh writes that it is necessary for the king to be informed of the circumstances of the people

12. Mirza Taqi Khan Farahani, also known as Amir Kabir and Atabak-e A`zam, was Prime Minister under Naser al-Din Shah between 1848 and 1851. He was a reformer, and among the measures that he took during his short tenure as Chief Minister was the founding of the first official gazette of the country, entitled *Vaqaye`e Ettefaqiyeh*. Years later, its name changed to *Iran*.

13. Mirza `Ali Khan Amin al-Dawleh was Prime Minister under Mozaffar al-Din Shah between 1897 and 1899.

of the nation, and to make use of the views of the scholars of the country. However since the king is only one person, no matter how vigilant or how much he devotes himself to hearing the news of the surroundings and getting informed about different parts of the country, he will still not become acquainted with a thousand and one matters. It is for this reason that the sages of the world have taken an important step and founded independent newspapers that can be the voice of the nations, and sources on governments. [Newspapers] present the views of all the scholars to His Imperial Majesty, reveal to the just king the grievances of the members of the nation from the smallest provinces and least-known villages, and uncover the behavior of the governors and ministers alongside the lowliest of the subjects. In short, the advantages of newspapers are so many that we cannot list them all in these pages.

It was the Egyptian newspapers that persuaded the Egyptian nation to reach an agreement with Urabi Pasha, made them think of protecting the independence of their country, and set them on expelling the British from Egypt. . . . *The Times* encouraged the British nation to conquer Transvaal. . . . *Qanun* newspaper published by Mirza Malkum Khan informed the Iranian nation of the term "*qanun*" [law], and made them aware of its advantages. The [Calcutta] *Habl al-Matin* demonstrated the corruption of the Court system to the people for several years, and made them think of [the need for] reform. *Adab* newspaper informed Iranians of the term "*mashruteh*" [constitutionalism]. . . . In short, whatever signs of progress there can be found in any part of the world, their starting point would have been newspapers.

This is why the first measure taken by the sages of the nation even before establishing a parliament, was the freedom of the press. The biggest pillar of Parliament is this principle. The first step is increasing the number of newspapers, and freedom of the pen, and the second step is the establishment of public schools and compulsory education, and after these two introductory steps, comes the establishment of the National Consultative Assembly which is the basis of the order of the country, the peace of mind of the nation and the prosperity of the country. There is no need for us to provide proof for this, since it is obvious that until such time that the people become informed about the way of progress, they will not think of useful measures, and until such time that ministers, deputies and other people of the nation fear newspapers that guarantee two issues, they will not behave in responsible ways. The first [of the two issues guaranteed by newspapers] is showing the paths to progress, and making use of the views of the thinkers on every subject, since no minister or deputy, no matter how wise, can be informed of all the necessary methods, and know the situation of the world. Second, if they don't fear that newspapers might uncover their shortcomings to the nation, then they won't be as bound by their duties....

2. "The Discussions of Molla Nasreddin with Shaikh Bohlul," *Neda-ye Vatan*, January 3, 1907[14]

Molla Nasreddin: Well, please, tell me, what is the meaning of these several words which the Europeanized (*farangi-ma'abha*) have recently spread among the people?

Bohlul: What should I start with?

Nasreddin: Well, as I said, tell me about constitutionalism (*mashruteh*).

Bohlul: Fine. The circle of humanity is in need of government.

Nasreddin: Buddy, that's not good enough! You were supposed not to use difficult language- what does the "circle of humanity" mean?

Bohlul: It means whenever humans get together in a place, one person has to become their ruler, leader, and their head of state, and the rest should obey his commands.

Nasreddin: And what will happen if they don't have one person as leader?

Bohlul: Inevitably, there will be disorder.

Nasreddin: Again, you are talking Arabic![15]

Bohlul: What I mean is that in the absence of a ruler or leader, wars, hatred, and grievances will come about, and peace of mind will disappear.

Nasreddin: I have something to say here. Will you let me say it, or will you be offended again?

---

14. *Neda-ye Vatan*, vol. 1, no. 2, 18 Zi al-Qa'dah 1324/ 3 January 1907, pp. 2-3. "The Discussions of Molla Nasreddin with Shaikh Bohlul" was the title of a series of columns that appeared in this weekly, which lasted for at least 47 issues. The choice of the two characters, namely Molla Nasreddin, a generally likeable, gullible, and naïve character, and Bohlul, an "archetypal wise fool" in Arabic, Persian, and Turkish literature, was one way this weekly made the discussion about constitutionalism not only more entertaining but also less abstract and therefore more accessible to a larger readership. See Negin Nabavi, "Spreading the Word: The First Constitutional Press and the Shaping of a New Era," *Critique: Critical Middle Eastern Studies*, vol. 14, no. 3, Fall 2005, pp. 307-321.

15. This is a Persian expression, a reference to someone speaking in a convoluted and incomprehensible way.

Bohlul: No, please, go ahead.

Nasreddin: Well, it is some time now that such and such a city has been without a ruler-in fact, it is almost a year that it has had no governor, and there has been no trouble there; neither a war nor a quarrel; everyone is at peace.

Bohlul: You are truly stupid, little fellow! The government that I speak of consists of the power to rule, and an organized administration, not the temporary governorship of provinces.

Nasreddin: First, I am not a little fellow. You, also, should understand what it is that you say. Secondly, you yourself say that in all the dictionaries, the word "government" has the same meaning. Where has this difference come from that I don't understand?

Bohlul: No, Your Excellency understands. You understand better than anyone else. Please let me go so that I can take care of my own affairs, and don't ask me any more questions.

Nasreddin: Please, for my sake, don't play hard to get, and answer properly! After all, our friendship goes back a long way. It should not be affected by such talk.

Bohlul: That's right. I am not offended, but why are you so dogged in wanting to know? How is any of this relevant to you?

Nasreddin: How wrong you are! It is of course relevant! These days, wherever I go, whatever gathering I enter, they talk about such things. I cannot sit still and say nothing. At the same time, I fear that I may say too much, and that rogues will make fun of me, and offend my dignity.

Bohlul: Then, don't go to any gatherings. What will happen then?

Nasreddin: You talk nonsense again! I have to go. Otherwise, I will not get to be part of any feast.

Bohlul: Why, are there feasts everywhere?

Nasreddin: Of course, I go wherever there is a wedding, or a funeral or a party. I don't waste my time going to any wretched person's place. So if you don't tell me, I won't be able to get to any feast.

Bohlul: Why do they speak of such things at weddings and funerals?

Nasreddin: May God bless your father! Are you foreign to this city? Nowadays, they talk of such things even in the bathhouse! So, please go ahead.

Bohlul: O.k. As I said, whenever a group of people gather in one place, inevitably they come in need of a government, meaning a cabinet and finally a monarch. The fact that they call the governors of provinces rulers is because they are representatives of the monarch and government. Otherwise, they have no authority of their own. In this way, their rule is of secondary importance and is beholden to the person of the monarch so that all their authority can be taken away from them and given to someone else with two words in a telegram. So if Shiraz or some other city were to be without a governor for ten years, it would still have a ruler, who is their actual ruler. At most, their functionary would change. . . .

Nasreddin: Very well, so what you are saying is that there is a government in Tehran, and that this must proceed at the command of the Shah and the Prime Minister.

Bohlul: Bravo! That's right; now you have understood.

Nasreddin: Well, if this is so, then why is it that the governors of provinces do not carry out the commands of Tehran properly?

Bohlul: This subject requires a separate explanation, for which I don't have time now. But perhaps, in the course of our conversation, it will become clear to you. Anyhow, there are three sorts of government in the whole world: independent, constitutional, and republican. Of these three, the best is the middle one. . . .

Nasreddin: I had wanted to understand the meaning of one term- now you mention two or three others! As women say, the problem has multiplied! Well, now then, explain the meaning of both.

Bohlul: There is no more time today. Let's continue our conversation tomorrow in Zargarabad coffeehouse.

Nasreddin: Fine, I accept. May your kindness increase! (goodbye!)

Bohlul: Prayers be with you! (goodbye!)

3. "Half an Hour at the Dar al-Fonun," *Sur-e Esrafil*, June 6, 1907[16]

In the first issue of the weekly *Sur-e Esrafil* . . . we put pen to paper with confidence and assurance and referred to the Office of Publications as an outdated and degenerate office. What we meant was that it was a dead office that had no external existence, since our country and government was now constitutional. So the press had to be free as it was in the rest of

---

16. *Sur-e Esrafil,* vol. 1, no. 2, June 6, 1907, pp. 7-8.

the constitutional states. [Similarly] the ominous word, "censorship," which means the inspection and surveillance of the press, together with other reviled terms which were souvenirs of the era of fear and terror had to be completely eradicated and wiped out from our country, so that later these words could only be found in history books, and history teachers would [have to] explain the meaning of these words in schools and colleges [*makateb*][17] for the benefit of our children and descendants when wanting to teach about the centuries before the constitutional era of the country. They would have to say, for example, that in the era of despotism, there were several offices like the Office of Publications which was a place that required anyone who wanted to publish a book or pamphlet, to abandon his work for several days, run here and there, go to the houses of the head of the Office of Publications, the deputy-head, the secretary, the copyist, and the janitor, give a thousand compliments, pay two *riyals*, and hand over two copies of the book so that the margins of the books could be signed and sealed.

Even though we had appealed to our publisher Esrafil to tell Ezra'il[18] to capture the soul of that demon with the steel fist of the fundamental laws,[19] it became clear that that Office of Publications still had some life, and made a point of being alive, for it had placed a complaint before the Ministry of Culture and Pious Foundations questioning the reason why the writer of the weekly *Sur-e Esrafil* had said that they accepted bribes.

Therefore, on Saturday, 19th [Rabi` I]/ [June 1, 1907], the Ministry of Culture and Pious Foundations summoned this author in writing to go to their office on Sunday, but the poor footman got lost in the city for a while, and did not find me. In the evening of that day, in the vicinity of the *majles*, I saw the footman asking this and that person who the writer of *Sur-e Esrafil* was. One person introduced me to him. I said, "Sir, did they not tell you where to take the envelope?" He replied, "No." I said, "But on the first page of the weekly *Sur-e Esrafil*, we had written the address for letters. Why did they put you to so much trouble?" I took the letter, and read what was written:

17. The word *makateb* (pl. of *maktab*) literally is a reference to traditional schools.
18. Ezra'il is the angel of death.
19. For the text of the Fundamental Laws, see "The 1906 Constitution (Fundamental Laws) and Its Supplement," above.

"The Ministry of Culture and Pious Foundations
The Office of the Press
No. 170
Dated 19 Rabi` II 1325/ [1 June 1907]

To Mirza Jahangir Khan, the manager of the newspaper *Sur-e Esrafil*, I have to trouble you to come to *Dar al-Fonun* school on the morning of Sunday, 20 [Rabi` II/ 2 June] for it is necessary to meet with you.
[Signed by] Mokhber al-Saltaneh"[20]

I went to the celebrated *Dar al-Fonun* school on Sunday, four hours before noon, and entered the small room assigned to the Ministry of Culture and Pious Foundations in the northern corner of the school. . . . A number of the Seyyeds from Qom were discussing the performance of the pious foundations in Qom. After a glance, the Minister of Culture began to talk to the author, as described below:

Q: Yesterday I went to the National Consultative Assembly, and spoke about *Sur-e Esrafil* newspaper. It was decided that you be reprimanded. But I tell you that from now on, you should abandon writing in this way.

A: At the time when you were talking in a private assembly, spirits from the other world told me the outline of the meeting. Nothing has been written for me to be reprimanded. Even if I get reprimanded, it will be an honor for me, since it would have all been for the sake of the peace and freedom of the nation, and for the good of the government. Our newspaper is historical. Important events of the world are written about there.

Q: I don't say that you should not write about historical events, but why do you write them in this way?

A: But I did not abandon the boundaries of civility. None of the constitutional countries address themselves to the "dust under the feet of their Emperor," whereas, we, for the sake of observing our respect to our own king, did not change our former views.

Q: I don't say that you should not address the king, but you should write in a gentle language.

A: As I said, nothing was written that was contrary to civility.

Q: What did you mean by mentioning these historical events?

A: What I meant was that perhaps someone, a loyal or personal servant, would let our crowned father know so that it can become clear to His Royal

---

20. Mehdi Qoli Hedayat, known as Mokhber al-Saltaneh, was the Minister of Culture.

Majesty that the nation has matured and come of age, and that whatever the treacherous sycophants say are all lies and have no basis. (In between our discussion, one of the sycophants who is present in all the ministries, said, "What business is it of yours, that you write such things?" I said, "I, too, am a member of the nation, and must write what I consider to be in the interest of the people and the state.") Although Your Excellency was not present at the National Consultative Assembly during those two days of general protest and excitement, most probably you must have heard how excited the crowd of thirty thousand people had been and what they were saying.

Q: His Imperial Majesty knows about all the events and developments and I, too, relay whatever I know to His Presence every day.

A: Your Excellency might tell His Imperial Majesty about the developments, but then, others, that is, the so-called devotees of government, or the self-sacrificing servants, who think of nothing other than duplicity and personal gain, deny all.

Q: Let's move on! What does *Charand Parand*[21] mean?

A: *Charand Parand* is the ethical section of *Sur-e Esrafil*.

Q: Can't ethics be written in a different manner?

A: Ethics have been written in specific ways. However, human nature is more inclined towards this kind of talk.

Q: It is up to you! The other issue concerns the article entitled "the responsibility of the pen."[22] Even though I have not read it carefully, I have heard what you have written there. I don't know in which column it has been published. (Then, he gave me the *Sur-e Esrafil* weekly, saying that I should find it.) I read him the column that he was talking about, where it said, "a huge frightening demon took hold of my arm, and said, give me my share of sweetmeats!"

Q: Why did you say that they wanted sweetmeats [a bribe]? Has anything [ever] been taken from you or the other newspaper managers?

A: Today, our country is constitutional. Why should people who want to publish books, have to give two *riyal*s in payment, together with two copies of their book to the Head of Publications? Books, too, are like news-

---

21. *Charand Parand* (translated as "Tittle-tattle") was the name of *Sur-e Esrafil's* regular and very popular satirical column by `Ali Akbar Dehkhoda.

22. This was the title of an article that was published in the first issue of *Sur-e Esrafil*. See *Sur-e Esrafil*, vol. 1, no. 1, 17 Rabi` II 1325/ 30 May 1907, pp. 4-5.

papers. There is no need for inspectors. Writers of books, like newspaper managers, will accept the same responsibilities.

Q: This payment of two *riyal*s together with the two copies of a book which people are to give is tantamount to a tax. After this, once the code of regulations of the Ministry of Education and Sciences is signed and put into effect, people will have to pay more than this.

A: What kind of taxation is this that it provides the daily bread of the Head of Publications? Don't you remember the night two or three months ago, when in the *Majles*, two thousand people protested in favor of the freedom of the press, and surrounded you at the bottom of the columns of the hallway [of the *majles*], and you reassured them? Other honorable deputies, too, reassured the people on behalf of the *majles*, and after two or three days, E'temad al-Saltaneh was removed from heading the Office of Publications, and the censorship of the press was stopped.

Q: The deputies said no such thing. Do you have anything in writing regarding this?

A: Ever since the establishment of the National Consultative Assembly until today, the people have protested and got excited repeatedly. Never has the *majles* produced a bill where something has been written on this subject. What I meant was why should this poor nation lose out and pay money that does not even make its way to the State Treasury, and instead goes towards paying 'Omar and Zayd?

Q: I don't listen to such talk. In the second issue of *Sur-e Esrafil* you must write an explanation regarding the word "sweetmeat," so that people don't think it means bribery. Otherwise, we will ban the newspaper. This is what I wanted to say. It is up to you.

A: Why should I consider this sum that the poor, long-suffering people pay to the Head of Publications for no reason whatsoever as tax? Whereas following the freedom of the press and the removal of E'temad al-Saltaneh, it was rumored that the Head of Publications had said to His Majesty that these two *riyal*s together with the two copies of books constitute the livelihood and daily bread of this [loyal] servant!

O honorable deputies of the nation! Are the government and country of Iran constitutional and in possession of a constitution or not? Does a constitution mean that the press should not be free? Was the fact that we wrote that they wanted "sweetmeat" [or a bribe] a lie and slander? Does the Head of Publications in Tabriz not take a sugarloaf and two copies of books in order to grant permission for the publication of books? Is sugar not sweet, or is it different from other sweet things?

O, you blessed members of the Finance Commission! On the divine sense of justice and on your own conscience and sense of honor, is this tax that the Head of the Publications extracts from this poor nation mentioned in the book of the expenditure of the country? Among the books of the state library, have you seen the list of those that have been published and have been taken from their authors? Since this is an issue of public concern that should be discussed in Parliament, we ask that you respond to the above questions in an open session in the presence of journalists so that it can be published in *Majles*[23] and other newspapers, and people can know where they stand.

Women "Going Public"

With the proliferation of newspapers that followed the promulgation of the constitution in 1906, women and women's issues gained more visibility in the pages of the newly emerging press. To begin with, an increasing number of letters were published in newspapers addressing the predicament of women. That many of these letters were published anonymously (or with signatures withheld) has led some scholars to doubt their authenticity, and speculate about whether they were in fact written by the editors of the newspapers themselves. Regardless of the actual authorship, however, the important point is that the plight of women was being aired publicly in the pages of newspapers. The three passages below provide examples of the different ways this was achieved. The first two letters, published in the constitutional press in 1907, not only object to patriarchy, the factor responsible for the challenges faced by women, in a blunt and forthright way, but also argue for girls' schooling and education—a theme that was much talked about and emphasized by women activists in the constitutional times—as a potential solution to this quandary. The final passage is the "Statement of Purpose" from Danesh, *the very first weekly published by a*

---

23. *Majles* was also the name of a newspaper that first appeared on November 25, 1906, soon after the opening of Parliament. Its aim was in part to publish the proceedings and debates that took place in this new legislative body.

*woman and addressed to a predominantly female readership in 1910. What
makes this of interest is its contrasting tone with the earlier letters; that is,
it presents girls' education in a very apolitical and non-threatening way,
arguing basically that better-educated girls make better mothers—an objective that no one should fear and everyone should be working towards.*

1. "The Letter of One of the Ladies," *Tamaddon*, April 30, 1907[24]

Friends, listen to my tale of distress
Listen to what I have to say and my bewilderment
Until when should one not talk about this heartrending tale?
Until when should one keep quiet about this pain?

I may be no more than a dim-witted and uneducated woman, but since
I am one of the sisters and friends of the nation, and feel some degree of
the passion and zeal of patriotism, I present to the fathers and brothers of
our nation a touch of the plight of us women, hoping that in the midst of
this, someone can be found to come to the relief of us, ill-fated lot.

First of all, our fathers whose daughters we were, used to send us to
maktabs[25] from the age of five—that did not even happen to all girls. Sometimes when we reached the age of nine, they would remove us from the
maktab. At that age, other than the love of play, we did not think of much
else, let alone our studies. Secondly, if we could read or write, our dear fathers would reproach us, take the book or the pen from our hands in extreme
anger, tear or break it up and throw it away, saying what does it mean that
a girl know how to write? Do you want to be a clerk? It is enough that you
know how to read the Qur'an. We, young children thought that things must
be this way.

Such was the story of us girls in our fathers' homes until they gave us
away in marriage. If we were among the elite, we would be assigned several
servants so that we wouldn't tire ourselves out working [at home], and give

---

24. *Tamaddon*, no. 12 (7 Rabi` I 1325/ 30 April 1907), pp. 3-4. Parts of this letter have been trans-
lated by Afsaneh Najmabadi, although the translation here is my own. See Afsaneh Najmabadi, "*Zanha-
yi millat*: Women or Wives of the Nation," *Iranian Studies*, vol. 26, nos. 1-2, Winter-Spring 1993,
pp. 65-66.

25. *Maktab* was a traditional school, typically taught by a low-ranking cleric or *akhund*. For a description of *a maktab* in late Qajar Iran, see chapter 1, "Schooling and the Role of *Akhunds* in Everyday
Life."

orders instead. If we were among the poor, then we would have to do nothing other than housework and childcare. If one night, our husband could not provide the little amount of bread for sustenance, we women did not have the ability to pay for the cost of the food for one night. We, Iranian women, did not know anything other than giving birth. And that was because you were our fathers, you brought us up in this way. Otherwise, we had intelligence, reason and understanding like other human beings. The only thing that was different about us was that we were women and you were men.

Now for what reason should those people who claim to be patriots and consider themselves to be among the devoted servants of the nation, talk ill of women from pulpits, in *Hosayniyeh*s,[26] and in public, saying that they are lazy, self-indulgent, and ignorant? These people are those same ones who did not let women progress. These people are those same ones who used to say that women should not leave the house. These people are those same ones who wasted all the intelligence, sensibility and strength of women. These people are those same ones who used to call women "the dim-witted weak sex." Finally, these people are those same ones who seeing the situation of the country change, go to *Hosayniyeh*s, and talk ill of women from pulpits, referring to them in vulgar and offensive terms, complaining about their laziness and self-indulgence while denying their own role in any of this.

These women who have such a bad name have always been a step ahead of men so that at the beginning of the [Constitutional] Revolution, it was women who covered their heads with mud following the murder of the martyred Seyyed 'Abd al-Majid,[27] prompting the men to take action out of a sense of honor, and leading to the revolution at large. It is these same women who are the protectors of the decrees of the National Assembly. Thus when the *Majles* decided to establish a national bank, it was women who sold their earrings and bracelets, whereas wealthy men who own much of the wealth of the country, put their money in foreign banks, and did not give any help or contribution in utmost mean-spiritedness.

---

26. A *Hosayniyeh* is a place where the ceremonies commemorating Husayn, the third Shi'i Imam, are held. However, they can also serve as locations for public sermons.

27. This is a reference to the killing of a young theology student in summer 1906 that had the effect of rallying a larger number of people to protest against the government, further enhancing the cause of the Constitutional Movement.

After all, we, too, are your compatriots. We, too, are your co-religionists. You who speak of the rights of the nation, you who speak of laws, you who claim to have a sense of honor and dignity, we, too, are part of this nation. We too have a share in these rights. Which school did you open for women that they withdrew from? Which field of learning and which skill was made available to women that they did not take advantage of? Don't women have rights in this country? Let us lament our misfortune since there is no one more unfortunate than us Iranian women. It is our fellow brothers and high-minded fathers who share our religion, that have made us into objects of mockery. They have made us women into a laughing-stock.

This is what you have done. This is a misfortune that you have created for your children. Don't say this is for the best.

I have a heart full of pain and sorrow

Don't you pour salt on my wound

If what you say is the truth, and you say all of this out of a sense of honor and dignity, and you believe that women are lazy and self-indulgent, then there is a very easy solution. Open a few schools, send your daughters there, let them study and learn a skill so that they don't become self-indulgent, illiterate, and uneducated like us. Then, we both will be able to hold our heads up high.

The signature has been withheld.[28]

2. "The Letter of One of the Ladies," *Habl al-Matin*, September 1, 1907[29]

To the respected manager of the honorable *Habl al-Matin* newspaper: Please be kind enough to include the letter below in the newspaper:

His Excellency, Hojjat al-Islam Mr. Shaikh Fazlollah[30]—In the newspaper that you have published and sent from the shrine of Shah ʿAbd al-ʿAzim to Tehran, these few words feature: "Learning for women is against religion

---

28. At the end of the letter, *Tamaddon* comments, "We approve of the complaints of our compatriot sister and hope to write about the measures that should be taken by the government and the nation in the next issue."

29. *Habl al-Matin*, vol. 1, no. 105, 22 Rajab 1325/ 1 September 1907, pp. 4-6.

30. Shaikh Fazlollah Nuri (1843-1909) was one of the leading *mojtaheds* of Tehran. He came to be a steadfast opponent of constitutionalism, and to represent a hardline conservative voice against equality, whether between Muslims and non-Muslims or Muslim men and women. See "Contending Visions Regarding Constitutionalism," below.

and faith." Since, I, the humble writer of this letter, am an ill-educated woman and do not understand these words . . . I thought it necessary to ask you to explain them to me. If what you meant was that women should not learn anything and remain unthinking beasts until they die and that this is God's decree, please state in which part of the Qur'an and *Hadith* has God Almighty said such a thing. And if this is correct, could you please explain the reason behind the lack of kindness on the part of God, the Prophets, and the Saints towards women who have been created in the shape of human beings, but have been banned from going beyond animal nature to the truth of humanity. Also despite this ruthlessness, why have women been made to commit to unbearable duties, and have been expected to worship, to have refined morality, and obedience towards their husbands and fathers? Why has God favored men, and even though he has not deprived them of learning, why hasn't he made them obedient—like he has made us, poor beings, obliged to obey husbands—to anyone other than God? If God's blessing is the same for everyone, in exchange for all our unbearable trouble, and difficult obligations, what reward and blessing has he given us that he has not given men?

Perhaps you will say that you have no right questioning God's acts. I will say that I am talking to a God that you have made needless of justice and have shown to be cruel towards us women whereas the God that we know and worship is much higher and greater than to want to discriminate in this way between men and women, and to decree anything without good reason.

The dear prophet of our Glorious and Exalted God has said that seeking knowledge is an obligation for all Muslims (male and female). There is thus a big difference between our God who has made seeking knowledge an obligation for women, and your God who, contrary to the precepts of religion, has declared knowledge unlawful for women.

Therefore, in order to avoid this *hadith* which has been related by successive contemporaries, Your Excellency will have to consider a particular type of knowledge to be appropriate for women. If this is the case, you would have to confess to the fact that you have lacked caution and have shown carelessness in your *fatwa*. . . . If you excuse me for saying so, it is in fact a *fatwa* against the message of God.

For since you have not specified the particular knowledge that is appropriate for women, I will have to trouble you and ask what knowledge do

you specifically have in mind which is unlawful to women? If it is literacy
and the ability to read books, including the Qur'an as well as letters, what
is the reason based on the *hadith*s and Qur'anic verses? Were any of the
wives of the household of the prophet and the pure Imams and the leading
`*ulama*, whether Muslim or non-Muslim, illiterate, and were they banned
from becoming literate? Are you capable of such slander? Are you able to
provide evidence for such a claim . . . ?

Other than that, you and all the people of Tehran and other cities of Iran
know and see that in most of the streets of Tehran and other cities, female
*molla*s (*molla-baji* or *mirza-baji*) have houses where they teach young girls
in utmost freedom, just as in the *maktab*s in alleyways and bazaars, where
male teachers teach both girls and boys. What is the reason that in all these
years, you have never objected to these schools, and [it is] only in these
last two months of your stay in the shrine of `Abd al-`Azim, that you have
gained this religiosity, and have considered this objection to be so necessary
that you have published it in a pamphlet? Perhaps you will say that the
opening of girls' schools is different from the *maktab*s in passageways, and
the room in *molla-baji*'s house. . . .

In this case, I will say that of course there are several differences; for
one, in proper schools, girls learn to read before reaching the age of puberty,
whereas in the room of *molla-baji*, they don't learn to read, even after having reached the age of puberty. Also often, *molla-baji*s admit one or two
rough boys and recently-married irreligious young men as well as several
men living in the neighborhood. If the girl's father is respectable, and brings
tutors home, he will cause the kind of immorality that all residents of
Tehran already are familiar with. So that sometimes a girl becomes preg-
nant in a *maktab*, and sometimes, she is wed to the teacher. What more can
I say? However, in girls' schools, the only man is an old man who does not
even have the right to enter the school playground, and if he lets a ten year-
old or even younger boy into the school, he will be punished. Also in [girls']
schools, all kinds of skills can be taught to girls, whereas in *maktab*s, the
most that girls can learn consists of the one or two defective skills that the
molla-baji knows.

Similarly, in girls' schools, girls are taught good manners, whereas in
the *maktab*, they will learn the acceptable or unacceptable behavior of the
molla-baji. In this way, in schools, girls will learn the way of looking after
a husband, household management, all kinds of cooking, and child care

according to these new books that have been published, whereas in *maktab*s, not only do girls not study such subjects, since the *molla-baji* knows nothing about such things, but they only learn her unbecoming behavior. She may teach books like that of Hafez which talks about nothing but praising the beloved, whereas in schools, they teach books of ethics. In short, there are thousands of other differences between girls' schools and *maktab*s, and an intelligent person understands most of them. But what does Your Excellency say? By God, I am at a loss to understand that in view of these obvious differences, what unconscionable and unjust irreligious person would recommend the *maktab* over schools . . . ?

I have another question regarding this matter: In view of the fact that according to your statement, women should not learn any literacy, what is an unfortunate girl who has no wealth, accomplishment, or beauty and not even a man willing to marry her, to do? What about a woman who in addition to having none of the three qualities mentioned above, has to feed two or three children, and is responsible for their livelihood? How is she to make ends meet?

. . . Do men who, in this day and age, have had a little bit of education and have acquired good taste, put up with uneducated and unaccomplished women? Must someone who has enough of an income to be able to fulfill the wishes of his daughters, regardless of their talent, be unaware of the predicament of other poorer and less fortunate girls? On top of that, must he become the cause of banning these girls from becoming accomplished and earning a living? What an injustice to have someone in authority, make learning, one branch of which is the Qur'an, not only unlawful but also present it as against religion. Dear God, save us from such people!

3. "Statement of Purpose of a Women's Weekly," *Danesh*, September 14, 1910[31]

In the Name of God, the Compassionate, the Merciful

It is not hidden from the knowledgeable and discerning people that the Creator of reason and learning, and the Provider of the daily bread of all creation, has placed the responsibility of the education of mankind, whether boys or girls, into the hands of competent and intelligent mothers. He has

31. *Danesh*, vol. 1, no. 1, 10 Ramazan 1328/ 14 September 1910, p. 2.

bestowed this blessing on women because all children, from the time of their birth until the approximate age of ten, learn their manners and morals from their mothers, and imitate their expressions and manners, especially girls who will be the future mothers. Whenever mothers do not have good morals, then their children will inevitably not have good morals either. So what must be done to enable mothers to fulfill this responsibility well? They must become knowledgeable since it is said that "seeking knowledge is an obligation on all Muslims, male and female" or "seek knowledge even if it be in China."

It is clear that the means by which children can get an education is schools, and thankfully, today, in this capital-city, a certain number of schools for boys and girls have come into existence. However, with regard to adults and people of discernment, there is no better means by which they can gain knowledge than newspapers which they can read in their free time, with full attention, and become informed about everything.

In order to teach the dear respected women and intelligent mothers of our country home economics, being a wife, and childcare, and to increase their knowledge, your humble servant, the daughter of the late Mirza Mohammad Hakim Bashi, Dr. Kahhal, presents this newspaper called *Danesh*, to the discerning and insightful people, once a week for now. In each issue, I will include translations of some novels . . . so that respected ladies can learn good morals, be amused and entertained. I hope that the dear gentlemen and ladies help this humble servant to carry out this service well. No help is better than encouragement, and no encouragement is better than becoming a customer, in order to avoid the imposition of a loss that cannot be compensated on this poor being. In fact, the subscribers to this newspaper can buy this newspaper with the intention of doing good. As for the women who do not know how to read, it is the duty of honorable gentlemen to read the newspaper to them every week, so that they, too, do not remain deprived of this blessing. In fact, perhaps this will mean that in this way, women will become literate.

Contending Views Regarding Constitutionalism

Perhaps the two most well-known contending views regarding constitutionalism were those of Shaikh Fazlollah Nuri (1843-1909) and Mohammad

Hosayn Na'ini (1860-1936). Both were religious scholars; Shaikh Fazlollah was one of the leading and most learned mojtaheds *of Tehran at the time, who became very critical of constitutionalism, and Na'ini was one of the most high-ranking religious authorities who wrote in favor of constitutionalism. The passages below represent each of their arguments: the first consists of excerpts from one of the several pamphlets that Shaikh Fazlollah published during his sit-in at the Shrine of Shah `Abd al-Azim in summer 1907, when he came out openly against the constitution and its provisions of equality before the law for both Muslims and non-Muslims. The second is an excerpt from Mohammad Hosayn Na'ini's treatise entitled* Tanbih al-umma wa tanzih al-milla ya hokumat az nazar-e Islam (Exhortation of the Faithful and Purification of the Nation, or Government from the Perspective of Islam) *from 1909, in the aftermath of the June 1908 bombing of the Majles and also in refutation of the arguments put forth by Shaikh Fazlollah.*

1. Shaikh Fazlollah Nuri and His Objections to Constitutionalism

Text: *A Collection of Treatises, Announcements, Writings, and the Newspaper of the Martyred Shaikh Fazlollah Nuri*[32]

Printed in the Holy Shrine of His Holiness `Abd al-`Azim, may peace be upon him, in order to remove any misunderstanding on the part of our religious brothers on Monday 18 Jumada II 1325/ 29 July 1907.

. . . Last year, some ideas spread[33] to our country from Europe to the effect that any state where its king, ministers and governors behave in an arbitrary fashion towards their subjects, will be the source of oppression, transgression and tyranny, and a country where the doors of oppression, transgression, and arrogance are open, will never become prosperous; it will rather continue to add onto the distress and suffering of the people until a time when suddenly that country loses its independence. . . . It was said that the cure for this terminal disease consisted of people getting together and asking the king that he change arbitrary rule and instead, incorporate some order in the governmental duties, the services and duties at

---

32. Mohammad Torkaman, ed., *Majmu`eh-i az rasa'el, e`lamiyyehha, maktubat . . . va ruznameh-ye Shaikh-e Shahid Fazlollah Nuri*. Vol. 1. Tehran: Mo'aseseh-ye Khadamat-e Farhangi-ye Rasa, 1362/ 1983, pp. 260-269.

33. The verb used in the original Persian is that used for the spread or contagion of disease.

court, so that henceforth, the behavior of the shah and his class of servants
and retinue does not transgress what has been agreed upon, and that wise,
correct and reliable people, from among the subjects should write this contract and have it approved by each other, and signed by the king, and then
published in the country. They said that in today's parlance, the name of
that arbitrary rule is "despotism," that of the contractual rule, "constitutionalism;" that of those who write the contract, "deputies" or "delegates,"
that of the center for discussion and deliberation, the "National Consultative
Assembly;" that of their contract, "the Law" [*Qanun*], and that of the book
where they write those contracts, "the Code of Laws." Once the honorable
`ulama and the Hojjaj al-Islam[34] became fully aware of this talk and order,
they repeatedly met with each other, and wrote articles, and all agreed that
this crumbling state of the country is because of lack of laws and the arbi-
trariness of the government, and that a National Consultative Assembly
should be demanded from the state, so that it can determine the duties of
the governmental departments and define them. Finally, thanks be to God,
the late king [Mozaffar al-Din Shah] agreed, and with the help of the honorable and praiseworthy `ulama, the Grand Islamic Consultative Assem-
bly[35] was opened. . . . So the basis of the discussions was the lack of order
in governmental departments, and what we, the people of Iran, needed was
limited to the establishment of principles and laws in the duties of the Court
and Court interactions. . . . However as soon as the deliberations of the *Majles* began, and questions regarding the principle of constitutionalism and
its limits were discussed, issues came to the fore in the course of the
speeches, pamphlets and newspaper articles that no one expected, and
caused horror and shock among the spiritual leaders . . . and all religious
people.

For example, when we saw that in the royal decree, it was written "the
National Islamic Consultative Assembly," we realized that the term "Islamic" had gotten lost, and had disappeared altogether. . . . Also at the time
when the decree granting the constitution was issued by His Majesty the
Shah . . . , in the *majles* they said openly in the presence of a thousand or
more people that "we don't want the *shari`a*." . . . Also since the inaugu-
ration of this *majles*, we have all seen with our own eyes how the group of

34. See chapter 3, footnote 9.
35. It should be noted that the *majles* is here deliberately referred to as the Grand Islamic Consultative Assembly as opposed to the National Consultative Assembly.

people who have no religion and are loose in morals, people who used to be known as Babis in the past, have all come to life together with those who disavowed the *shari`a* and believed instead in nature. . . . Next, there emerged newspapers and night-letters, most of which insulted the distinguished `*ulama* and reproached the laws of Islam, arguing that modifications had to be made in the *shari`a*, that certain laws had to be changed, improved and made more apt; that those laws which had been set 1300 years ago, had to be adjusted to the needs of today. These laws included things such as the legalization of alcoholic drinks, the propagation of brothels, and the opening of schools for the training of women, and primary schools for girls; spending the money that would be otherwise used for preaching and the visiting of holy shrines [now had to be used for the purposes of] setting up factories, leveling of roads, and opening railways. . . . It was said how today in Europe, there existed philosophers who were much more learned, wiser, and greater than prophets and God's messengers . . . and that all the countries on earth had to have equal rights, so that the blood of the *dhimmi*[36] and that of the Muslim were one and the same, that they [could] mingle together, and give and take wives from each other. (Long live equality!).

Next was the emergence of chaos all over the Guarded Domains, and the lack of security, order, and the spread of bloodshed, and corruption . . . especially the incidents that have occurred in Azarbaijan and the border region there, as well as the killings in Kermanshahan, Fars, and the borders of Nahavand. Since you and I are all in Tehran, I only ask you about Tehran. Since the term "freedom" has spread in this city, to what extent has the weakness of the faith of the people, and the degree of depravity and debauchery grown? . . . You all have seen that the . . . preachers say that this year, the gatherings in commemoration of and mourning the martyrdom of Husayn, and the participation of people in this worship which is among the great customs of Shi'is have been reduced to half what it used to be. Had you ever expected such a result? Had you ever heard that some person in the world has said or written . . . that God's divinity is conditional? . . .

36. *Dhimmi* is an Arabic term that refers to non-Muslims living in an Islamic state. In the early centuries of Islam, the *dhimmi*s did not enjoy all the rights that Muslims had, and had to pay *jizya* or tax in return for being allowed to practice their own religion.

The agreement was that the Consultative Assembly make laws to address those matters that had to do with the arbitrary nature of the government and the Court, and to limit the powers of the king and the Royal Council, and to close the way to oppression, tyranny, and transgression. However, today we see that in the Consultative Assembly, they bring books of law from Europe, and that they have expanded the areas where new laws are thought to be needed, without paying attention to the fact that European nations have never had codified *shari`a*. This is why the Europeans have written codes of law concerning every matter, and have put them into effect, whereas we, Muslims, have *shari`a* that is divine and eternal, and that is so firm, correct, complete and solid that it will never be done away with. . . . Furthermore, *shari`a* has a law for every matter and has determined a duty for every situation. Therefore, we, the people of Iran only need laws that are exclusive to the royal affairs, and which by chance happen not to be covered by the *shari`a*. . . .

Yes, after the Hojjaj al-Islam and other Muslims from among the founders of the *Majles* became aware of these intrigues and the appearance of all this corruption . . . they decided to put an everlasting stop to the changes made by the irreligious. . . . To this end, several points have to be considered: in the Fundamental laws passed by the *Majles*: first, after the term "constitution" [*mashruteh*], the term "*mashru`eh*" or "religiously lawful" should be written. [Second], the clause about observing the compatibility of the laws passed by the *majles* with those of the holy *shari`a*, and the oversight of a committee of just *mojtaheds* on the *majles* in every age, as described and written by us all, should be added to the clauses of the Code of laws. Furthermore, the Consultative Assembly will have no right whatsoever to interfere in choosing the members of this committee of wise *mojtaheds*. Rather the right to choose and determine . . . the members of that committee will be all in the hands of *the `ulama-ye moqalledin*[37] of every age and no one else. [Third], in the interest of stopping irreligious sects, especially heretics from religions such as the Babis and its deviations, His Excellency, Hojjat al-Islam Mirza Akhund Molla Mohammad Kazem . . . has asked that another clause be added. It is clear that his decree should be obeyed, and that a clause should be written into the Fundamental Laws

37. This is a reference to *maraje`-e taqlid* or scholars of high learning and standing who become sources of emulation to their followers.

with regard to carrying out religiously legal decrees about the Babis, and other atheists and unbelievers.

[Fourth], since the fundamental laws of the *majles* have been copied from laws that have been external to our religion, and in the interest of observing the *shari`a* and preserving its Islamic character, a number of modifications have been made to some clauses in the presence of all the Hojjaj al-Islam. Those clauses, too, must be written bearing the same modifications and corrections that everyone has made. . . . Let us give an example of such modifications and corrections so that all our religious brothers learn what the clause was like to begin with, and what it became. For example, one of the European laws that was translated stated that the press was completely free (meaning that no matter what anyone published, no one had the right to dispute it). This law is not compatible with our *shari`a.* As a result, the honorable `*ulama* changed and corrected it, since the publication of sacrilegious books and the spread of obscenity are banned in Islam. From the perspective of the *shari`a,* no one has the right to publish books that mislead people, or that say bad things and use abusive language about Muslims, and disseminate them among the people. So the publication of the books by the Frenchman Voltaire, which consist of nothing but insults to the prophets, may peace be upon them, the *Bayan* by Seyyed `Ali-Mohammad Bab Shirazi, and the writings of Mirza Hosayn Ali Takeri[38] and his brothers and sons, who represent the Gods, or the prophets or the Imams of the Babis, are banned in newspapers or pamphlets that consist of unbelief. . . . [Similarly], insults to the `*ulama* of Islam are all completely banned and unlawful in Qur'anic laws. The irreligious want this door to be open so that they can do such things.

Yes, the aim of the migrants to the holy shrine [of Shah `Abd al-`Azim] is nothing but furthering these above-mentioned points . . . which are in the interest of preserving Islam and the *shari`a.* . . . Whenever the respected deputies who all talk of their adherence to Islam, religion, and piety, abandon their refusal, and obtrusive attitude with regard to these four points, and accept them, then not one of the `*ulama* of Islam and the Muslim classes will have any trouble with them, and the Grand National Islamic Consultative Assembly will then become truly deserving of the title "holy" and the prayer "May God strengthen its foundations."

---

38. Mirza Hosayn-Ali Takeri (Nuri), also known as Baha'ullah, was the founder of Baha'ism.

2. Mirza Mohammad Hosayn Na'ini and His Arguments in Favor of Constitutionalism

Text: *Exhortation of the Faithful and Purification of the Nation, or Government from the Perspective of Islam*[39]

Introduction: An Analysis of the Nature of Tyranny, Conditionality of the Government, Achieving a Constitution and a Consultative Assembly of the People, and an Explanation of the Meaning of Liberty and Equality

"Be aware of the notion that all sages of Islam and of the nations of the world agree that some form of polity and government is necessary for the constitution of the society and the life of humankind, whether it be personal or group rule, legitimate or illegitimate government, freely elected, hereditary, or dictatorially imposed. Also, it is necessarily true that the maintenance of the honor, independence, and nationality of every nation, be it in religious or national affairs, is contingent upon their own endeavors. Otherwise, their privileges, the honor of their religion, the integrity of their country, and the independence of their nation will be utterly destroyed, regardless of how wealthy, progressive, and civilized they may be. That is why the pure *shari`a* of Islam has designated the protection of the 'essential constitution' of Islam as the highest of duties, specifying Islamic government as a holy duty invested in the institution of the imamate. (A detailed explication of this issue is outside the scope of this essay.) It is evident that all worldly affairs are contingent upon government, and that the protection of every nation's honor and nationality is contingent upon self-rule, based upon two basic principles:

1. Protection of domestic order, education of the citizenry, ensuring that rights are allotted to the rightful, and deterring people from invading others' rights—these are among the internal duties of government.
2. Protection of the nation from foreign invasion, neutralizing the typical manoeuvers in such cases, providing for a defensive force, and so on—these are what the experts in terminology call the 'protection of the essential constitution' of Islam.

---

39. This text has already been translated by Mahmoud Sadri, and published in Charles Kurzman, *Modernist Islam, 1840-1940: A Sourcebook*. Oxford University Press, 2002, pp. 117-125. (Reprinted with permission of Oxford University Press.)

The *shari`a* canons concerning the upholding of these two holy duties are known as political and civilizational laws and are considered as the second subdivision of 'practical reason.' This is why the greatest kings and emperors of Persia and Rome were adamant in choosing competent sages in theoretical and practical disciplines for the management of societal affairs. Three sages realized the necessity and legitimacy of discharging such duties, and this realization persuaded them to accept such responsibilities, despite their abhorrence of tyrannical rule. One can even surmise that the reason for any government, any system of taxation, any organization of forces in society, whether initiated by divine prophets or by sages, was to uphold these principles and discharge such duties. The pure *shari`a* too has endeavored to remedy the shortcomings [of government] and to stipulate its conditions and limitations.

The nature of the ruler's domination, in terms of the extent of the exclusiveness of its rule, can only be conceived as one of two kinds. It is either 'possessive' or 'preservative.'

The possessive form of government is the case in which a prince considers the nation his personal property to dispose of as his whims and desires dictate. He treats the nation like a stable full of animals meant to satisfy his passions and wishes. He rewards or punishes people insofar as they aid or impede him in realizing his ends. He does not hesitate to imprison, banish, torture, or execute his opponents, tear them to pieces, and feed them to his hounds. Or to encourage his pack of wolves to spill their blood and plunder their property. He can separate any proprietor from his property, and give it to his entourage. He upholds or tramples people's rights as he sees fit. He considers himself the sole possessor of the right to expropriate any holdings, to sell, rent, or give away any part of the nation or its rights, or to exact any taxes for his personal private use. His attempt to maintain order and to defend the nation is like that of a farmer toward his farm. If he wishes, he keeps it. If not, he gives it away to the obsequious bunch around him. On the slightest suggestion, he sells and mortgages national rights to finance his silly and hedonistic trips abroad.[40] He doesn't even hesitate to give himself leave for open sexual debauchery at the expense of his subjects, and still, he adorns himself with divine titles worthy of God. His courtiers help him identify his powers of tyranny, domination,

---

40. "This jab is meant particularly for the late-nineteenth and early-twentieth-century shahs who sold exorbitant concessions to foreign corporations in order to finance lavish trips to Europe.—Trans."

passion, and anger with those of the nation. They help him to arrogate to himself God's attribute: 'He cannot be questioned about what He does, but they will be questioned.' [Qur'an, Sura 21, Verse 23]

This form of government, because it is autocratic and arbitrary, is known as possessive, tyrannical, enslaving, imperious and dictatorial. It is clear why each of these titles would be appropriate for such a form of government. The head of such a form of government is known as an absolute ruler, 'owner of the yokes,' dictator, and so on. The nation that is subject to such rule should be called servile, downtrodden, and oppressed. And insofar as they are alienated from their own resource and wealth, like little orphans, they may be called 'children' as well. And insofar as their use for their rulers is like the use of crops for the farmer, they may be called 'vegetative.' The degrees of dictatorship exerted by this form of government varies according to the personal attributes and rational faculties of the princes and their courtiers, as well as the degree of the awareness of nations of their rights, and the rights of their rulers, and the degree of their devotion to monotheistic or polytheistic religions. (For this affects the leave they give to their rulers to lord over them as the sole arbiter and proprietor of their rights.) The most extreme form of tyranny is where the ruler declares himself God. Its power will be limited to the extent to which those subject to such a rule resist it. The rule is absolute if the citizens acquiesce to it, as happened under the rule of the pharaohs. And according to the old adage: 'People follow the religion of their princes.' They in turn treat their subordinates as petty tyrants. The root of this sprawling, degenerate tree is none but the nation's ignorance of its own rights and the rights of its rulers, and a general lack of responsibility, accountability, watchful deliberation, and checks and balances.

The second form of government is that in which rule does not belong to an absolute arbiter. Government is based on discharging the aforementioned legitimate responsibilities. It is a limited form of government, and the ruler's authority is rule-bound and conditional to the same extent.

These two forms of government are distinct both in their true nature and in their effects. Because the former is, in all its manifestations, based on domination and possession, the nation is hostage to the whims of the leaders. National resources are at the mercy of the ruling group. They are not responsible to anyone for what they do, so whatever they refrain from doing deserves profuse thanks. If they killed someone but didn't mutilate him and feed him to their hounds, they should be thanked. If they expropriated property but didn't rape the women, they should be thanked. Everyone's relationship with the ruler is that of a slave to his master—even lower than that! It is the relationship of the farm animal to the farmer. It is even lower than that: it is the relation of the crop to the crop owner. They have no independent right to their own life and existence. In short, their relationship is like the relationship of creation to the Creator. On the other hand, the nature and essence of the latter form of government are stewardship, service, upholding domestic order, and protecting the nation. This form of government is committed to using the nation's resources to meet the nation's needs, not to satiate the passions of the rulers. Therefore, the authority of the government is limited to the above-mentioned matters, and its interference in its citizens' affairs is conditional upon the necessity of reaching those [national] goals. The citizens are partners with government in the ownership of the nation's powers and resources. Everyone has equal rights, and the administrators are all stewards, not owners. They are responsible to the nation, and the slightest infraction is punishable by law. And all citizens share the national right to question the authorities safely, and are safe in doing so. Nor does anyone protesting the government bear the yoke of servitude of the sovereign prince or his courtiers. This kind of government is called limited, just, conditional, responsible, and delegated. And it is evident why each of these designations would be appropriate for such a form of government. Those in charge of such a government are called protectors, guardians, just arbiters, responsible and just rulers. The nation that is blessed by such a government is called pious, emancipated, gallant, and alive. (And again, it is evident why each of these designations applies to such a nation.) The nature of this government is analogous to loaning and delegating, and it can survive only in the absence of usurpation and violations of trust. That which protects this form of government and prevents it from degenerating into an absolute and arbitrary rule is none other than the principle of accountability, vigilance, and responsibility.

The most exalted means of ensuring that a government will not betray the trust of the nation in any way, is, of course, having infallible rulers. This is the same principle that we Shi'is consider as a principle of our religion. It is necessarily evident that anyone who partakes of the exalted status of an infallible leader will be innocent of base passions, blessed with wisdom, and endowed with many moral attributes (whose explanation falls beyond the scope of this essay). Due to divine protection, such a leader is immune even to the slightest oversight and neglect. In short, this is a status 'whose true nature is incomprehensible for ordinary human beings.'

However, given a lack of access to such divine leaders, seldom does it happen that the king is just and virtuous and happens to choose a perfectly wise and chaste supervisor of the affairs of the state, as happened in the case of Nushirvan [Khosrow, king of Iran, r. 531-579] and [his vizier] Buzarjumihr a long time ago. The level of vigilance, accountability, and responsibility and the partnership, equality, and honesty of the people and the government achieved under Nushirvan's rule was an exception, not a rule, in history. It is indeed rarer than the rarest of jewels. It is impossible to expect it to happen with frequency in history. Thus in the absence of divine leadership and the exceedingly rare incidents of just kingship, nations may attempt a pale likeness of such a rule only under two conditions:

First, by imposing the aforementioned limits so that the government will strictly refrain from interfering in affairs in which it has no right to interfere. Under these conditions, governmental powers are stipulated in degree and kind, and the freedoms and rights of all classes of the people are formally guaranteed, in accordance to the requirements of religion. Violating the trust of the nation on either side and in any form, whether by excess or penury, is punishable by permanent termination of the service and other penal measures applicable to betrayal of trust. Since the written document concerning political and civil affairs of the nation is analogous to 'practical treatises' [compendia of ritual duties issued by a religious scholar], in that it sets limits and the penalty for exceeding them, such a document is called the constitutional law or the constitution. There should be no doubt about its universal application, with no conditions, except in areas of conflict with religious laws. Other considerations concerning this issue, and the points that must be observed in order to maintain the integrity of the constitution will be mentioned later, God willing.

Second, strengthening the principle of vigilance, accountability, and complete responsibility by appointing a supervisory assembly of the wise, the well-wishers of the nation, and the experts in internal and external affairs, so they can discharge their duties in preventing violation and wrongdoing. The people's representatives are comprised of such individuals and their formal seat is called 'the Assembly of National Consultation.' True accountability and responsibility will preserve the limits on power and prevent the return of possessive government only if the executive branch is under the supervision of the legislative branch, and the legislative branch is responsible to every individual in the nation. Slackening either of these two responsibilities will lead to the deterioration of the limits on power and reversion of constitutional government to absolutism in the first case, and to oligarchic autocracy of the legislature in the second. The legitimacy of the supervision of the elected legislative assembly rests conclusively on the will of the nation's selection, according to the principles of Sunni Islam, which relies on the contractual powers of the *umma* [Muslim community]. But according to Shi'i Islam, this legitimacy rests in the principle of the supervision of 'the public representatives' of the Hidden Imam during his occultation. Thus the legislature should either include some of the experts in religious law or be comprised of people who are given leave by such personages to adjudicate on their behalf. The correction and confirmation of the representative assembly's decisions by the grand experts in religious law will suffice, as we shall, God willing, explain later.

From what we have explained so far, it is clear that the foundation of the first form of government [tyranny] is absolute power, possession of the nation, inequality of the citizens with the government, and irresponsibility of the leaders. And all of these stem from a disregard of the above two principles. All of the devastation and atrocities in Iran; all that has ruined religion, government, and the nation in the land, knowing no limits, is of this sort. 'There is no need for explanation after exhibition!'

The foundation of the second [constitutional] form of government, as you have learned, is limited to delegation in affairs beneficial to the nation. Contrary to the first form, this government is based on partnership, liberty, and rights, including the right to financial accountability and supervision of administrators. All these, as well, are the results of the application of the above two principles. These two principles and their corollaries were constituted by the founder of the religion. So long as they were protected, and Islamic government did not degenerate from the second to the first form, the pace of the expansion of Islam was mind-boggling. After Mu`awiya [r. 661-680] and the children of al-`As came to power, and all the principles and corollaries of Islamic government were transformed into their diametrical opposites, the situation changed. Still, so long as other nations too were enslaved in tyrannies of their own, nothing much changed, and Islam continued to enjoy a measure of stability despite its tyrannical leaders.

However, as soon as other nations realized the natural foundations of progressive government, it was inevitable that they would prosper and that the
Islamic nation would become their inferiors, and worse, be returned to the
pre-Islamic savagery and ignorance, like animals, even plants in their degree of their servitude.

At any rate, since the basis of the former is thralldom and of the latter
liberty, the text of the holy Qur'an and traditions of the holy infallible ones
have on several occasions likened the servitude of the tyrants to idolatry,
the opposite of liberty. They have guided Muslims to free their necks from
the yoke of wretchedness. . . .

The difference between these two forms of obedience is that political
tyranny is based on naked force, while religious tyranny is based on devi-
ousness and chicanery. The difference leads us to believe that, in truth, the
former is based on the control of bodies while the latter stems from the
control of hearts.

This argument confirms the astuteness and accuracy of the argument of
some of the experts of this science who divide tyranny into political and
religious kinds. They consider them interrelated and mutually protective
of each other! It is also evident that uprooting this evil tree and liberation
from this abject slavery—possible only through the heedfulness and awakening of the nation- is relatively easy in the case of political tyranny, thus
complicating resistance to the former form of tyranny as well.

The dismal condition of us Iranians is living testimony to the mutual
support of these two forms of tyranny and slavery. The two are allied and
mutually confederated. Thus the difficulty of getting rid of political tyranny
is rooted in religious tyranny's support of the political order. This will be,
God willing, further explicated in the discussion of the methods of resisting
the forces of absolutism.

We can conclude that obedience to the autocratic orders of the rebellious
tyrants of the *umma* and the bandits of the nation is not only an injustice to
one's own life and liberty, which are among the greatest endowments
granted by God, holy be His names, to human beings. In addition, according to the explicit text of the worthy Qur'an and the traditions of the infallible ones, it is tantamount to idolatry, taking associates with God, for God
only deserves the attributes of ultimate possession of creation, and unques-
tionable authority in whatever He deems necessary. He alone can be free
of responsibility in what He does. All of these are among His holy attrib-

utes. He who arrogates these attributes for himself and usurps his status is not only a tyrant and usurper of the station of stewardship, but also, according to holy texts, a pretender to the divine mantle and a transgressor to His inviolate realm. Conversely, liberation from such an abject servitude not only releases the soul from its vegetative state and animal status into the realm of noble humanity; it also brings one closer to monotheism and the worship of God and His true and exclusive names and attributes. That is why liberating the imprisoned and usurped nations from the yoke of slavery and abject servitude and leading them to their God-given rights and liberties has been among the most significant goals of the prophets, peace be upon them. . . .

From the Prophet's biography, one recognizes the equality of a nation's people with their leaders in all laws and obligations and the great efforts of the Prophet, God's greetings be upon him, to establish this principle, thus guaranteeing the well-being of the *umma*.

Let us cite an example for such a case. First the principle of equality in property is evident in the incident in which [Muhammad's step]-daughter, Zaynab [died 629], came to Medina and offered an heirloom in order to purchase the freedom of her husband, Abu'l-'Asi [ibn al-Rabi`, a non-Muslim who had been captured by the Muslims in battle]. When she approached with the heirloom, an ornament that she had inherited from her mother Khadija [the Prophet's wife, died 619], may peace be upon her, the Prophet wept and announced that he would free her husband without payment. Yet he was careful to ask whether all the Muslims would forego their share of the payment before he returned the heirloom [to Zaynab]. Second, the principle of equality in decrees is evident in the case in which [the Prophet] did not discriminate between his uncle `Abbas [ibn `Abd al-Muttalib, died 652], his cousin `Aqil [ibn Abi Talib, died ca 670], and other prisoners of war, when they were brought in front of him. They were given no special privileges, even in the binding of their hands and arms. Third, the principle of equality in punishment is evident in [the Prophet's] last sermon, when he asked all the faithful to exercise their right of just retribution if he has unfairly injured any of them. Someone claimed that [the Prophet's] riding crop had accidentally touched his shoulder during one of the campaigns. The Prophet of Islam bared his shoulder and asked the man to retaliate if he wished. But the man was satisfied to kiss [the Prophet's] shoulder. Also, the Prophet once said in public that if my only daughter, Fatima, ever commits a crime, her punishment would not differ in the slightest from the punishment of any other wrong-doer.

It was for the revival of such a blessed tradition of leadership, and in order to abrogate the apostasy of discrimination in the distribution of favors, and to reverse the endowment of fiefs, and to uphold the principle of equality, that the commander of the faithful `Ali encountered so many enmities and disturbances during his rule. . . .

All these endeavors served to preserve this central pillar of Islam and discharge the great responsibility of leadership in Islam. It was with a similar motivation, and in order to follow the glorious example of the praiseworthy prophets and their trusted stewards, that the godly jurisconsults and leaders of the Ja`fari [Shi'i] religion have resolved to free the faithful from the servitude of the tyrants in this auspicious age—which is, with God's help, the age in which the enslavement and decline of the Muslims are being terminated. They have resolved as well that in accordance with the maxim 'He who can't accomplish all should not abandon all,' they ought to convert the form of government from possessive back to delegative. While the possessive form has caused the ruin of Islamic societies and the decline of Islamic states, the delegative form will protect against most forms of corruption and prevent the dominion of the infidels over the country. In this path [the religious leaders] have engaged in a struggle needed to protect the essence of Islam. Recognition of the need for change, and the brave, sober, and earnest attempt to bring about the end of absolutism and to replace it with limited government, has clearly sparked a backlash. The religious form of absolutism, in conformity with its ancient and ongoing duty to protect the evil tree of tyranny in the name of protecting religion, did its best to describe the life-sustaining principles of limited and responsible government in the most grotesque and reprehensible disguises—contrary to the Qur'an's warning: 'Do not mix the false with the true, and hide the truth knowingly' [Sura 2, Verse 42]. It portrayed the liberation of the nation from the clutches of unjust tyrants as illusory. (The reader of this essay knows such liberation to be the goal of all prophets and their just successors, and the origin of Islamic government, which was distorted by the evil tree of autocracy planted by the family of al-`As.) The proponents of religious despotism went farther and declared this struggle a denial of all moral limits and an attempt to spread apostasy. They even attributed the outward appearance of women in the West (allowed by Christianity in places such as Russia, France, or Britain) to the political change from absolutism to constitutionalism, though this is as irrelevant to constitutional government as could be. Further, they mischaracterized the principle of equality of rights and powers, which the reader has learned from this essay to have been the practice of the Prophet of Islam and his just successors, for which `Ali was martyred, as was his son Husayn. They said that this principle will erase all differences between Muslims and non-Muslims in affairs such as inheritance, marriage, even penal law: and that it denies any difference between children and adults, sane and insane, healthy and sick, the free and coerced, the able and the disabled, and so forth, in terms of their rights and duties. All of these issues, which are further from the quest for constitutionalism than the sky is from the earth, they attached to the essence of this noble endeavor.

Because the salvation and prosperity of the nation, and the preservation of its essential rights, is contingent upon the limitation and responsibility of the government, they have mobilized to cloak this divine beneficence with ugliness. They do not realize that the sun cannot be covered with mud, nor the Nile delta dammed with shovels. The Iranian nation—no matter how ignorant of the requirements of religion it is imagined to be, regardless of how unaware it may be of the evils of slavery and the advantages of liberty and equality—at least understands this much: Its sages and brave compatriots—be they clergymen, heroes, businessmen—would not have risen in order to achieve that which the proponents of religious despotism attribute to constitutionalism, but to attain freedom and equality. The leaders of the Ja`fari religion, too, had no motivation in authenticating this movement with such explicit edicts and orders, and in calling its enemies the enemies of the Imam of the age [the Hidden Imam], except to protect the essence of Islam and the integrity of the Islamic countries. This bunch of tyrants and oppressors of the *umma*, these depreciators of the *shari`a*, know full well that spreading corruption, anarchy, and debauchery can only strengthen the position of irresponsible, absolutist autocrats. They have no other objective in mind but to help their masters by committing these heinous acts. They know full well what we mean when we say that these so-called clerics 'do more harm to the downtrodden Shi'is than the cursed troops of Yazid did to Husayn, peace be upon him'! They know how much we are hurt by their alliance with tyrants. They recognize that the blessed verse of the Qur'an [Sura 3, Verse 187] speaks of them: 'And remember when God took a promise from the people of the book, to make it known to humankind, and not keep back any part of it, they set aside [the pledge] and sold it away for a little gain; but how wretched the bargain they made.' They must realize that in this world and in the Hereafter, nothing but scandal and damnation will result from their support of tyranny. This is God's unchanging tradition, as stated in the Qur'an: 'Such was God's tradition among those before you, and you will not find any change in God's tradition.' [Sura 33, Verse 62].

It is time to rein in our pen, to describe this scandal no further, for it is sure to affect its own kind [that is, even pro-constitutional clergy will suffer.] We shall postpone revealing their fallacies to appropriate sections in our five chapters."

Expressions of Disillusionment with the Constitutional Experiment

The mood of optimism that had played a major role in inspiring the struggle for the constitution soon turned to that of disillusionment when the promises and expectations that were anticipated to result from constitutionalism were not fulfilled. The two passages below convey two very different expressions of disillusionment. The first is an entry from the memoirs of `Ayn al-Saltaneh, a member of the elite and Qajar Court, concerning the hanging of Shaikh Fazlollah Nuri, "one of the most senior of three mojtaheds in Tehran,"[41] who rose up in opposition to the constitution, and who therefore was executed by the supporters of the constitution on 31 July 1909 following the defeat of the royalist forces. What is interesting about this first entry is not only the expression of disbelief that something like this could have happened in an Islamic country—this was, after all, the first time in the history of Iran that such a senior member of the `ulama was being hanged— but also the deep sense of unease at the absence of due process that constitutionalism had otherwise promised. While `Ayn al-Saltaneh does not know what the consequences of such an action will be exactly, he realizes that it does not bode well for the future. The second passage is an excerpt

41. Ervand Abrahamian, *A History of Modern Iran*. Cambridge: Cambridge University Press, 2008, p. 50.

from an editorial in Amuzegar, *a weekly with socialist leanings published in Rasht in 1911. While the aim of this editorial is first and foremost to encourage readers not to give in to despair, it points to the link between the lack of improvements in the everyday life of the people and the growing disenchantment with the constitutional experiment.*

1. The Hanging of Shaikh Fazlollah

Text: *The Diaries of `Ayn al-Saltaneh*[42]

They killed the Shaikh [Fazlollah]. It was a big deal. They thought that Iran would then become orderly, but they were wrong. . . . Once this news reaches the `Atabat,[43] and other cities in Iran, or even in this same city of Tehran, it will cause a lot of trouble. If Molla Qorban `Ali[44] hears of it, he will raise much uproar. Everyone was certain that the Shaikh would be sent to exile. No one thought it possible that he would be murdered so openly in public, without a trial and interrogation in a court of justice. The Shaikh, himself, had said that he would not go to a [foreign] embassy to seek refuge; that he would be ready for questioning if there were to be one; that he would prove all his services to Islam, [including] the addition of that clause to the Fundamental Laws according to which five people from the first ranks of the *mojtaheds* should be present to propagate the laws; and that in the case of force, he would have no choice but to surrender.

They questioned him for half an hour at the *Komiteh-ye Jang* [War Committee]. That consisted of them telling him that he was guilty, and that he had spoken against the Constitution, even though the Shaikh was not a military man and had not killed any troops. He should have been questioned openly in a court of justice, in keeping with the Constitution and the Fundamental Laws, and the verdict for his murder should have been issued by more learned *mojtaheds*, and signed by the *Nayeb al-Saltaneh*, not by

42. Qahraman Mirza Salur, *Ruznameh-ye Khaterat-e `Ayn al-Saltaneh.* Tehran: Entesharat-e Asatir, 1377/ 1998. Vol. 4, pp. 2709-2710.

43. `Atabat is a reference to the holy shrine cities of Karbala, Najaf, Samarra, and al-Kazimayn (also known as al-Kadhimiya) in Iraq.

44. Akhund Molla Qorban `Ali Zanjani (d. 1911) was a leading religious scholar who opposed constitutionalism.

45. Yeprem Khan and `Abd al-Hosayn Mo`ezz al-Sultan were constitutionalists who had fought the royalist forces of Mohammad `Ali Shah, and thus played a role in helping the constitutionalists take Tehran in 1909. Following this victory, Yeprem Khan was appointed the Police Chief of Tehran.

Yeprem and Mo'ezz al-Sultan.[45] This was nothing but revenge, a personal and collective grudge. However, it will soon lead to decay and disintegration.

Yes, the Shaikh's son had wanted to go and visit his father a few days earlier, but he had been stopped. His brother had gone into hiding. He only saw his mother and sister, who had fallen on his feet, pleading with him, saying that it was enough-that he should not consent to the murder of his father. . . . He did not listen, and instead did what he had to do. The War Committee gave this son all that the Shaikh possessed. This was while his father had disinherited this son when he had been alive.[46]

I had no intimate friendship with the Shaikh. . . . He was learned, and a source of emulation. In Iran, there were no two people like him. His classes would be attended by six hundred students. But what I feel sorry about is that such acts will result in the disintegration of the country and the weakening of religion.

When the Shaikh was coming out of the *Komiteh*, he had said, "If I have been a burden, I am leaving now." He had pleaded that he be killed there, but had been told that that was not possible. So then he had turned to the people and said goodbye. "May your trial and mine be fifty thousand years from now!" Then he began to say his prayers until he reached the square, and he was praying when he died.

2. "The Lack of Progress towards the Objectives of the Nation," *Amuzegar*, July 18, 1911[47]

From the time that the Iranian nation has come into possession of a democratic state and a constitutional government, it has expected numerous benefits and good results so that every day it has promised itself good fortune, and every hour, it has expected things to improve and gain better organization. Indeed, it should be so too! Constitutionalism is the basis for all kinds of progress for the country and the people. We must anticipate many results and benefits.

However, unfortunately, what has become apparent until now has been the opposite of the objectives of the nation. That is, no one has seen a proper

---

46. Shaikh Mehdi Nuri, the son of Shaikh Fazlollah Nuri, was a constitutionalist and thus was considered to have turned against his father.

47. *Amuzegar*, vol. 1, no. 7, 21 Rajab 1329/ 18 July 1911, p. 1.

judiciary, a lasting sense of security, a protection against transgression, whether external or internal, a proper ministry of culture, an organized school . . . a proper system of cleaning and sweeping of streets, or an effective system of hygiene which has been among the utmost wishes of the long-suffering nation. Rather, to the contrary, with every day that passes, the people have become further troubled, incurring losses and suffering all sorts of wrongdoings.

It is for this reason that many people of the nation have become tired and despondent. In fact, they have lost hope and despaired of constitutionalism. Perhaps they even have become nostalgic about despotism. At the time of elections, they have objected, and have refused to participate in choosing delegates [for Parliament.]

These objections originate from either not knowing about the evils of despotism, or having forgotten them, while at the same time belittling the advantages of constitutionalism and a democratic state. These objections and refusal to participate are tantamount to the actions of that enslaved man who in all his stubbornness to oppose his master, kills himself, all in the hope of bringing injury onto his master. . . .

O Iranian nation! Who is there who is more sympathetic towards you than yourselves! Do not become exasperated at the cheating and thieving of swindlers! The more they cheat, the more serious and active you should become [in your fight against them] . . . so that you can choose a representative according to your wishes, and who will bring about the key to your prosperity! . . .

We write this in order to remind our dear readers of some of the evils of the old despotism and the benefits of constitutionalism, so that they snap out of their disastrous weariness and disillusionment.

PART TWO

1911–1978

4

War, Coup D'État, Hopes, and Disillusionment

The 1919 Anglo-Persian Agreement and Reactions to It

In the aftermath of the First World War in 1918, Britain sought to maintain its influence in Iran by concluding a secret agreement with the Iranian government (in return for payment to certain individuals within the cabinet) and without the knowledge of the Iranian Parliament or public. Known as the 1919 Anglo-Persian Agreement, it guaranteed Britain the "sole right to provide Iran with loans, arms, advisors, military instructors, customs administrators and even teachers. . . In return, Britain was to provide Iran with a loan of £2 million [and] was also to have the monopoly right to help the country build railways, combat famine, find entry into the League of Nations and seek damages suffered in WW1."[1] However, once the terms of the agreement became known to the Iranian public, opposition and resistance to the agreement grew, in due course making it untenable. The two passages below consist of parts of the actual text of the agreement, and the reaction that it provoked once its details became clear. As stated in the second passage, taken from the memoirs of Yahya Dawlatabadi, a liberal nationalist, one of the major critiques of the treaty at the time seems to have been the manner in which it was concluded, that is, with utter disregard for public opinion or the democratic institutions of the country.

1. Ervand Abrahamian, *A History of Modern Iran*. Cambridge: Cambridge University Press, 2008, p. 60.

1. The Text of the 1919 Anglo-Persian Agreement[2]

"THE POLITICAL AND MILITARY AGREEMENT

Preamble: In virtue of the close ties of friendship which have existed between the two Governments in the past, and in the conviction that it is in the essential and mutual interests of both in future that these ties should be cemented, and that the progress and prosperity of Persia should be promoted to the utmost, it is hereby agreed between the Persian Government on the one hand, and His Britannic Majesty's Minister, acting on behalf of his Government, on the other, as follows:—

1. The British Government reiterates, in the most categorical manner, the undertakings which they have repeatedly given in the past to respect absolutely the independence and integrity of Persia.
2. The British Government will supply, at the cost of the Persian Government, the services of whatever expert advisers may, after consultation between the two Governments, be considered necessary for the several departments of the Persian Administration. These advisers shall be engaged on contracts and endowed with adequate powers, the nature of which shall be the matter of agreement between the Persian Government and the advisers.
3. The British Government will supply, at the cost of the Persian Government, such officers and such munitions and equipment of modern type as may be adjudged necessary by a joint commission of military experts, British and Persian, which shall assemble forthwith for the purpose of estimating the needs of Persia in respect of the formation of a uniform force which the Persian Government proposes to create for the establishment and preservation of order in the country and on its frontiers.
4. For the purpose of financing the reforms indicated in clauses 2 and 3 of this agreement, the British Government offer to provide or arrange a substantial loan for the Persian Government, for which adequate security shall be sought by the two Governments in consultation in the revenues of the customs or other sources of income at the disposal of

2. J. C. Hurewitz, *The Middle East and North Africa in World Politics: A Documentary Record*. New Haven: Yale University Press, 1975, pp. 182-183.

the Persian Government. Pending the completion of negotiations for such a loan the British Government will supply on account of it such funds as may be necessary for initiating the said reforms.

5. The British Government fully recognizing the urgent need which exists for the improvement of communication in Persia, with a view both to the extension of trade and the prevention of famine are prepared to co-operate with the Persian Government for the encouragement of Anglo-Persian enterprise in this direction, both by means of railway construction and other forms of transport; subject always to the examination of the problems by experts and to agreement between the two Governments as to the particular projects which may be most necessary, practicable, and profitable.

6. The two Governments agree to the appointment forthwith of a joint Committee of experts for the examination and revision of the existing Customs Tariff with a view to its reconstruction on a basis calculated to accord with the legitimate interests of the country and to promote its prosperity.

THE LOAN AGREEMENT

Art. 1. The British government grant a loan of £2,000,000 sterling to the Persian Government, to be paid to the Persian Government as required in such instalments and at such dates as may be indicated by the Persian Government after the British Financial Adviser shall have taken up the duties of his office at Tehran, as provided for in the aforesaid agreement.

Art. 2. The Persian Government undertakes to pay interest monthly at the rate of 7 per cent per annum upon sums advanced in accordance with article 1 up to 20th March, 1921, and thereafter to pay monthly such amount as will suffice to liquidate the principal sum and interest thereon at 7 per cent per annum in twenty years.

Art. 3. All the revenues and Customs receipts assigned in virtue of the contract of the 8th May, 1911, for the repayment of the loan of £1, 250,000 are assigned for the repayment of the present loan with continuity of all conditions stipulated in the said contract, and with priority over all debts other than the 1911 loan and subsequent advances made by the British Government. In case of insufficiency of the receipts indicated above, the Persian Government undertakes to make good the necessary sums from other resources, and for this purpose the Persian Government hereby assigns to the service of the present loan, and of the other advances above mentioned, in priority and with continuity of conditions stipulated in the aforesaid contract, the Customs receipts of all other regions, in so far as these receipts are or shall be at its disposal.

Art. 4. The Persian Government will have the right of repayment of the present loan at any date out of the proceeds of any British loan which it may contract for."

2. Critique of the 1919 Anglo-Persian Agreement According to Yahya Dawlatabadi

Text: *The Life of Yahya*[3]

On Sunday 13 Zi al-Qa`dah 1337/ [10 August 1919], people woke up to read the text of this Treaty together with its appendix in the two newspapers, *Ra`d* and *Iran*, both of which supported the thinking and actions of the government. The [people] sank into a state of amazement and disbelief.

It is true that people who are not involved in politics, do not [necessarily] detect the scent of the death of Iranian independence that this Treaty entails, but within two or three days, the elite get excited, and the masses, too, follow. A group of the members of government get together and speak out against the Treaty. A group from among the clergy bluntly expresses their dissatisfaction in gatherings and meetings. A number of preachers talk against the Treaty in public congregations, at times indirectly, and at times, directly and openly. Gradually, there is uproar. The Americans and the French who are resident in Tehran, also, make the people understand that their governments are not in agreement with this Treaty, and this in itself provides reassurance to the Nationalists.

In the face of all this pandemonium, *Ra`d* newspaper whose publisher is Seyyed Zia al-Din Tabataba'i, one of the individuals who worked for bringing about the Agreement . . . publishes one article after another, arguing for the need to conclude this Treaty and listing its advantages. *Iran* newspaper also states its support of the Agreement. Since the publisher [of *Iran* newspaper], Malek al-Sho`ara Bahar, considers himself among the

3. Yahya Dawlatabadi, *Hayat-e Yahya*. Tehran: Entesharat-e Ferdawsi, 1361/ 1982. Vol. 4, pp. 126-131.

Nationalists, he writes that the columns of [his] newspaper are open for the publication of articles both in favor and against the Treaty. . . .

A few days have passed since the conclusion of the Treaty. One day, Sir Percy Cox[4] comes to see the author. At the outset he says, "The Treaty was good for Iran. It was in fact very good. All is now in the hands of Iranians."

The author does not respond.

The ambassador asks the reason for my silence, and says, "Wasn't it good?"

I say, "No."

"Why? Didn't you say that the politics of Iran and Britain have to become clear?"

I say, "Yes, I used to say that it must become clear, but I didn't say that it should get more murky."

The ambassador gets agitated, and says, "Which of the Articles of the Agreement are bad?"

The author: "We have not yet considered the Articles, but the way in which it was issued is bad. Our country is constitutional. It is not acceptable that two or three ministers conclude such a Treaty with a foreign government in the absence of Parliament and against the constitution of the country. A Treaty [concluded] in this way will darken not only the politics of Iran and Britain, but also that of India and Britain. Mr. Ambassador, just as the twentieth century will not allow an illiterate and uninformed person to become a statesman holding the reins of a country, similarly, this same century will not allow that in a country with a constitutional government, such a Treaty be concluded, while even its elite had no idea about it let alone the ordinary people."

The ambassador: "What is to be done now?"

The author: "Since this has happened in the absence of the National Assembly, a council must be held, to gauge people's opinions or to try to consult them. Of course the subsequent ratification of the National Assembly will also be an important condition."

The ambassador leaves with the heavy burden that has been put on his shoulders as a result of these discussions.

---

4. Sir Percy Cox (1864-1937) was the British Chargé d'Affaires and Acting Minister in Tehran between 1918 and 1920, and in this capacity he played a major role in negotiating the Anglo-Persian Agreement of 1919.

As a result of the tumult caused by the people, or perhaps in consequence of the discussions of this council, the British ambassador reminds the Prime Minister to involve a group of Nationalists in this task, and get their hands dirty. The Prime Minister invites twelve of the distinguished men and chief merchants to his summer house in Solaymaniyeh to discuss this issue. He explains his obligations vis-à-vis the events leading to the signing of this treaty. However, the audience see themselves before a *fait accompli*, and for whatever reason, they do not say anything that is clearly in opposition. However, everyone displays their dissatisfaction and anxiety by means of either brief statements or subsequent silences. The Council adjourns without reaching a resolution.

. . . In short, a big tumult is raised against the Treaty [first] in Tehran, and gradually all over Iran. Outside the country, especially in Istanbul and India, protests are made against the Treaty by Iranians living abroad. Foreign newspapers especially those in France write articles against the Anglo-Persian Treaty.

Expectations and Initial Optimism in the Early Years Following Reza Khan's Coup d'État

Following the coup d'état carried out by Reza Khan and Seyyed Zia al-Din Tabataba'i in February 1921, there seems to have been an initial phase of optimism among people regarding the possibility for change. The excerpts below reflect from different perspectives the high expectations people had of the new government. The first is from an editorial in Nameh-ye Banovan *(The Ladies' Paper), a fortnightly newspaper first published in Tehran on July 23, 1920, by Shahnaz Azad (1901-1961), a female journalist and activist. In response to a request put forth by the Prime Minister of the time, encouraging people to send in their list of proposals for reform, the editorial in the thirteenth issue of* Nameh-ye Banovan *published its own list of suggestions. This "wish list" is interesting because it is wide-ranging; while not necessarily political, it shows that the newspaper was at least of the opinion that much was going to change in society to ameliorate the lives of ordinary people, both men and women. The second excerpt is from the memoirs of `Ali Akbar Siyasi, the long-time chancellor of Tehran University (between 1942 and 1954), who also held the portfolio of Minis-*

*ter of Culture (1942-1944) and, in later years, that of the Minister of For-
eign Affairs (January-February 1950). In this excerpt, he recalls a meeting
that he and his friends had with Reza Khan in the 1920s—when they were
ambitious twenty-somethings—in their capacity as members of the* Anjo-
man-e Iran-e Javan *(Association of Young Iran), an association with progressive[5] leanings, which they had recently founded.*

1. "Proposals Once Again," *Nameh-ye Banovan*, June 12, 1921[6]

To the Honorable Cabinet: After expressing our congratulations on the occasion of the reshuffle of the honorable cabinet, we have stated below a
short list of the proposals that was published in the previous issues, and
followed it with [a set of] new proposals in order to carry out our service
to [both] the government and the nation;

1. The establishment of an assembly consisting of the people of Tehran
    in order to exchange ideas and prepare the necessary grounds for the
    development of schools for women and granting them the rights that
    have been denied them, since this is the basis for the progress of Iran
    and humankind;
2. The appointment of good and suitable men to teach in women's schools
    as a result of a shortage of good female teachers;
3. The establishment of easily-accessible factories appropriate for women
    in order to prevent abandoned women from being forced into prostitu-
    tion as it was discussed at length in issue no. 11 [of *Nameh-ye
    Banovan*];
4. To write and act upon the Employment laws so that [both] the govern-
    ment and the nation can be free from the endless troubles of people
    looking for jobs, and [wanting to] occupy government positions;
5. To prepare the groundwork for the publication of a low-priced maga-
    zine on [issues relating to] health and hygiene;
6. The commitment of the Tramway Company not to treat Iranians like
    animals, and not to admit more than 24 people at any one time;

---

5. This is how Sa`id Nafisi, another original member of *Iran-e Javan* described this Association.
See Sa`id Nafisi, *Beh ravayat-e Sa`id Nafisi: khaterat-e siyasi, adabi, javani*. Tehran: Nashr-e Markaz,
1381/ 2002, p. 407.
    6. *Nameh-ye Banovan*, no. 13, 5 Shavval 1339/ 12 June 1921, pp. 1-2.

7. To give an adequate salary to postal and telegraph workers so that henceforth, they will no longer discriminate when delivering telegrams and letters on the basis of the payment of bribes;

8. To change the dates of the postal stamps from the Gregorian to the Islamic calendar, at least for those that are to be used inside the country (to learn more about the details of the 8 points above, please consult previous issues [of *Nameh-ye Banovan*]);

9. The endorsement and preservation of the correct measures taken by the former Prime Minister, Mr. Seyyed Ziya al-Din, such as the banning of alcoholic drinks, begging, and the expulsion of opium addicts from government offices, as well as the establishment of a contemporary municipality, and so on;

10. To impose heavy taxation on celibate men and to allot the income to the poor with large families;

11. To transform ruins in the city into public places for recreation;

12. To invite competent Zoroastrians from India and Europe to work in government and other offices;

13. To make telephone communication widespread throughout the day and night, as is the practice in other countries, even in Tabriz;

14. To ban physicians from writing non-Persian prescriptions;

15. To set up a commission to exchange ideas, and to prepare the groundwork for standardizing the units of weight throughout all of Iran;

16. To incorporate Esperanto in the curriculum of schools in Iran;

17. To found an academy under the leadership of Haj Mirza Yahya Dawlatabdi[7] for reforming the alphabet and reviving the Persian language;

18. To institute freedom of the Press by establishing a Court for the Press;

19. To sell small portions of crown lands to the peasants who can in turn pay for them in small instalments. This will cause a large number of people looking for government jobs to turn to agriculture, thus bringing about the blooming of idle lands and the prosperity of the country;

20. To encourage the nation to use home-produced goods—such that to begin with, the ministers and the elite themselves do so in their own households;

---

7. Yahya Dawlatabadi was a liberal nationalist. For more on his views, see "The 1919 Anglo-Persian Agreement and Reactions to It," above.

21. To invite companies from all foreign states to build railways and to work the mines so that both the people without jobs and the country can benefit;

22. To impose and implement a law for compulsory education for both men and women throughout Iran.

2. An Account of a Meeting between *Iran-e Javan* and Reza Khan in the 1920s

Text: *The Account of a Life*[8]

Not much time had passed since the establishment of [the association of] *Iran-e Javan* (Young Iran), when *Sardar Sepah*, the Prime Minister,[9] invited representatives from *Iran-e Javan* to meet with him. The Association accepted *Sardar Sepah*'s invitation-of course it had no choice but to do so! . . . [We were] standing in the garden when he appeared from a distance, with a cape on his shoulders, tall and erect. He sat on a bench, signaled to us that we approach and sit on a bench that was close to him. Then he said, "You young men who have been to Europe, what do you want? What are you after? What is the meaning of this Association of *Iran-e Javan*?" I said, "This association is made up of a group of patriotic young men. We feel pain at the backwardness of Iran and the huge gap which has separated us from the European countries. We wish to remove this gap and to bring about the progress and development of Iran. The platform of our association is on this same basis and principle." He said, "What platform?" I gave him the printed version of the constitution of the association. He took it, and read it slowly and with care. Then he turned to us with his penetrating and captivating eyes, and said with utmost affability, "What you have written is good. I see that you are patriotic and progressive young men, and that you have big and heart-warming wishes. There is no harm in spreading your platform, and thus opening the eyes and ears of the people and familiarizing them with these matters. You do the talking but leave the action to

---

8. `Ali Akbar Siyasi, *Gozaresh-e yek zendegi*. London: Paka Print Ltd., 1366/ 1987. Vol. 1, pp. 76-77.

9. *Sardar Sepah* literally means Army Commander. This was the title given to Reza Khan following his coup d'état in 1921. In 1923, Reza Khan became Prime Minister, a post he held until 1925, at the end of which year he deposed the last Qajar king and became the first king of the newly founded Pahlavi dynasty.

me. . . . I assure you, but more than assurance, I promise you that I will fulfil all these wishes. Your aims are also my own. I will implement them from beginning to end. . . . Leave this copy of the constitution [of the Association] with me. . . . You will hear about it in several years."

Unveiling and Its Consequences

Mandatory unveiling was introduced as a state policy in 1936. The argument for unveiling, namely, to bring the otherwise invisible half of the nation into the fold of the nation, thus advancing renewal and progress, had already been articulated in the writings of late-nineteenth-century reformers like Mirza Malkum Khan and Mirza Fath `Ali Akhundzadeh, as well as by women like Taj al-Saltaneh, and women's publications like Danesh *and* Shokufeh *in the early twentieth century. However, what made unveiling controversial when it was introduced as a state policy in 1936 was the fact that it was mandatory and was implemented through coercive means. The four passages below shed light on unveiling from different perspectives: that of Reza Shah, who presents unveiling in nationalistic terms; those of Reza Baraheni (b. 1935), a writer and critic of Reza Shah, and Maryam Firouz (1914-2008), the founder of the Women's Organization of the Tudeh Party, whose short accounts both focus on the creative and humorous ways in which ordinary people circumvented mandatory unveiling in the late 1930s; and that of Sadiqeh Dawlatabadi (1882-1961), a women's rights activist who, writing in 1944, not only supported unveiling but also considered the pressure for re-veiling—from certain factions in the 1940s, following the abdication of Reza Shah—as a threat not only to women but also to the independence of the country.*

1. Reza Shah's Statement on the "Day of Unveiling," January 8, 1936[10]

I am very pleased to see that women have become acquainted with and learnt about their rights and privileges as a result of their wisdom and knowledge of their situation.

---

10. The "Day of Unveiling" was 17 Dey 1314/ 8 January 1936. The text of the original statement in Persian is available on Iran Press News http://www.iranpressnews.com/source/139941.htm.

Just as Mrs. Tarbiyat[11] has pointed out, women in this country could not show their innate talents and competence because they were marginalized from society. Rather I must say that they could not pay back what they owed their dear country and homeland, and carry out their duties and acts of devotion as they should, whereas now, in addition to the privilege of motherhood, they are about to benefit from other advantages offered by society.

We should not forget that half of the population of our country was not taken into account. This means that half of the work force of the country was idle. Women were never included in the census, as if women were these other people who were not part of the population of Iran. It is unfortunate that the one occasion when it was possible for women to be included in the census was when the food situation fell into difficulty. In that case, a census was taken in order to supply provisions.

I have no desire to pretend and do not want to express happiness with the measures that have been taken. I do not want to make a distinction between today and the other days. However, you, ladies, should consider this day a great day and take advantage of the opportunities that you have [before you] to bring about the progress of the country.

I believe that for the progress and prosperity of the country, we must all work from the bottom of our hearts.

But one should not squander the opportunity because the country is in need of work and activity, and every day, better and additional steps should be taken for the prosperity and good fortune of the people.

Now that you, my sisters and daughters, have entered society, and have stepped out for your own prosperity and that of your country, you should know that it is your duty to work for the sake of your country. You are the educators of the next generation. Our expectation from you, learned ladies, is that you be content in life, work hard, and abstain from extravagance and wastefulness.

---

11. Hajar Tarbiyat was the director of *Kanun-e Banovan* (Women's Association), which had been established with the support of the state, under the auspices of the Ministry of Education in 1935. See Camron Amin, *The Making of the Modern Iranian Woman: Gender, State Policy and Popular Culture, 1865-1946*. Gainesville: Florida University Press, 2003, p. 85.

2. The Experience of Mandatory Unveiling

A TRIP TO THE BATHHOUSE

Text: *The Crowned Cannibals: Writings on Repression in Iran*[12]

" . . . In the mid-thirties Reza Shah tried to unveil the Iranian women by brute force. Whenever a woman walked outside, his police would tear the veil from her face and figure. Women, not yet ready socially or psychologically for such an action and as a result of their economic, political and legal subservience to a masculine society, were forced to stay home. But difficulties arose. Since there were no showers in Iranian homes, women had to go to a public bath. The husband would put his wife in a large sack and carry her like a bale of cotton to the bath.

I remember from my childhood, when my father would carry his mother in the sack, empty his load in the bath and then come back for his wife, my mother. He once told me that Reza Shah's policeman had asked him what it was that he was carrying. He had improvised an answer: pistachio nuts. The policeman said, "Let me have some," and started tickling Granny. First she laughed, and then she wiggled her way out of the sack and took to her heels. My father was arrested."

VISITING INMATES IN PRISON

Text: *Brilliant Portraits*[13]

She laughed and told the story.[14] Many years ago, when I used to go to visit my son-in-law [in prison], Reza Khan had ordered that women be unveiled. What was I to do without a veil, and how could I go to the street and the bazaar with a bare head and uncovered hair? It was for this reason that I would always wrap a headscarf around my head in such a way that other than my face, nothing would show. I was not alone. In that year, most of

---

12. Reza Baraheni, *The Crowned Cannibals: Writings on Repression in Iran*. With an Introduction by E. L. Doctorow. New York: Vintage Books, 1997, p. 52.

13. Maryam Firouz, *Chehrehha-ye derakhshan*. 5th ed. Tehran: Entesharat-e Hezb-e Tudeh, 1359/1980, p. 27.

14. In this passage, Maryam Firouz features a woman of 60 or 70 years of age whose son-in-law had been imprisoned under Reza Shah for his left-wing activities.

the women who used to come to prison were like me.

One day, the soldiers and guards got strict and said that unless you wear a hat, you won't be able to go [to prison] for a visit!

Where were we to find a hat? We had come all the way from the city to the Qajar Palace[15] and how were we to return without a visit and stand the prisoners up? One of the women was wearing a hat. We all turned to her and asked her for help. We arranged that she go and see her prisoner first, and that after her, we all take our turn, and one by one, put on her hat so that they let us in. This is exactly what we did. All of us took her hat, put it on our headscarves, and went for our visit. . . .

What a tumult this big or small and most probably ugly hat . . . must have caused! What hearts had it soothed! "Mother" was happy that on that day, the women had been able to laugh at the government and the bullies with such a trick. They had managed both to keep their headscarves on their heads and to visit [their loved ones]. She ended by saying, "Dear Child! We would have put anything on our heads, even if it had been a bed-pan, let alone a hat!"

3. Sadiqeh Dawlatabadi's Speech Regarding the Veil, October 1944[16]

. . . Today, the provocations regarding the return of the veil increase by the day and reactionaries are in the process of reaching their sinister aims and they don't know where they are going with their extremist actions.

Unfortunately, women who know nothing about anything follow in their footsteps. I promise you that in order to shut women up, that is, half of the body of the Iranian people, different individuals in different places, have put up their . . . sleeves and opened their pockets to stifle you and me. After they have killed our right to independence and freedom, and it has become clear that half the body of the Iranian is paralyzed, they will cross out the right to Iranian independence at the peace negotiations. They are right, too.

15. Originally a palace built by Fath `Ali Shah, the second Qajar king, in 1798-1799, it fell into disuse by the late nineteenth century. During Reza Shah's rule, a prison was built on its grounds. It thus came to be known as *Zendan-e Qasr* or the Palace Prison.

16. The text of this talk originally appeared in *Zaban-e Zanan*, a journal published by Sadiqeh Dawlatabadi, a women's rights activist, in October 1944, pp. 2-7. Reprinted in Afsaneh Najmabadi and Mahdokht San`ati, eds., *Sadiqeh Dawlatabadi: namehha, neveshtehha, yadha* (Sadiqeh Dawlatabadi: letters, writings, reminiscences). New York: Negaresh va Negaresh-e Zan, 1998. Vol. 2, pp. 376-377.

Here is a nation where one half fights each other with the pen and other measures, and the other half is like a table. I, who exercise authority over it, may one day feel like removing the table cloth, and another day, putting it back on. What right does this nation have and how does it expect to be counted among the living people of the world? . . .

Dear honorable ladies! Admit that we have both a pressing need and a heavy duty. The need can be eliminated on the condition of real unity, so that we carry out our duty and not allow that we be treated like tables or wooden doors by the world. We still have another need and that is the unity of enlightened men with us. Otherwise, you can't clap with one hand. It is essential that we step into the battlefield together and united, in order to fight the formidable . . . and walking shrouded men. What kind of fight, [you ask]? A rational fight, not a fanfare. Today, we are very few in number whereas the number of old-fashioned and misled women is large. Are you ready to be trampled upon under the feet of the ignorant?

It is rumored that those who have made it their task to be sycophantic . . . and demagogic are waiting to get reassurance from the relevant authorities that once they start with their activities, there will be no complaints. Then, they will openly attack the honorable unveiled women in the streets and alleyways. Let me now conclude my remarks.

First rest assured that my statements . . . are not baseless. Secondly, I cannot make the decision for you ladies. My duty is only to investigate any actions that there may be against the character and social rights of women, and to make you aware of them. The little house whose name is *Kanun-e Banovan* (Women's Association)[17] is the right of every Iranian woman, and until now, it has only taken the path of good, and it has never sought chaos and disorder. However, if in very dark times, it chooses silence, and a return to the age of Shah Sultan Hosayn[18] . . . , it would be preferable that it shuts its doors, and that another meaningless name not exist. So I will repeat to you again that I am not making the decision for you, but what I consider my duty is that if the day comes when the obscurantists and the ignoble want to openly rise up against the progress and advancement of women, and take away the freedom that we have gained in the past ten years, and

17. See chapter 4, footnote 11.
18. Shah Sultan Hosayn (r. 1694-1722) was the last Safavid Shah. He is remembered not only as an impressionable and incompetent king but also one with a reputation for piety, superstition, and puritanism.

to blemish the dignity of the Iranian woman, believe me, that without look-ing back . . . or hesitation, and with a white banner and in the name of the freedom of women, I will go amongst these men who do not understand that blinding and deafening their mothers, sisters, wives and daughters is a huge crime and who don't want to understand that if their mothers are not wise and educated, then the purity of Islam will not remain protected, and that this veil of dishonor that they want to impose on women is in fact a veil of immodesty with which they cover the acts of prostitutes—it has nothing to do with the religion that they have fabricated for themselves. . . . Yes, I will go amongst these same men and with a loud voice will make the world understand that women are present in Iran.

Years of Increasing Autocracy in the 1930s

In the 1930s, as Reza Shah became more autocratic, he also became in-creasingly intolerant of any form of criticism and suspicious of all, whether leftist members of the intelligentsia or his own close advisers. In fact, he famously turned against his most loyal advisers and members of his cabi-net, arresting and imprisoning them—which often resulted in their myste-rious deaths. Among them were men like `Abdolhossein Teymourtash, the Minister of Court between 1926 and 1933, and Sardar As`ad, the Minister of War between 1927 and 1933. Needless to say, such decisions not only led to further alienation and disillusionment among his former early sup-porters but also further undermined Reza Shah's authority as a rational ruler. The passages below are taken from the memoirs of two very ideolog-ically different individuals: the first two excerpts are from the prison mem-oirs of `Ali Dashti, a writer and former supporter of Reza Shah, and the third, from that of Bozorg `Alavi, a Marxist intellectual, short-story writer, and member of what became known as the "group of fifty-three."

1. Disillusionment with Reza Shah in the Words of `Ali Dashti

`Ali Dashti (1894-1982) was a writer, journalist, parliamentarian, and scholar who was detained twice under Reza Shah: first, in the aftermath of the 1921 coup d'état carried out by Reza Khan and Seyyed Zia al-Din Tabataba'i, and then in 1935. This second stint was to consist of fifty-nine

days in jail, followed by five months at the Najmiyeh clinic and a final eight months at his home under house arrest.[19] *Dashti himself does not seem to understand the reason behind his detention—he was, in fact, never charged, tried, or sentenced officially. What is of interest for our purposes, however, is the clear manner in which he expresses his disillusionment with Reza Shah. As an influential journalist whose newspaper,* Shafaq-e Sorkh (Red Twilight), *had supported Reza Shah since 1922, he first lists all the different reasons that had compelled him to see Reza Khan as a savior, and a "Garibaldi" of Iran, and then he explains that if he had now fallen victim alongside others, it was not because he had violated any laws but because of the "Shah's mysterious and abstruse psychology."*

Text: *Prison Days*[20]

19 KHORDAD 1314/ 10 JUNE 1935[21]

. . . How happy were those days! Those days when I did not have to wait for an act of kindness; those days when I was not waiting for the good news of a royal favor or pardon in the manner of one condemned to death. There was no king around; the *Sardar Sepah*[22] was a patriotic military man, a dynamic man, full of fervor and patriotic zeal and enthusiasm, the Iranian Garibaldi. I thought that I had found Ardeshir Babakan.[23] A country which was on the verge of destruction and extinction, a country which had fallen apart as a result of weakness and anarchy, and which had become helpless and dark because of poverty and unemployment, wants to wake up from a deep sleep in the shadow of good thinking and foresight, sacrifice, and willpower of one its sons; it wants to shake off the stupor. The surface of its sacred soil will be cleansed from the foreign domination and intervention, the land of the forefathers will be liberated from dismemberment and the occupation of foreigners, the capitulation and concession of the Imperial Bank will be cancelled . . . Iranian women will gain their rights and social

19. See J. E. Knorzer, *Ali Dashti's Prison Days: Life under Reza Shah.* Costa Mesa, CA: Mazda Publishers in association with Bibliotheca Persica, 1994, p. 119.
20. `Ali Dashti, *Ayyam-e mahbas.* Tehran: Bongah-e matbu`ati-ye Safi `Ali Shah, 1952, pp. 190-195.
21. Ibid., pp. 190-191.
22. See chapter 4, footnote 9.
23. Ardeshir Babakan was the founder of the pre-Islamic Sasanid dynasty (224-651 C.E.).

position, education with become universal and compulsory; the script will be reformed, these things and many other things will be secured under the protection of this patriotic soldier. In those days, I spent all my youthful energy, and every drop of my blood in support of him, endorsing his ideas and policies and I was happy that I was serving the revival and renewal of the greatness of Iran. I did not want anything from him in return. . . . Whereas now, in return for this generous leap of a soul that was full of faith and enthusiasm, I cannot even breathe freely, the way a street-porter can. . . .

21 KHORDAD 1314/ 12 JUNE 1935[24]

. . . From the morning until then, I had done nothing but smoke—fifty to sixty cigarettes. My mouth had become bitter and dry. My nerves, like the strings of an instrument that had been stretched to the point of breaking, were ready to cry out loud. . . . The policemen looked at their new client with curiosity. The prison warden asked one question after another, with an ironic, reproachful and prying tone. At a time when anger and sorrow had put pressure on me like an iron coffin, and did not give me the chance to move, these questions landed on my head like a hammer.

"Why you? You who were his standard-bearer and his swordsman? You who were one of the ring leaders? What have you done? Why did you begin to oppose him? You knew the situation; so why did you throw caution to the wind? What has Rahnama done? What trouble has Tajaddod caused?[25] How did the cautious and wise Dabir-e A`zam[26] get caught?"

These continuous questions made me despondent, but at the same time, they made me realize one thing. It became clear that other than me, three other people had also been arrested. Now, the conspiratorial minds of these people who are not at all familiar with the mysterious and abstruse psychology of the Shah will speculate and make up stories. They, all, will imagine that the four of us had [formed] committees and were making plans, but the shah laughs at all their reasoning. . . . These different ques-

24. Dashti, *Ayyam-e mahbas*, pp. 193-195.
25. Zayn al-`Abedin Rahnama (1893-1989) and Reza Tajaddod (1888-1973), a journalist, and a parliamentarian, respectively, counted themselves among the supporters of Reza Shah. However, they both fell out of favor in 1935, at which time they were imprisoned and later exiled by Reza Shah.
26. Farajollah Bahrami (1882-1951), also known as Dabir-e A`zam (literally "Great Secretary"), had been Reza Shah's bureau chief.

tions that were asked by the prison warden and this look of his in which you could find a combination of pity, mockery and prying; worse of all, thinking about what kind of suspicion, and dark imagining had made the shah take on such an aggressive method, and wondering about the kind of mental and physical torments that awaited me, as well as the terrifying and bloody fates of Teymourtash, Sardar As'ad,[27] Mirza Karim Khan Rashti, [and] 'Abdol-Hosayn Diba . . . passed through my fevered and anxious mind, alongside the thought that one must survive, and put up with all this fear and wait. Are all these worth a transitory miserable life?

2. Bozorg 'Alavi and the "Group of Fifty-Three"

The "group of fifty-three" consisted of fifty-three leftist students and intel-lectuals who had come together as part of a secret study group organized by and centered around Taqi Arani, a Marxist professor of physics. This "group of fifty-three" became famous because its members were arrested by Reza Shah's police in 1937 and tried for breaking the law against prop-agating socialism and communism. Upon the abdication of Reza Shah, with the exception of Taqi Arani who had died in prison, the "group of fifty-three" became the founding members of the communist Tudeh party, which came into being in September 1941. The excerpt below, from the memoirs of Bozorg 'Alavi (1904-1997), one of the "group of fifty-three," is of inter-est because it points to the baselessness of the accusations.

Text: *The Group of Fifty-Three*[28]

We had been under arrest for eight months without any official documents confirming our sentence. In most cases, our arrest warrants had been signed by J. R.[29] The Prison Service, in keeping with the unnumbered memoran-dum of the political division of the Police had detained us in temporary prison cells. During all this time, long discussions used to take place be-tween the fifty-three people concerning the fate that awaited us. [Whereas]

---

27. Ja'farqoli Khan Sardar As'ad III (1878/79-1934) had been an early supporter of Reza Shah and had held various ministerial positions during Reza Shah's rule. However, in 1933, like a number of others, he, too, fell out of favor, and as a result he was arrested and jailed. He died in prison in 1934, allegedly of heart failure, although there were rumors that he had been poisoned.

28. Bozorg 'Alavi, *Panjah-o seh nafar*. Tehran: Amir Kabir, 1978, pp. 71-72.

29. In the Persian text, 'Alavi rarely mentions full names; instead he uses initials.

the optimists believed that this case could not be sent to any legal source, the pessimists believed that our cases would be sent to the military courts. Some thought that we would be kept without charge like other political prisoners, since the people whose cases had remained pending in Qasr prison, and who had spent years in prison were the remainder of groups that had got arrested on the same charges as us. Therefore, some believed that a number from the group would be held in detention without charge, and the majority would either be released or exiled.

We had been in prison for seven months and still did not know how many we were. Even more strange was the fact that the Iranian judiciary and parliament, too, had been officially unaware of the arrest of these people; the police itself, even the political office which had issued our arrest warrant, had not yet decided on the number of people that they should link to an imaginative organization. The strongest basis for the accusation of the fifty-three people was that they knew Dr. Arani,[30] but in some cases, this accusation was not quite true either. For example, the reason for the arrest and conviction of Dr. H. S. was that years before the arrest of the "fifty-three," he had sent a letter from Isfahan to his brother, in which he had said that "the people of Isfahan were very uncivilized." Since the brother who had received this letter had been among the students of Dr. Arani, the political branch of the Police had concluded that both brothers were communists. The Tehran prosecutor and the criminal court had interpreted the sentence "the people of Isfahan were uncivilized" to mean "the people of Isfahan were not communists." Such reasoning is plentiful in the case of the group of fifty-three. Dr. R. Sh. had had no links with the group of fifty-three. He had even got arrested before them, but since in due course, it became clear that he had met Dr. Arani once in his house, they conspired against him as well, and considered him among the followers of Dr. Arani's ideology. In short, the group of fifty-three had at first consisted of fifty-two people, and then they almost became fifty-four people.

---

30. Taqi Arani (1903-1940) was a German-educated professor of physics who espoused Marxist ideas. On his return from Germany in 1930, he initiated a secret discussion group made up of leftist intellectuals, and later founded a Marxist theoretical journal entitled *Donya* (The World). Arani was arrested in 1937 and later tried, convicted, and sentenced to ten years in solitary confinement. However, he died in prison sixteen months later, at the age of thirty-eight. See Ervand Abrahamian, *Iran between Two Revolutions*. Princeton: Princeton University Press, 1982, pp. 156-162.

5

State-Building, the Politics of Modernization, and Its Discontents

The 1940s and the Tudeh Party

Reza Shah abdicated soon after the Allied invasion, in September 1941, leaving Iran and the throne to his young son, Mohammad Reza Shah, who at the time was no more than twenty-one years old. As a result, censorship was lifted and there was a general opening in the political atmosphere, which in turn led to a proliferation of political parties and newspapers. Perhaps the most influential of these political parties was the Tudeh (or Masses) party, which came into being almost "as soon as Reza Shah had gone."[1] While it was originally set up as a social democratic party, within a few years it became openly aligned with the Soviet Union. In its early years, however, it counted among its ranks many of the young educated Iranians, writers, and intellectuals—the crème de la crème of society. The two passages below characterize the party in the 1940s from different perspectives: the first is an excerpt from the memoirs of Khalil Maleki (1901-1969), a disillusioned former member of the Tudeh,[2] explaining, in retrospect, the appeal that the Tudeh had for young educated Iranians in

1. Michael Axworthy, *Revolutionary Iran: A History of the Islamic Republic*. Oxford: Oxford University Press, 2012, p. 46.
2. Khalil Maleki seceded from the Tudeh in 1948 over the party's openly aligning itself with the Soviet Union in the Azarbaijan crisis.

the 1940s. The second is from the recollections of Maryam Firouz (1914-2008), a female activist member and founder of the Women's Organization of the Tudeh Party, describing the extent to which the Tudeh owed its existence and persistence, in times of adversity, to ordinary people, in this case, women, who sacrificed much without asking for anything in return.

1. Excerpts from the Political Memoirs of Khalil Maleki

Text: *Political Memoirs*[3]

Everyone considered the experience of September 1941[4] as the chime heralding freedom. From some time before, the eyes and the ears of the intellectuals and young generations had opened. They did not approve of the black past and the abhorrent present state of things, and wanted to bring about a bright and brilliant future. They had grown tired of all that was linked to the worn-out and decayed past and wanted to put into place a new world, with modern types of people bearing a fresh mentality and psychology. . . .

Without having a particular ideology, the intellectuals and young generations were intent on changing and reforming the situation. Many among the ardent youth did not know whether they were fascists or communists, but they knew one thing for certain, and that was that everything had to change and a new world had to come into being, a world according to the wishes of all. At the threshold of the fateful September, an enthusiastic young man who had come to Damghan to see me while I was in internal exile said something that almost ten years earlier I had heard from a German girl. That young man told me, "I have ideas; I don't know exactly if they are fascist or communist, but I do know that things must change completely." . . .

In the first half of the twentieth century, and especially on the threshold of the Second World War, and even after the war, the young generations all over the world had been inspired by ideas of revolution. . . . Following September 1941, the intellectuals, young generations, and the conscious working classes were in a transitional situation. They were ready for self-

---

3. Khalil Maleki, *Khaterat-e siyasi*. Edited and with an introduction by H. Katouzian. Tehran: Sherkat-e Sahami-ye Enteshar, 1367/ 1989, pp. 309-312.
4. In September 1941, Reza Shah abdicated in favor of his son.

sacrifice. . . . In that period, the only center that responded positively to such expectations or at least did so in the domain of talk and theory, and satisfied the thirsty, was the Tudeh party. By virtue of having a global criterion and paradigm, and showing the example and blueprint of the Soviet Union (about the reality of which few people knew much at the time), the leaders of the Tudeh attracted different forces without any competition. This time, if it was not all the *crème de la crème*, it was at least most of the *crème de la crème* of Iranian society that turned to this unique wave and school of thought. As a result of the twenty-year despotism and strangulation, no other school of thought which had had a global and historic paradigm, or deep national roots, had been allowed to grow in Iran.[5]

2. Excerpts from the Memoirs of Maryam Firouz

Text: *Brilliant Portraits*[6]

In Baharestan square, opposite the *majles*, a room on the upper floor had been rented to print *Mardom* newspaper.[7] However, after some time, when the Party became stronger, the room was leased to the women's organization. Several times a week, especially on certain days, we would go there enthusiastically. Every time, we would see a new face with curious eyes. . . . [These women] constituted the core that laid the grounds for the [women's] organization. They were the first women who had accepted our invitation.

One day, I saw a young woman who not only was a new face but also had much charisma. . . . She was a pleasant woman called Safa. She was always ready to take part in any work that we had. Since in those days, we held different classes for the purpose of both learning ourselves, and teaching others, and we asked everyone to teach to others what they knew, Safa suggested that she set up sewing classes.

What good days they were! How excited and enthusiastic we were! Everyone had a thirst for learning and a readiness to teach. We learnt the

5. Parts of this passage have also been translated in N. Nabavi, *Intellectuals and the State in Iran: Politics, Discourse and the Dilemma of Authenticity.* Gainesville: University Press of Florida, 2003, pp. 7-8.

6. Maryam Firouz, *Chehrehha-ye derakhshan.* 5th ed. Tehran: Entesharat-e Hezb-e Tudeh, 1359/1980, pp. 215-216.

7. *Mardom* was the organ of the Tudeh party, and its first issue appeared on January 31, 1942.

basics of the struggle and tried both to benefit from the great movement that had begun, and to help others. . . .

Soon after, Safa left. . . . We all thought that she had got scared and no longer wanted to work with us. . . . The inauspicious February 1949 came about.[8] The prisons became full. . . . The homeless took refuge in any house and corner. . . . The government searched for everyone one by one with iniquity and forcefulness. . . . I found out that in all these years, Safa had not only not withdrawn from the course of events but had in fact continued to help the Party with her work. Her ostensible leaving the Party had been for the purpose of helping the Party all the more, assisting with clandestine activities, in the guise of a woman who was not affiliated to anywhere, and who led an ordinary life.

Safa had sacrificed her life for the Party without making the slightest demand in the way of money. . . . Even before the Party got banned, her house had been the refuge for the convicted members of the Tudeh. Her life had become so mixed and entangled with clandestine activities that for me, the name Safa became permanently associated with clandestine activity, serenity and resistance. . . .

After the Party was banned, despite much anxiety and apprehension, Safa would go to work every day without any pretension or change in her usual manner. In her own house, she tried as much as she could to host the [Party member] runaways who came to her.

Little by little, the Party became strong and had to have a newspaper. Different publications were necessary, both to inform the people, and to teach those who were turning to the Party.

Safa's house and person had been chosen for this purpose. She accepted this big responsibility with that same composure, and found a place for the printing-workers and the printing machine in the basement of the house that had been rented in her name. In the rooms upstairs, she took care of guests, and in the basement, she kept an eye on the printing machine. Little by little, she, herself, became familiar with the printing-machine, and learnt how to work it. Neither her family nor relatives knew anything about this difficult and dangerous . . . life. Perhaps one or two people suspected something, but no one truly knew what went on in her house, and what she did in general.

---

8. In February 1949, an assassination attempt was made on the life of the Shah, allegedly by a member of the Tudeh party. As a result, the Tudeh party was banned.

The Electoral Law of 1952 and the Question of Women's Enfranchisement: The Letter of Sadiqeh Dawlatabadi to Mohammad Mosaddeq (ca 1951)[9]

In December 1952, the government of Prime Minister Mohammad Mosaddeq[10] presented its draft electoral law to Parliament. Contrary to the expectations of a number of women's rights activists, who also counted themselves among Mosaddeq's supporters, women's suffrage was not included in the document proposing changes to the electoral law, despite demonstrations and heated debate regarding this subject in the preceding years. It was therefore not surprising that the days and months that followed the electoral law of 1952 saw the debate in support of and against the question of the women's right to vote continue in the pages of the Iranian press.[11]

Sadiqeh Dawlatabadi (1882-1961), the founder of the newspaper Za-ban-e Zanan *and an advocate of women's education, was perhaps among the most influential women's rights activists in twentieth-century Iran. As is pointed out in the letter below, she was also a devoted supporter of Mohammad Mosaddeq. This letter seems to have been a confidential exchange that she had with the Prime Minister. While we don't know if her letter received any response, it is of interest for two reasons: first, it is an example of the kind of arguments that supporters of women's suffrage made at the time, and second, it shows that some supporters, even if silent in public, continued to advocate quietly and in private for women's right to vote.*

His Excellency, Dr. Mossadeq, the Prime Minister,

With all due respect, and with your permission, I am writing confidentially to ask about the electoral law and the fact that women are absent from it. Do you personally believe that in comparison to the laws of the first constitutional period, women today should be presented as more ineffectual

---

9. The Persian text of the letter is available at www.qajarwomen.org. See "Sadiqah Dawlatabadi to Muhammad Musaddiq [ca 1951]," *Women's World in Qajar Iran Digital Archive*. www.qajarwomen. org/en/items/1017A14.html. (The original document is held at the International Institute of Social History, Amsterdam.)

10. For more on Mohammad Mosaddeq, see the following section in this chapter, entitled "Mohammad Mosaddeq and the Nationalization of Iranian Oil."

11. Janet Afary, *Sexual Politics in Modern Iran*. Cambridge: Cambridge University Press, 2009, pp. 192-197.

and subordinate in the eyes of outsiders? If you answer in the affirmative and say that this is in the interest of the country, I will obey, and will keep the more than 2000 women who are in my constituency quiet to safeguard the interest of the times. But you should pay attention to the rights that have been given to women in three stages in the last fifty years:

1. The Fundamental Laws of the first constitutional period had considered women to be among the same rank as the insane and children.
2. The amendment to the law that was made in the Constituent Assembly in 1949 (which [also] created the Senate), removed women from among the ranks of the insane and the children. On the surface, therefore, women seemed to be in a better place. However, at that time, I asked for an explanation regarding this same issue from His Imperial Majesty, the Shah via the good offices of Mr. Jam, the Minister of Court at the time. He answered that the Senate would resolve this matter and that women would reach their legitimate rights.
3. The existing law which is to be approved by the people, has not only deprived women of the right to vote without any reason, but has also placed them in the category of those denied the right to vote that also include murderers, people of immoral views, criminals, the bankrupt and so on. In view of all the importance that has been given to the growth and maturity of the Iranian nation in matters of justice, will a share be given to women, or is everything specific to men?

Your Excellency, the beloved Prime Minister, I do not want to waste your valuable time, but I want to understand this matter so that I will be able to give an answer or at least do the right thing for the women in my constituency. If growth and development is specific to men . . . then in such a case, it is better that it be written in law (that for however long, women will be deprived from voting); that no mention should be made of women and that they should be dealt with in silence. However, if women, too, are part of the Iranian nation, and have a share in the national growth, then is it right that in the law that has been signed by Your Excellency, women be placed in the rank of the most shameful and notorious people? It would be good if Your Excellency ordered that some rights be recognized for women. If the United Nations were to ask you these same questions, what would you answer? If I were to know the answers to these questions in advance, I would be in a better position to silence educated women.

In the end, as a matter of conscience, I would like to defend my own personal right. I, who am among those same women mentioned in the law, other than having served in the cultural field for forty years, have also spent eighteen years in administering the Women's Association (*Kanun-e Banovan*) and working towards the progress and training of women's culture. Despite a limited budget, I have pursued my only noble aim of training capable mothers for the next generation in the best manner that I knew and with the help of God, have sustained a demanding organization, and every year, have managed to serve society and my fellow human beings more than the year before.

I ask that you compare my services with those of any one of the high-ranking and good managers of this country and consider which one of us has carried out our humane duties better and more competently? I leave the judgment with regard to this comparison to the person of Your Excellency. If I, for the sake of the interest of the time and the order of the person of the beloved Prime Minister, have remained silent today and have kept others silent too, this was once again an act of devotion, which will be judged by the world in the future. I have nothing more to say.

Mohammad Mosaddeq and the Nationalization of Iranian Oil: Mohammad Mosaddeq's Testimony at the Hague Tribunal Defending the Nationalization of Oil in Iran[12]

Mohammad Mosaddeq (1882-1967) was the Prime Minister of Iran between 1951 and 1953. He has come to be remembered for his instrumental role in nationalizing the Iranian oil industry as part of his greater aim of gaining total independence from foreign powers. The British government which had had control of the Iranian oil industry since 1914, when it bought 51 percent of the shares in the Anglo-Persian Oil Company (founded in 1909), had no intention of surrendering what it considered to be its rightful property, and fought this decision through different means,

---

12. For the Persian text of Mohammad Mosaddeq's speech, see Sa'id Fatemi, "Matn-e notq-e doktor mohammad mosaddeq dar dadgah-e Laheh," Andishesara, http://mossadeq.com/farsi/mos-notghlaheh.html.

ranging from negotiations and diplomacy to organizing a covert operation that ultimately helped to unseat Mosaddeq in August 1953. In June 1952, the British government appealed to the International Court of Justice to protect its rights in Iran. The passage below is the text of Mosaddeq's testimony before the International Court of Justice at the Hague. It is of interest because it explains and contextualizes the decision to nationalize Iranian oil.

Mr. President, Honorable Judges: For some time Humanity has been pondering over solving its differences through truth and justice and by means of the International Courts of Law rather than resorting to force and pressure. The origins of this blessed and exalted thinking lay in the bitter and bloody experiences of the past which have taught mankind that force and pressure will never remain immune from terrifying and radical reactions. The intellectual growth of Humanity decrees that one's differences should be resolved through peaceful means. Rest assured that the wish to fulfil these aspirations has taken root in the hearts of the Iranian nation which joined the League of Nations, and after that, the United Nations from the very first day [these organizations came into being].

The honorable judges of this International Court will certify that a nation can surrender its fate completely to the ruling of international institutions only when it has complete faith not only in the utter impartiality and independence of the individuals in charge of such high positions, but also in their grasp of the course of events, as well as their experience and their ability to arrive at a vote. Therefore, if we admit this truth that as yet no such widespread trust and strong faith exists in any part of the world, then we should not consider the lack of such trust as an offense towards the organizations of the United Nations especially since in all the declarations, conventions and agreements which have been made about the international organizations, governments have tried to determine the limits of the powers of these new assemblies. . . .

At a time when the governments of great powers like the United States and France have exercised caution to the degree of having postponed determining the limits of their national competence to their own judgment, how is one to blame a small nation like Iran if it has limited the jurisdiction of the Court within the boundaries of the declaration of the United Nations, and not allowed it to transgress these boundaries.

I should not hide this truth from the gentlemen present that for us Iranians, the uneasiness of stopping any kind of action which is seen as interference in our national affairs is more intense than other nations. There is a reason for this too, namely that we nations of the East, have, for many years, experienced the bitter taste of exceptional organizations that have come into being specifically to serve the interests of foreigners, and we have seen with our own eyes how our country became the battlefield for the competition of imperialist policies. We have also realized that unfortunately despite all those hopes, neither the League of Nations nor the United Nations have been able to put an end to the regretful situation that had been created in the last fifty years, and of which the former Anglo-Iranian Oil Company was its most manifest representation.

The Iranian nation which had grown tired of this situation put an end to foreign domination in one go, in a manly movement, by nationalizing the oil industry and accepting the principle of paying compensation. At that time, the British government resorted to a series of threatening and intimidating operations. It sent its parachutists to the vicinity of Iran's borders, and its warships to our coastal waters. Then it set out to impose an economic embargo, and tried to fulfil this by means of economic pressure and the confiscation of the foreign currency that we had in Britain. At the same time inside Iran, it put into effect a number of intrigues against the government and the National Movement through its agents and mercenaries . . . encouraging obstruction in our industrial, economic and financial matters. Outside the country, it set into motion propaganda in order to lay the grounds for our ill-repute in [both] international circles as well as other countries. In the end, since it did not achieve its aim through such sinister activities, it put on the face of a victim and complained to the organizations of the United Nations such as the International Court of Justice and the Security Council. Perhaps this turning away of the British government from the previous course and resorting to international organizations appears like progress on the surface. However in view of the unfortunate track record that British policy has in Iran, the effect of this change on the thinking of the Iranian people is such that they conceive of this act as a new trick: that is, resorting to the judicial and peaceful means is another way for this same old political and economic rival whose presence we had put an end to, to be imposed back on us. However, the Iranian people will never again be prepared to revive the old situation.

In view of the full trust that we have in the rightfulness of our cause and especially since our trust cannot be dented, we cannot risk to put a matter which is existential for our nation to an unfavorable vote even if it be unlikely.

In view of what has been said, I beg the gentlemen not to find fault with our way of thinking, and if it is possible, to acknowledge it, or at the very least, to understand our thinking.

It was for this reason that despite my poor health . . . which is the result of old age and the hardships that I have had to bear on the path of the struggle for freedom . . . I have travelled the long distance to come to this country. It is so that on the one hand, by virtue of my presence here, I prove the sense of complete respect that the Iranian government and people have towards international institutions, and on the other, to demonstrate to the gentlemen present that other than the legal objections that we have with regard to the jurisdiction of the Court, we have been put in a position that we can no longer discuss the subject of the nationalization of oil either ethically or politically.

The history of the Anglo-Iranian relations is too long for me to discuss it in detail here. Suffice it to say that in the nineteenth century, Iran was the object of rivalry for the imperialist politics of Russia and Britain. Sometime later, in 1907, the two rivals reached an agreement and divided up our country into two spheres of influence. Then, when the Tsarist empire collapsed and the Soviet Union became entangled in a domestic revolution, Great Britain which had come out of the war as a victor, and had no rivals or adversaries left in the Middle East, took the opportunity and wanted to take exclusive control and gain political and economic domination by means of the 1919 Agreement,[13] which entrusted the reins of the civil and military affairs to British officers and experts. In the end, since that Treaty was faced with intense resistance on the part of patriots and progressives, British diplomacy fulfilled its aims by a different means, namely by bringing to power the dictatorial regime which it supported for twenty years.[14] By going to such lengths, the economic aims of British policy were to gain exclusive possession of our oil. In this way, that which could have led to our national wealth became the cause of our various afflictions and unbearable misfortunes. This domination took place by means of the concession-

13. See "The 1919 Anglo-Persian Agreement and Reactions to It" in chapter 4.
14. This is a reference to Reza Shah's rule.

aire company.[15] This meant that in addition to taking our oil to Britain, it provided Britain with many financial benefits at the expense of Iran.

It is not possible to verify the extent of these benefits since Iran was never able to investigate the items mentioned in the balance sheet of the Company, nor was it able to find out the extent and the price at which oil was sold to the British navy-either very cheaply or even for free. Similarly, it could not work out the benefits that Britain gained through its monopoly over maritime transport or the exemption from custom tax of its goods that were imported into Iran. If we were to consider the figures of the Company balance sheet as evidence, we will see that for example, during 1948, out of 61 million pounds sterling that constituted the net income of the Company, the Iranian Government only received 9 million pounds sterling, whereas the British Treasury collected 28 million pounds sterling as income tax alone.

In addition to the aforementioned losses, Iranian workers and employees have always been in an unfavorable situation in comparison to foreign workers. Tens of thousands of Iranian workers were given accommodation in places that looked more like animal cages. They also prevented Iranians from doing any kind of technical work for fear that one day they may gain the skills that would prepare them to run the installations. From another side, the Company under the pretext of safeguarding security had created a true secret police which with the help of the "Intelligence Service"[16] was firmly rooted not only in Khuzestan, the region where oil was extracted, but also in all parts of the country. . . . It also influenced the press and public opinion, and encouraged British agents, whether merchants or political representatives to interfere in the internal affairs of the country. In this way, without encountering any resistance from a Parliament whose members had been elected as a result of the plots and political influence of Britain, and a government whose members had been appointed by them too, the Anglo-Persian Oil Company which in reality had established a government within a government, took the fate of the country into its [own] hands. . . .

In 1951, the nationalization of the oil industry put an end to this deplorable situation. It should be said that a few years prior, the National Assembly had passed a special law as a result of which it had obligated the

15. This is a reference to the Anglo-Persian Oil Company.

16. This is a reference to the Secret Intelligence Service, otherwise known as MI6, which supplies the British Government with foreign intelligence.

government to demand that the Company recognize the rights of the Iranian people through negotiations. In 1949, in an attempt to preempt the imminent danger [of losing control], the Company was prepared to increase the royalty paid to the Iranian Government, and on this basis, made a proposal to Parliament. However, the Parliament did not ratify it because this proposal was too little too late. . . .

What they want to do today is to have that action put to your judgment and consideration. What right do they have?

The principle of nationalization is among the absolute rights of any nation, and until now, many states in the East and West have taken advantage of this right. Britain's insistence to have us held hostage to a classified Treaty, about whose illegitimacy there is no doubt, is very surprising. This is so especially since Iran has expressed its readiness to pay compensation, and the British government, too, has recognized the nationalization of the oil industry in a formal document known as the "Harriman formula," about whose text the Court has become notified. According to this document, the British government, in its own name as well as [in the capacity of] a representative of the Company, has recognized the principle of nationalization according to which all the operations of exploration, extraction and exploitation must be in the hands of the Iranian government. . . .

Therefore, in view of this development, it is no longer possible for the former Company or the British Government to avoid recognizing the principle of the nationalization of the oil industry as it has been stated in the "Harriman formula." In such a situation, the only point of discussion and difference remains that of compensation. As we will see, there is no ambiguity left in this matter either. . . .

On 19 September 1951, the Iranian Government made a proposal to the British Government concerning the details of the compensation. I will mention the text of it below:

1. The Iranian government is ready to extend the rightful claims of the former Anglo-Iranian Oil Company in one of the three ways mentioned below while mindful of the claims and demands of the Iranian government:

    a. on the basis of the price of the shares of the former Anglo-Iranian Oil Company (at the price before the nationalization of the oil industry);

    b. on the basis of the laws and regulations that have been implemented in each of the countries regarding the nationalization of
industries, and that the former Anglo-Iranian Oil Company considers it to its advantage;

    c. in any other way that both sides can agree upon.

In addition, in order to safeguard the means of paying the compensation, it is stated in that same proposal that:

2. In the future, the Iranian government is prepared to sell that same
amount of oil that the British government used to buy before, at the
fair international price and deliver it at the Iranian port on the basis of
a long-term treaty. . . .

If these proposals did not get accepted by the British government, it was
because their efforts were focused on something other than the question of
compensation. Instead, under the pretext that the Iranian government won't
be able to pay the compensation unless the exploitation is managed in a
useful way, it, once again, wanted the Iranian government to commit to a
new British company which would take over the exploitation of oil either
in the industrial or commercial sense. There is no doubt in my mind that
the aim behind resorting to the Security Council and the International Court
[on the part of Britain] is to gain similar commitments from us once again.
What they don't realize is that the bitter memories and extortions of the
1933 Monopoly have still not faded from people's minds, and if we had
wanted to surrender the management of national industries once again to
foreigners, why would we have needed to nationalize the oil industry?

The course of action taken by the Iranian government and people in this
tragic story was in the way that I have explained. In all honesty, one has to
acknowledge that our course of action has been moderate and just. What I
find difficult to understand is why it is that the issue of people's claims regarding the losses caused by the nationalization of industries has become
all the talk in the case of Iran, whereas in many other countries including
Britain which have nationalized their own industries, no such problem has
occurred. We have acted in such fairness, yet unfortunately, we see that the
international Trusts have attacked and boycotted us, causing great damage
to our country.

Honorable Judges, I have no doubt that if you had been given the task
of investigating the main issue at hand, you would have attested to the right-

fulness of our cause, and would have considered the proposals that we have made to the Anglo-Iranian Oil Company as fair. However, as I explained at the outset of my statement, this issue is so existential and sacred for us that we cannot, in any way, place it in danger of a foreign investigation, even if that danger be no more than imaginary.

The decision to nationalize the oil industry is the result of the political will of an independent and free nation. I implore you to pay attention to this point that our request to you is to refrain from interfering in this matter, based on the rules of the Declaration of the United Nations.

Mr. President, when I left Tehran, I was hoping to be able to tell the gentlemen present of the injustices that had been imposed on Iran. I wanted to present before you the numerous documents that I have in my possession regarding this matter, and of which I have only brought the attention of the Security Council to a number in the past, only so that you can have a better understanding of the intense interventions of the Anglo-Iranian Oil Company in our internal affairs. However, since you limited me to talking about no more than the lack of the jurisdiction of the Court, I have no choice but to follow your request and to refrain from presenting the documents that I have in hand. I will end here, and even if I was not able to put forth the rightfulness and innocence of Iran thoroughly before the public opinion of the people of the world, I hope that at the very least, the rightfulness of our cause has been proven to the Court.

Perspectives on the White Revolution

The "White Revolution" was a series of reforms that was first put into effect, following a national referendum, in January 1963. Initially, it consisted of six principles, namely land reform, nationalization of forests, sale of state-owned factories, profit-sharing for industrial workers, women's suffrage, and creation of literacy corps. Later, in the 1960s and 1970s, another eleven points were added, making a total of seventeen principles by 1977. Perhaps the most controversial parts of these reforms were the land reforms and women's suffrage, both of which encountered much resistance from the more conservative members of the society, including landlords as well as the `ulama. The excerpts below represent a number of different perspectives on the White Revolution.

1. The Statement of the National Liberation Movement Regarding the White Revolution

The National Liberation Movement was a political movement that had come into being in 1961, and had among its ranks religious laymen like Mehdi Bazargan, Mahmoud Taleqani, and Yadollah Sahabi. As the passage below attests, this political party took an oppositional stance to both the White Revolution and the national referendum, arguing that this series of reforms was neither revolutionary nor authentic; rather, the party believed that the reforms all originated from the United States, whose agenda at this time was to stop the spread of communism. The statement below was issued on January 23, 1963, only three days before the actual referendum took place.

Text: *The Memoirs of Bazargan: Sixty Years of Service and Resistance, in Conversation with Major Gholam Reza Nejati* [17]

The agent of this revolution is neither the peasant nor the city dweller; it is neither the nation, the Parliament, nor even the government; it is one person, the person of the king! This revolution is a novel phenomenon indeed! After all, there tend to be two sides to a revolution; the revolutionaries [usually consist of] the persecuted, the suffering, and the angry and oppressed of society, [who] carry out the revolution against the unjust, powerful and tyrannical ruling class. Today, however, the revolutionaries consist of the ruling class, which until yesterday . . . was itself the one and only supporter of the system of landlord and peasant, and feudalism. In short, it was the beneficiary of the extortion of landownership and capitalism . . . and ultimately, it was the source of all the [societal] pressures and corruption. . . . There can be no bigger revolution than one where within a short period of time, the assailant, himself, becomes the voice of the voiceless victim!

. . . American policy has no interest in the individual or the social class. They wanted a program; they demanded land reform and a fight against corruption, in order to prevent the spread of communism. . . . Therefore a trip took place to Europe, and another to America. Promises were made that the first person of the country becomes the first, middle, and last person

17. *Khaterat-e Bazargan: shast sal khedmat va moqavemat, goftogu ba sarhang Gholam Reza Nejati.* Tehran: Entesharat-e Rasa, 1375/ 1996. Vol. 1, pp. 388-389.

of the country, as well as the apparent and actual administrator of the program. . . .

A Prime Minister left and was replaced by a slave-like vassal. . . . Every ordinary individual asks himself: if a referendum or consulting public opinion is permissible, and the right thing to do, then why is it that this same regime condemned and sentenced Dr. Mosaddeq to prison in its own so-called legal courts on charges of organizing a referendum?[18] Why did Dr. Eqbal, the devoted, loyal servant, deprive the nationalists of Iran[19] of the right to become representatives in Parliament by charging them of having been agents of the referendum? If this is a bad thing and is against the law, how is it that the king of the country can become the agent of the referendum?! . . .

The Iranian revolution must be from within, not from without. . . . You peasants and farmers who are familiar with the [nature of] sheep and wolves, don't be deceived! Recognize the wolf when you see it! . . .

2. Mahmoud `Enayat on the White Revolution

This passage consists of a commentary by Mahmoud `Enayat, a journalist and essayist and the editor of Ferdawsi, an influential weekly with a "liberal leaning" in the early 1960s. It is of interest on two levels: first, because it shows that, at least in 1963, a secular liberal essayist like Mahmoud `Enayat found himself in the awkward and uncomfortable position of being in agreement with some of the principles of the White Revolution, and second, because, from his perspective, the reaction of the religious classes to the White Revolution was risky behavior in terms of its consequences for the future of religion and faith. In other words, while secularists like `Enayat did not see themselves as sharing much with the religious, they believed that the clergy's public position against the White Revolution would result in people's losing their belief in religion as a progressive force. That this proved to be the opposite of what actually transpired in 1978 is an indication of how complex and unpredictable the 1978-1979 revolution was!

---

18. This is a reference to the national referendum that took place in July 1953 to legitimize the dissolution of the Parliament by Mosaddeq.

19. Manuchehr Eqbal was Prime Minister between 1957 and 1960.

Text: "Find Faith," *Ferdawsi*, May 3, 1963[20]

Recent events in our society have come into open confrontation with a faction among the religious. The faithful have risen in opposition to some of these changes. Those supporting the abolition of the system of landlord and peasant as well as the participation of women in political and social activities, among whose ranks we, too, willy-nilly, and by virtue of keeping consistent with the positive developments of the times, count ourselves, have rejected the hostility [of the religious] with indignation.

At this juncture, a fear has come into being for every realistic and patriotic person. It is not a fear of a return to the system of landlord and peasant since this is irreversible. Nor is it a fear from more serious developments because we believe that the changes that have happened until now in the context of social relations, while necessary, do not go far enough. Our fear, instead, concerns the destruction of faith. In a society where even the phenomenon of political parties has never been realized in its real and authentic sense, and what is left of political and social beliefs—whatever that may be—is exclusive to a minority of the intellectuals and the literati . . . the destruction of religious belief will be a catastrophe.

This belief, willy-nilly, will be shaken in the course of the struggle between the supporters of social change and its opponents. Each side will, in some way, be effective in reinforcing its fragility. Fighting against the clergy who consider the abolition of the system of landlord and peasant, or the granting of the right to vote to women to be contrary to the principles of religion, alone, will not weaken the religious belief; rather, it is the illusion of being able to use religion as a sharp weapon against the interests of the disadvantaged classes that will endanger this religious belief. In other places, at least the strength of the belief in the system of political parties is such that it can fill in the place of lost belief but here . . . ?

If we had something other than this belief, there would be no fear, but the fear is that there is nothing, and that gradually, a terrifying vacuum will envelop everything around us.

Regressive systems are irreversible. With full knowledge of this point, the opponents must come forward to fill this vacuum.

20. *Ferdawsi*, no. 115, 13 Ordibehesht 1342/ 3 May 1963, p. 2.

3. Ayatollah Khomeini on the White Revolution

The `ulama, by and large, opposed the White Revolution, especially the land reforms and women's enfranchisement. They also—in particular, Ayatollah Khomeini—had taken a stance against the idea of a national referendum, arguing essentially that a referendum was not valid in Islam. The regime reacted against this opposition, sending paratroopers to the theological Faiziyeh school in Qom, where Khomeini taught. The ensuing confrontation resulted in a number of young theology students getting beaten, with several killed. This altercation only exacerbated the hostility between Khomeini and the regime, as seen in the passage below, which includes excerpts from the famous speech that Khomeini gave on June 3, 1963— the speech that became the basis for his reputation as an uncompromising individual.

Text: "The Afternoon of `Ashura": Excerpts from Ayatollah Khomeini's Speech Regarding the White Revolution, June 3, 1963[21]

"It is now the afternoon of `Ashura. Sometimes when I recall the events of `Ashura,[22] a question occurs to me: If the Umayyads and the regime of Yazid ibn Mu`awiya wished to make war against Husayn, why did they commit such savage and inhuman crimes against the defenseless women and innocent children? What was the offense of the women and children? What had Husayn's six month-old infant done? It seems to me that the Umayyads had a far more basic aim: they were opposed to the very existence of the family of the Prophet. They did not wish the Bani Hashim[23] to exist and their goal was to root out this 'goodly tree.'

A similar question occurs to me now. If the tyrannical regime of Iran simply wished to wage war on the *maraji*,[24] to oppose the `ulama, what business did it have tearing the Qur'an to shreds on the day it attacked the

21. The translation of this text has been published in Hamid Algar, *Islam and Revolution: Writings and Declarations of Imam Khomeini.* Berkeley: Mizan Press, 1981, pp. 177-180. (Reprinted with permission of Hamid Algar.)

22. `Ashura is the tenth day of the month of Muharram in the Islamic calendar, when Shi'i Muslims mourn and commemorate the death of Husayn, the third Shi'i Imam and the son of Ali, who was killed at the battle of Karbala in 680 C.E. at the hands of Yazid b. Mu`awiya, the second Umayyad Caliph.

23. Bani Hashim was the Meccan clan to which the Prophet belonged.

24. *Maraji*` is the plural of *marja*` and refers to learned scholars who have achieved the necessary standing to issue rulings on religious matters.

Fayziya Madrasa? Indeed, what business did it have with the madrasa or with its students, like the eighteen- year-old sayyid who was killed? What had he done against the Shah, against the government, against the tyranni- cal regime? We come to the conclusion that this regime also has a more basic aim: they are fundamentally opposed to Islam itself and the existence of the religious class. They do not wish this institution to exist; they do not wish any of us to exist, the great and the small alike. . . .

Respected people of Qum! On the day that mendacious, that scandalous referendum took place—that referendum contrary to all the interests of the Iranian nation and conducted at bayonet point—you witnessed a gang of hooligans and ruffians prowling through Qum, on foot and riding in cars, going down the streets and thoroughfares of this center of religious learning that stands next to the shrine of Fatima, the Immaculate One (peace be upon her)! They were shouting: 'Your days of parasitism are at an end! Your days of eating *pulao* are over!'

Now, these students of the religious sciences who spend the best and most active part of their lives in these narrow cells, and whose monthly in- come is somewhere between 40 and 100 tumans—are they parasites? And those to whom one source of income alone brings hundreds of millions of tumans are not parasites? Are the `ulama` parasites—people like the late Hajj Shaikh `Abd al-Karim, whose sons had nothing to eat on the night that he died; or the late Burujirdi,[25] who was 600,000 tumans in debt when he departed from this world? And those who have filled foreign banks with the wealth produced by the toil of our poverty-stricken people, who have erected towering palaces but still will not leave the people in peace, wishing to fill their own pockets and those of Israel with our resources—they are not parasites? Let the world judge, let the nation judge who the parasites are!

Let me give you some advice, Mr. Shah! Dear Mr. Shah, I advise you to desist in this policy and acts like this. I don't want the people to offer up thanks if your masters should decide one day that you must leave. I don't want you to become like your father.

Iranian nation! Those among you who are thirty or forty years of age or more will remember how three foreign countries attacked us during World War II. The Soviet Union, Britain, and America invaded Iran and occupied our country. The property of the people was exposed to danger and their

25. Ayatollah Hosayn Burujirdi (or Boroujerdi) held the position of the sole source of emulation, or *marja`-e taqlid,* from the 1940s to his death in 1961.

honor was imperiled. But God knows, everyone was happy because the Pahlavi had gone!

Shah, I don't wish the same to happen to you; I don't want you to become like your father. Listen to my advice, listen to the `ulama of Islam. They desire the welfare of the nation, the welfare of the country. Don't listen to Israel; Israel can't do anything for you. You miserable wretch, forty-five years of your life have passed, isn't it time for you to think and reflect a little, to ponder about where all this is leading you, to learn a lesson from the experience of your father? If what they say is true, that you are opposed to Islam and the religious scholars, your ideas are quite wrong. If they are dictating these things to you and then giving them to you to read, you should think about it a little. Why do you speak without thinking? Are the religious scholars really some form of impure animal? If they are impure animals, why do the people kiss their hands? Why do they regard the very water they drink as blessed? Are we really impure animals? I hope to God that you did not have in mind the `ulama and religious scholars when you said, 'The reactionaries are like an impure animal,' because if you did, it will be difficult for us to tolerate you much longer, and you will find yourself in a predicament. You won't be able to go on living; the nation will not allow you to continue this way. The religious scholars and Islam are Black Reaction! And you have carried out your White Revolution in the midst of all this Black Reaction! What do you mean, a White Revolution? Why do you try to deceive the people so? Why do you threaten the people so?

I was informed today that a number of preachers and speakers in Tehran were taken to the offices of SAVAK and were threatened with punishment if they speak on three subjects. They were not to say anything bad about the Shah, not to attack Israel, and not to say that Islam is endangered. Otherwise, they can say what they like! But all of our problems and all our differences with the government comprise exactly these three! If we overlook these three subjects, we have no dispute with the government. Even if we do not say that Islam is endangered, will that mean that Islam is not endangered? Or if we do not say, 'The Shah is such-and-such,' will that mean that he is not in fact such-and-such? And what is this tie, this link, between the Shah and Israel that makes SAVAK consider the Shah an Israeli? Does SAVAK consider the Shah a Jew?

Mr. Shah! Maybe those people want to present you as a Jew so that I will denounce you as an unbeliever and they can expel you from Iran and put an end to you! Don't you know that if one day, some uproar occurs and the tables are turned, none of those people around you will be your friends? They are friends of the dollar; they have no religion, no loyalty. They are hanging responsibility for everything around your miserable neck!

. . . There is much to be said, far more than you can imagine. Certain things are happening that endanger our country and our Islam. The things that are happening to this nation and those that are about to happen fill me with anxiety and sorrow. I feel anxiety and sorrow at the state of Iran, at the state of our ruined country, at the state of this cabinet, at the state of those running our government.

I pray to God Almighty that He remedy our affairs."

The Women's Organization of Iran and the Parameters of Its Activities in the 1970s

The Women's Organization of Iran (WOI) was an umbrella organization that came into being in 1966 with the support of Ashraf Pahlavi, Moham-mad Reza Shah's twin sister, who in turn became the WOI's Honorary President. The aim of this organization was to bring together and unite a number of women's organizations that had emerged in the 1950s so that they would be more effective in promoting the rights of women in Iran. The excerpt below is an account by Mahnaz Akhami, the Secretary-General of the Women's Organization between 1970 and 1979. Its interest lies in its being an insider's perspective on how the approach of the Women's Organization of Iran in the 1970s was different from that of women's movements in earlier times.

Text: *Women, State and Society in Iran: An Interview with Mahnaz Afkhami*[26]

In the 1940s, 50s and 60s, the activities of women's movements were concerned primarily with charitable projects, and often consisted of more

---

26. Gholam Reza Afkhami, ed., *Women, State, and Society in Iran, 1963-1978: An Interview with Mahnaz Afkhami.* Bethesda, MD: Foundation for Iranian Studies, 2003, pp. 94-97. (Translated with permission of the Foundation for Iranian Studies.)

affluent women trying to assist the disadvantaged and less fortunate women. Their emphasis on education was based on this rationale that education would help women become better wives and mothers. However, with a growing number of educated women looking for employment [outside of the house], the terms of the discourse changed direction: [the idea, now, was that] women had the ability to carry the burdens of being responsible for both the household as well as holding a job, while also being good mothers and wives. It was emphasized that having an education and a job enabled women to bring up healthier children while also improving the financial situation of the family. However, rapid change in the situation of women, especially in view of their joining growing numbers in a professional workforce, soon made it clear that carrying the burden of responsibility for both the household and the workplace would not be possible for most women without a fundamental change taking place in the perception that men had of women, and in their behavior [towards women] in society. The intellectual turning point towards this issue was the General Assembly [of the Women's Organization] in 1973 which resulted in a revision in the constitution of the Women's Organization. . . .

In the inaugural meeting of the Organization, a number of women activists spoke about the advantages of education and employment for women, as well as the indisputable ability of women to carry out the roles of good wives and mothers and that of a modern working woman at one and the same time. Another member of the Central Committee made a reference to the proverb that "one half of an apple completes the other half," and argued that women had a complementary role to men. Following this speech given by my colleague, I went to the microphone. . . . I knew that in any case, I had to discuss the main issue. I said, "Sisters, it is time for us to recognize our problems and their solutions. We all know that we are in no way women with extraordinary powers, and no one should expect us to be so. No one can possibly carry out all these different and demanding tasks. No one should expect us to shoulder all the responsibilities at home while having full-time jobs. . . . We are each a complete person in our own right; we do not constitute one half of anything or anyone." The crowd was silent for several seconds and then, the sound of applause, and cheering . . . filled the big room.

We had reached a stage when we could express our own views clearly and emphasize that our situation, role, and needs had changed. We no longer felt obliged or indebted to anyone to do things under circumstances that were not in our interest. We were in search of a change in the make-up of society and the relations between members of the family in order to reach a just balance in the distribution of rights and responsibilities. We challenged not only the political configuration of the family, but also the social hierarchy of which the family was at the center.

. . . We were worried about both how our discussions would get reflected in the press and how society and the authorities would react to them, yet there was no going back. The Assembly took the necessary decisions including a revision in the constitution of the Women's Organization. The most important change [in this revision] was the first part of the second article [of the constitution]. This article had described the aim of the organization to be "Assistance to women in carrying out their social responsibilities as well as fulfilling their roles as mothers and wives in the changing Iranian family." However, the revised text no longer referred to women's roles in the family. Rather it inserted the question of rights and duties in two separate articles in which the question of rights was described in two paragraphs before that of duty. The revised text was as follows: "Defending the personal, family and social rights of women in order to safeguard women's complete equality in society and before the law." The other major change in the constitution [of the women's organization] had to do with the selection of the members of the Central Council [of the organization]. Whereas in the older version of the constitution, half of the members of the Central Council were elected, and the other half were appointed by the honorary President [Princess Ashraf], in the new version of the constitution, all the members of the Central Council were to be elected.

After this change, as the legal work of the [Women's] Organization progressed gradually, certain accomplishments were made in the domain of passing laws, resulting in a broadening of the parameters of the work that was being done [by the Organization]. One of the important issues, for example, concerned the family and the laws pertaining to it. We tried to make women aware of their rights, because the family laws and other laws which were associated with it and had passed, had broadened the parameters of women's rights, and had led to the development of their opportunities. But passing laws was one thing, informing women of the existence of such laws, and making them aware of how they could use these laws to their advantage, was something else. For example, the Family Court could decide on issues relating to divorce or child custody, and social workers associated with the Women's Organization worked in these family courts and helped women. From our perspective, one of our most important tasks was to inform women that such means existed; that there was a Family Court, with a social worker to help women. Many women did not know such things, and for years, had gotten into the habit of a man telling them "I divorce you." By means of this phrase alone, [a man could] put an end to their shared life, without bearing any responsibility, whether with regard to taking care of the children or assisting the woman with her daily expenses. The Family Protection Law and the establishment of family courts changed this situation.

This change was huge; getting used to it, learning and becoming informed of the rights that women had gained, needed [not only] lots of time, but also extensive informative programs. One of the more successful and interesting programs [of the Organization] consisted of drawing up pamphlets to teach [women's] rights in a simple and accessible language, as well as the establishment of meetings to teach rights to women with little education and low incomes, with the help of a broad group of women lawyers.

The Establishment of the Rastakhiz Party

The Rastakhiz (or Resurgence) party was established in early March 1975. It was intended to replace the existing political parties, and membership in it was a requirement for most government and university employees, and for anyone who wanted to move up in society. However, it was short-lived: it was dissolved in late 1978 once the anti-government demonstrations had intensified. In fact, in retrospect and while in exile, the Shah admitted that the creation of Rastakhiz had been a mistake. The passage below is an excerpt from an interview with `Abdolmajid Majidi, who, by virtue of his position as director of the Plan and Budget Organization, had frequent meetings with the Shah. It is of interest because it gives an account of where the idea of creating a single party had come from. It also shows that individuals such as `Abdolmajid Majidi who were highly positioned in the establishment were aware of the kind of grievances and dissatisfactions that people harbored.

Text: *Memoirs of `Abdolmajid Majidi, Director of the Plan and Budget Organization*[27]

. . . I remember that in . . . February 1975, I came to St. Moritz[28] in order to present the budget report . . . to His Majesty. . . . In fact, the step before sending the budget to the *majles* was to present it to His Majesty. . . . After I had finished reporting [on the budget], and the Shah had instructed me with what to do and what not to do. . . . I wanted to leave. I asked for permission. He said, "Sit, I have something else to say." I sat down, and His Majesty said, "We want to make some changes in the political set-up of the country because there is not much criticism of the system in the way that there should be, and as a result, the system cannot reform itself [from within]. Therefore, we have thought that we should establish a system whereby there can be criticism from within, so that the system can reform and better itself on a regular basis. So we want to change the political system of the country, and make it such that the system can itself take on a critical approach." From His Majesty's description, I thought that what was intended was a single party, since there had been much discussion regarding this issue in the past . . . and I was familiar with this idea."

Q: How had this idea come about? Where had it been proposed for you to have discussed it?

A: Well, it had been discussed in the political office of the Iran-e Novin party[29] of which I was a member. Whenever the late Hoveyda[30] came across problems, he would say, "It seems that the only way forward is a single party, because we cannot proceed in this way." This was the case especially following the elections in Shahsavar when there was a confrontation between the opposing groups, namely the People's Party and Iran-e Novin Party, and it did not look good. Hoveyda [then] said, "The People's Party also follows the policies of His Majesty. In fact, we are all after the same thing. Such apparent quarrels which take place on the electoral scene of a

27. Habib Ladjevardi, ed., *Memoirs of Abdolmajid Majidi, Director of the Plan and Budget Organization (1973-1977)*. Iranian Oral History Project. Center for Middle Eastern Studies, Harvard University, 1998, pp. 61-70. (Translated with permission of the Center for Middle Eastern Studies, Harvard University.)

28. St. Moritz is a favorite holiday destination in Switzerland for skiers. In the 1970s, the royal family would spend their winter holidays in St. Moritz.

29. The Iran-e Novin (or New Iran) party had been founded in December 1963, replacing the Melliyun (or Nationalists) party.

30. Amir Abbas Hoveyda was Prime Minister of Iran for thirteen years from January 1965 to August 1977. He had also been the Secretary-General of the Iran-e Novin party between 1965 and 1975.

city or an electoral district are a little meaningless. We must all have one single party, rather than having quarrels between two parties both of which say the same thing. [Instead], we should have a [genuine] argument between two people in order to see which one makes more sense . . . and which one is more patriotic. . . ." This was the logic.

Q: Did Mr. Hoveyda discuss this logic? What I mean is, was he in agreement with this view?

A: Since Mr. Hoveyda was in contact with His Majesty more than us, and came across such issues, he knew what the views of His Majesty were. He would try to reflect the views of His Majesty both in the party as well as the government. [Having said that], I cannot say that Hoveyda, himself, believed in this. Hoveyda had been educated abroad . . . and had gained experience there. [As a result], he was familiar with electoral politics and procedures, and how western democracy worked. Naturally, he could not have had such an inclination from the bottom of his heart. But perhaps he pointed to this issue because he felt that there was a preference for this from the top.

In any case, when His Majesty told me that "we want to change the political set-up of the country, and create a system where there can be criticism from within," I told him, "Sir, I don't think that this is good for our country. The problem in our country is that people do not trust the decisions or the actions and measures taken by the government as they should. One main reason for this is corruption. If we could fight corruption, reduce or eliminate it, people would become much more satisfied than if we changed a multi-party system to a single-party one. At present, there is the Iran-e Novin Party, the People's Party, and the Pan-Iranist party.[31] If they are few in number, let other parties come into being. If they are enough in number, allow those that are weaker now to become more active so that some form of alternation can come into being . . . and another party can take the matters into its hands. At the moment, people have other worries. . . .

Of course, His Majesty did not like what I said. He asked, "What do you mean by corruption?" I said, "What I mean by corruption is that a number of people who are close to the government or to the Court and the royal family, take certain advantages from what they do that is not logical. I even gave examples. "A contract is signed; a project is put into effect, between 5 to 10% and sometimes even more than 10% will be pocketed by some

---

31. The Pan-Iranist party was a nationalist party that had been founded in 1951.

person who either initiated the project or was the middle-man. This is not right. It is for this reason that people get angry. They are upset that such corruption exists in the country, or that they see that some people suddenly become millionaires without deserving it, or having done anything. . . ."

Well, this discussion was not methodical or systematic. His Majesty had one view, and I was trying my best to dissuade him. My aim was not to talk of social justice. Rather, I wanted to convince the Shah that changing the political system into a one-party system did not solve anything.

His Majesty told me, "When you go to Tehran, tell the Prime Minister all that we have talked about." What the Shah meant indirectly was that I should pass this on to the Prime Minister so that when [the Shah] goes back, a single party can be established.

. . . His Majesty came back in mid to late February 1975, and it was in early March that Rastakhiz Party was established. That is, it still did not have a name then—the Shah would refer to it as the "all-encompassing party. . . . An all-encompassing party has to come into being." We asked Hoveyda, the Secretary-General of Iran-e Novin Party and Prime Minster, to put this into effect. Soon after, the Rastakhiz Party came into being. . . . Mr. Jamshid Amuzegar[32] was very influential in creating [the Party] and establishing its specifics. Fortunately, I had no involvement in any of this until the time when its constitution was written. Its constitution stated that the Minister of Planning was a member of the political office [of the Party] and . . . in this way, I became a member of the political office of the Rastakhiz Party until Mr. Amuzegar became the Secretary-General of the Party.

One day, Mr. Amuzegar, himself, came to me and said, "I was with His Majesty this afternoon, and he told me that now that you are becoming the Secretary-General of Rastakhiz, let Majidi be in charge of the progressive wing."[33] I said, "But sir, His Majesty knows what I think [about Rastakhiz]." Amuzegar said, "No, this is what His Majesty said. And anyway, the progressive wing is a very liberal, progressive and worthy part of Rastakhiz and it will be very good for you to manage it. Hoveyda also came later and congratulated me, saying His Majesty has chosen you for the progressive wing." And so it was that I became the co-ordinator of the progressive faction until the time that I retired from it.

32. Jamshid Amuzegar was Minister of Labor (1958-59), Minister of Agriculture (1959-60), Minister of Health (1963-65), Minister of Finance (1965-74), Minister of the Interior (1974-76), Secretary-General of the Rastakhiz Party (1976-77), and Prime Minister (1977-78).

33. The Rastakhiz party was divided into two wings, the Progressive and the Constructive wings.

CHAPTER

6

Intellectuals, Islam, and the Search for "Cultural Authenticity"

Jalal Al-e Ahmad

Jalal Al-e Ahmad (1923-1969) was a short story writer, essayist, and jour-nalist. He has become perhaps one of the most well-known intellectuals of 1960s Iran, in part because of his treatise called Gharbzadegi *(translated as "westoxication" or "occidentosis"), which captured the mood of the time in Iran when third-worldism and nativism were on the rise in intellec-tual circles. Even though the term had not originated with Al-e Ahmad, the concept came to be identified with him because he politicized and popu-larized it. The two passages below consist of excerpts from Al-e Ahmad's two most celebrated works:* Gharbzadegi (Occidentosis) *and* On the Service and Betrayal of Intellectuals, *respectively. In the first, he defines what he means by* gharbzadegi *or "occidentosis," and in the second, he expresses his ambivalence towards the clergy. That is, while on the one hand, he seems to have much esteem for clergy members in view of both their con-nection with everyday people and their oppositional stance to the state—and thus advises that secular intellectuals join forces with them in order to sustain a more effective front against oppression—on the other, he thinks that the clergy are in need of reform in order to maintain their relevance to society and not become obsolete.*

1. Excerpts from *Gharbzadegi*[1]

"I speak of 'occidentosis' as of tuberculosis. But perhaps it more closely resembles an infestation of weevils. Have you seen how they attack wheat? From the inside. The bran remains intact, but it is just a shell, like a cocoon left behind on a tree. At any rate, I am speaking of a disease: an accident from without, spreading in an environment rendered susceptible to it. Let us seek a diagnosis for this complaint and its causes—and, if possible, its cure.

Occidentosis has two poles or extremes—two ends of one continuum. One pole is the Occident, by which I mean all of Europe, Soviet Russia, and North America, the developed and industrialized nations that can use machines to turn raw materials into more complex forms that can be marketed as goods. These raw materials are not only iron ore and oil, or gut, cotton, and gum tragacanth; they are also myths, dogmas, music, and the higher worlds. The other pole is Asia and Africa, or the backward, developing or nonindustrial nations that have been made into consumers of Western goods. However, the raw materials for these goods come from the developing nations: oil from the shores of the Gulf, hemp and spices from India, jazz from Africa, silk and opium from China, anthropology from Oceania, sociology from Africa. These last two come from Latin America as well: from the Aztec and Inca peoples, sacrificed by the onslaught of Christianity. Everything in the developing nations comes from somewhere else. And we—the Iranians—fall into the category of the backward and developing nations: we have more points in common with them than points of difference.

. . . All I will say here is that "East" and "West" are no longer geographical or political concepts to me. For a European or an American, the West means Europe and America, and the East, the USSR, China, and the Eastern European nations. But for me, they are economic concepts. The West comprises the sated nations and the East, the hungry nations. . . . Western nations generally have high wages, low mortality, low fertility, well-organized social services, adequate foodstuffs (at least three thousand calories per day), per capital annual income of at least 3000 tumans, and nominal

---

1. Jalal Al-e Ahmad, *Occidentosis: A Plague from the West*. Translated by R. Campbell, with an introduction by Hamid Algar. Berkeley, CA: Mizan Press, 1984, pp. 27-35. (Reprinted with permission of Hamid Algar.)

democracy (the heritage of the French Revolution). The second group of nations has these characteristics: low wages, high mortality, even higher fertility, social services nil (or for hire), inadequate foodstuffs (at most one thousand calories per day), annual income less than 500 tumans, and no notion of democracy (the heritage of the first wave of imperialism).

. . . Our age is one of two worlds: one producing and exporting machines, the other importing and consuming them and wearing them out. The stage for this conflict is the global market. The weapons, apart from tanks, guns, bombers, and missile launchers, themselves products of the West, are UN-ESCO, the FAO, the UN, ECAFE, and the other so-called international organizations. In fact, they are Western con artists come in new disguises to colonize this other world: to South America, to Asia, to Africa. Here is the basis for the occidentosis of all non-Western nations. I am not speaking of rejecting the machine or of banishing it, as the utopianists of the early nineteenth century sought to do. History has fated the world to fall prey to the machine. It is a question of how to encounter the machine and technology.

The important point is that we the people of the developing nations are not fabricating the machines. But, owing to economic and political determinants and to the global confrontation of rich and poor, we have had to be gentle and tractable consumers for the West's industrial goods or at best contented assemblers at low wages of what comes from the West. And this has necessitated our conforming ourselves, our governments, our cultures, and our daily lives to the machine. . . .

Let me consider Iran. We have been unable to preserve our own historico-cultural character in the face of the machine and its fateful onslaught. Rather, we have been routed. We have been unable to take a considered stand in the face of this contemporary monster. So long as we do not comprehend the real essence, basis, and philosophy of Western civilization, only aping the West outwardly and formally (by consuming its machines), we shall be like the ass going about in a lion's skin. We know what became of him. Although the one who created the machine now cries out that it is stifling him, we not only fail to repudiate our assuming the garb of machine tenders, we pride ourselves on it. For two hundred years, we have resembled the crow mimicking the partridge (always supposing that the West is a partridge and we are a crow). So long as we remain consumers, so long as we have not built the machine, we remain occidentotic. Our dilemma is that once we have built the machine, we will have become mechanotic, just like the West, crying out at the way technology and the machine have stampeded out of control. . . .

If we define occidentosis as the aggregate of events in the life, culture, civilization, and mode of thought of a people having no supporting tradition, no historical continuity, no gradient of transformation, but having only what the machine brings them, it is clear that we are such a people. And because this discussion will relate primarily to the geographic, linguistic, cultural and religious background of its author, I might expand on the definition by saying that when we Iranians have the machine, that is, when we have built it, we will need its gifts less than its antecedents and adjuncts.

Occidentosis thus characterizes an era in which we have not yet acquired the machine, in which we are not yet versed in the mysteries of its structure. Occidentosis characterizes an era in which we have not yet grown familiar with the preliminaries to the machine, the new sciences and technologies. Occidentosis characterizes an era in which the logic of the marketplace and the movements of oil compel us to buy and consume the machine.

How did this era arrive? Why did we utterly fail to develop the machine, leaving it to others to so encompass its development that by the time we awakened, every oil rig had become a nail driven into our land? How did we grow occidentotic? Let us turn to history to find out."

2. Excerpts from *On the Service and Betrayal of Intellectuals*[2]

. . . Each of the tasks of the [Muslim] clergy—from the person issuing the *fatwa* (legal judgment) to the itinerant preacher and the religious leader of such and such a village—is tantamount to the tasks of the intellectual, in terms of the intellectual work that is involved in it, the teaching that it entails, and the fact that it is related to the word. In my opinion, the freethinking clergy issuing fatwas and the *mojtahed*s (that are not superstitious) . . . should be placed, if not in the actual central nucleus of intellectualism, then, in the first circle around the central nucleus of intellectualism. This is by virtue of the fact that the people issuing *fatwa*s are authors of written works, without any intention to profit or to proselytize, in addition to the fact that, at times, their works result in creativity. I am referring to the one or two *fatwa*s that I mentioned in the previous pages, including the *fatwa*

2. Jalal Al-e Ahmad, *Dar Khedmat va khiyanat-e rawshanfekran.* Rev. ed. Tehran: Entesharat-e Ferdaws, 1372/ 1993, pp. 292-296.

regarding radio and television as well as the *fatwa* advocating investment in state banks and banning it in private banks which implies a certain socialist perspective. Even though the *fatwas* issued by His Excellency [Mr.] Khomeini and Mr. Hakim were considered to be [too late in the manner of] the antidote after the death of Sohrab,[3] they were still godsends. . . .

In confirming the educational impact of the job of the clergy, I should make the point that at present . . . there are two hundred Islamic schools (at both primary and secondary levels) with 50,000 students all over the country, which in addition to official cultural programs also have religious instruction. In addition, the educational impact of the job of the clergy will become clearer when we realize that for 80 percent of the illiterate population that has no access to schools, classes, or modern culture, their only link to the news, sciences, and culture is through the clergy on the one hand and the radio on the other. If we consider that everyday people get half of their information orally from the radio, the other half comes from the clergy who in the months of Muharram, Safar, and Ramazan[4]—that is, three months of each year—make themselves the subject of a large part of the people's preoccupation. In addition to the fact that the clergy have also begun to gain a foothold on the radio, in those same months that I mentioned, there are many days (at least twenty days) where other than political news, there are no other programs broadcast from the radio except religious programs. In this way, until such time that, as in the Middle Ages, a large part of the transmission of culture and the traditional heritage remains on the shoulders of the clergy—without [secular] intellectuals being able to replace them in such domains—one cannot disregard the power of the clergy in social movements. This is especially the case here where both the intellectuals and the clergy find themselves in the realm of imperialism, whose first phase of plunder concerns culture and religion. Also, the situation of the intellectuals is in no way similar to that of the intellectuals and the clergy in the countries of the *metropole* where at times they stand in opposition to each other. [This is the case] especially since the [Iranian] constitution states the religion of the country to be Shi'ism and considers five members of the high-ranking clergy to play a necessary role in super-

3. This is a reference to the story of Rostam and Sohrab in the *Shahnameh* or *Book of Kings* by Ferdawsi, in which the antidote reaches Sohrab too late to save him from death.

4. Muharram, Safar, and Ramazan, the first, second, and ninth months of the Islamic calendar, respectively, are considered holy months and thus why the clergy are said to play a more perceptible role during these months.

vising the legislature.[5] Regardless of the fact that in the course of these past sixty years of constitutionalism, this Article of the constitution has not been acted upon even once, and that the clergy maintain the right to object to the illegitimacy of all the laws that have been passed by all the past constitutional parliaments, at present, in view of the strict measures taken towards the clergy (such as exile and imprisonment, monitoring the pulpits, reducing the days of mourning, and rewarding only those among the clergy who know how to serve the state . . .), there is no option other than choosing one of the following three options:

1. The state should either provide the clergy with appropriate responsibilities together with an appropriate budget according to the constitution, or it has to have the courage to remove its dependence on religion. . . . This means that it should modify the constitution of Iran, and announce Iran to be a secular state where no one religion is official while all religions are recognized.

2. The clergy should either fundamentally reconsider their positions—with regard to officially recognizing unveiling, and denouncing any advocacy for reform . . .— or they will become isolated and cut off from having any social impact, and will turn more ossified by the day.

3. Or intellectuals should either reach a compromise with the clergy, [enabling them to] join together and become a united front against the state so that in sensitive situations they can keep an eye on the actions of the state in terms of injustice and repression, or they should take over the duties that the clergy have at present. If they do not proceed in any of these ways, then inevitably they will have to cope with the situation that they have before them—that is, act as two-sided agents, in the way of both weakening themselves and the clergy, to the advantage of the state.

5. This is a reference to Article 2 of the Supplementary Fundamental Laws ratified in 1907.

`Ali Shari`ati

`Ali Shari`ati (1933-1977) has been regarded as the "main ideologue of the Iranian revolution"[6] and thus the intellectual par excellence of Iran in the 1970s. A university professor and gifted speaker, he captured the imagination of a generation of young educated Iranians by blending a revolutionary interpretation of Islam and Shi'ism together with Marxism. The two passages below represent excerpts from perhaps two of his most well-known lectures, delivered at Jondishapour University in Ahvaz, Iran, in 1976 and at Hosayniyeh-ye Ershad in Tehran in September 1972, respectively.[7] In the first passage, he defines what he means by "Return to the Self," a theme that gained much popularity in the Iran of the 1970s, and in the second, he delineates his understanding of revolutionary Shi'ism.

1. Excerpts from *Return to the Self*[8]

. . . The fundamental issue that is currently being discussed among intellectuals, whether African, Latin-American, or Asian, and recently, it has been discussed in Iran too . . . is the issue of "Return to the Self." Before anything, I should explain . . . that if you have heard that I emphasize religion, that I emphasize Islam, my emphasis is on a reformed and reconsidered Islam . . . an Islamic renaissance movement. I did not achieve this religious insight by sitting and considering different sects and religions, and studying each one of them, and finally coming to the conclusion that Islam is the "best religion," but I have taken another route. If I talk about that course here, it is [so that I can point out] that it is not only religious intellectuals and students who can listen and accept my invitation; rather anyone who is an intellectual, has an independent mind, wants to serve his/her society, and feels his/her own intellectual mission vis-à-vis his/her generation and age, can follow this same path that we have taken.

. . . Yes, the issue of "Return to the Self" is not a slogan that the religious have suddenly put forward in the world. Rather, it tended to be mostly non-

---

6. Mehrzad Boroujerdi, *Iranian Intellectuals and the West: The Tormented Triumph of Nativism.* Syracuse, NY: Syracuse University Press, 1996, p. 105.

7. The texts of these lectures were later published and made widely available.

8. `Ali Shari`ati, *Bazgasht beh khishtan: konferansi dar daneshgah-e jondishapur-e Ahvaz.* Solon, Ohio, 1977, pp. 13-41.

religious progressive intellectuals who put it forth for the first time—intellectuals like Aimé Césaire, and in Africa, Frantz Fanon, Julius Nyerere, Jomo Kenyatta, Senghor de Senegal, Kateb Yacine, the Algerian writer, and Jalal Al-e Ahmad in Iran. It is such people that have put forth the motto "Return to the Self," and none of them are religious types. Rather, they are outstanding figures in the world intellectual movement and among the anti-imperialist leaders in the Third World and accepted by all factions. . . . On this basis, when the issue of "Return to the Self" is put forth, for I who am religious, and you who are not, but we, both, share our social responsibility and have reached a common understanding, the issue changes from "Return to the Self" to "Return to One's Own Culture," and learning about that self. It is in this line of study that we reach "the return to Islamic culture and ideology," where Islam is not a tradition, a heritage or a belief system in society, but an ideology, a faith that brought awareness and created a miracle in this same society. In truth, the emphasis is not on the basis of an inherited religious feeling, or a dry pious feeling; rather, it is on the basis of an intellectual motto which is put forth by all intellectuals on a global scale. . . .

But which self should we return to? . . . We have an ancient self, belonging to the periods of the Achaemenids, Sassanids, Arsacids, and those before them.[9] Should we return to them? . . . That self is ancient; it is old; it is the self that has been recorded in history, but whose ties with us have been broken as a result of the interval of many centuries. That Achaemenid and ancient self is the self which historians, sociologists, scholars, and archaeologists can discover, read about and understand, but our nation does not feel that "self" as its own. The heroes, personalities, geniuses, glories and myths from that period neither live nor have a heartbeat among our people. The scissors of the Islamic civilization have come and have created a distance between our pre-Islamic and post-Islamic self so that our pre-Islamic self can only be seen and studied by scholars and experts in museums and libraries, and the masses among our people don't remember anything from them. Consider what feelings our people have towards the rock inscriptions, how do they know them? They say that jinns have written the inscriptions. This makes it clear that they have no link to them. . . . In short, this historical return to the self that we talk about is not a return to

---

9. The Achaemenids (550-330 B.C.), Arsacids, also known as the Parthians (247 B.C.-224 C.E.), and Sassanids (224-651 C.E.) were dynasties that ruled Iran in pre-Islamic times.

nostalgia or to antiquity, or to worshipping stones. . . . Rather, it is a return to the self that is actual and present in the conscience of society. Therefore, it can be dissected and extracted by the intellectual and made to come alive. . . . It is the self . . . that is based on the deep feeling of our spiritual and human values; it is the spirit and mental disposition which is present in our nature. Ignorance and alienation from the self are what have made us neglect it, and having become attracted to another, has left it unknown. But at the same time, it is still living and has movement. It is not the dead classicism of the archaeologist; rather, that self rises up from the midst of the masses. Is that self religious? Is it Islamic? And if so, which Islam? . . . Which religion? . . . Is it the one that is there now? . . . Returning to that on the basis of which our people live and practice is of no use. In fact, that is one of the reasons for their stagnation. . . . That which is called religion now not only stops people from assuming their present responsibilities, but it also stops them from feeling that they constitute living beings in this world. . . . It is this same religion that has deferred thinking and reflection from the time before death to that after death, and has nothing to do with this world. It is with this religion that mankind does everything for his afterlife and feels no sense of responsibility or duty for the world, whether for the sake of his own growth or social life. . . . It is this same religion that any socially-conscious intellectual is weary of and flees. So in one word, I say: our emphasis is on our Islamic cultural self. We must make the return to this same self our motto, because this is the only self that is closer to us than anything else, and is the only culture and civilization that is alive now. It is the only soul, life and faith that lives and has a heartbeat in the society where the intellectual has to work. However, Islam has to be put forth [not] in the form of the repetitious and ignorant traditions which have been the biggest cause of decline, but in the shape of a progressive and dissident Islam, an enlightening ideology that brings awareness. . . . It has to change from a collection of customs, symbols, and actions which are carried out only for the sake of rewards in the afterlife to the biggest force that gives mankind a sense of responsibility, a will to act, and a sense of sacrifice before death. . . . In this way, both religious and non-religious intellectuals will return to their powerful, humane, and sentient conscious selves, stand against the cultural imperialism of the West, and awaken their [own] society, which has been mollified as a result of religion, with the power of religion.

2. Excerpts from *Red Shi'ism*[10]

"Islam is a religion which makes its appearance in the history of mankind with the 'no' of Mohammad, the heir of Abraham, the manifestation of the religion of the Unity of God and the oneness of mankind—a 'no' which begins with the cry of Unity, a cry which Islam reinitiated when confronted by aristocracy and compromise.

Shi'ism is the Islam which distinguishes itself and determines its direction in the history of Islam with the 'no' of the great `Ali, the heir of Mohammad and the manifestation of Islam of justice and Truth—a 'no' which he gives to the council for the election of the caliphate in answer to `Abdul Rahman[11] who was the manifestation of Islamic aristocracy and compromise.

This 'no' up until pre-Safavid times, is recognized to be part of the Shi'ite movement in the history of Islam, an indicator of the social and political role of a group who are the followers of `Ali, known for their attachment to the kindness of the family of the Prophet. It is a party based upon the Qur'an and the Traditions, not the Qur'an and the traditions proclaimed by the dynasties of the Umayyads, Abbasids, Ghaznavids, Seljuks, Mongols and Timurids, but by the one proclaimed by the family of Mohammad.

. . .

And Shi'ism which begins with a 'no,' a 'no' which opposes the path chosen by history, rebels against history. It rebels against a history which, in the name of the Qur'an, Kings, and Caesars, follows the path of ignorance and in the name of tradition, sacrifices those brought up in the house of the Qur'an and the Traditions!

Shi'ites do not accept the path chosen by history. They negate the leadership which ruled over history and deceived the majority of the people through its succession to the Prophet, and then, supposed support of Islam and fight against paganism. Shi'ites turn their backs on the opulent mosques and magnificent palaces of the caliphs of Islam and turn to the lonely, mud house of Fatima.[12] Shi'ites who represent the oppressed, justice-seeking

---

10. This passage is reproduced from Ali Shari`ati, *Red Shi'ism*. Translated from the Persian by Habib Shirazi. Houston, TX: Free Islamic Literatures, 1980, pp. 7-11.

11. `Abdul Rahman was the cousin of `Uthman, the third caliph.

12. Fatima was the Prophet's daughter who married `Ali, the Prophet's cousin and the first imam of the Shi'ites.

class in the caliphate system find, in this house, whatever and whoever they have been seeking:

Fatima: The heir of the Prophet, the manifestation of the 'rights of the oppressed' and, at the same time, symbol of the first objection, a strong and clear embodiment of the 'seeking of justice.' In the ruling system, these are the cries and slogans of subject nations and oppressed classes.

`Ali: The manifestation of a justice which serves the oppressed, a sublime embodiment of the truth who is sacrificed at the altar of anti-human regimes which lie hidden in the layers of the formal religion of the rulers.

Hasan: The manifestation of the last resistance of the garrison of "imamate Islam" who confronts the first garrison of 'Islamic Rule.'

Husayn: Bears witness to those who are martyred by the oppression in history, heir of all the leaders of freedom and equality and seekers of justice from Adam to himself, forever, the messenger of martyrdom, the manifestation of the blood revolution.

Zainab: Bears witness to all of the defenseless prisoners in the system of executioners, the messenger after martyrdom, and the manifestation of the message of revolution!

Shi'ites find their slogans in the embodiment of the tribulations and the hopes of the masses of the oppressed. . . . Like a revolutionary party, Shi'ism had a well-organized, informed, deep, and well-defined ideology, with clear-cut and definite slogans and a disciplined and well-groomed organization. It led the deprived and oppressed masses in their movements for freedom and for the seeking of justice.

It is considered to be the rallying point for the demands, pains and rebellions of the intellectuals seeking to gain their rights and the masses in search of justice.

Because of this, throughout history, as their might grew, the pressures, injustices, usurpations and extortions of the rights of the people and exploitations of the farmers increased. Contrasts became more pronounced, through the system of aristocracy, class-inequalities . . . the attachment of the theologians to the temporal rulers, the poverty and privation of the masses, and the power and wealth of the rulers.

When this occurred, the Shi'ite front became stronger, the basic slogans of the movement more potent, and the struggle of the Shi'ites more acute and more weighty. It changed from a school of thought, a way of study and religious sectarianism reserved for the intellectuals and the chosen few, to a way of correctly understanding Islam and the culture of the people of the house of the Prophet, when confronted by Greek philosophy and oriental Sufism, to a deep-rooted and revolutionary, socio-political movement of the masses, especially the rural masses. . . ."

Mahmoud Taleqani

Ayatollah Mahmoud Taleqani (1911-1979) was a religious scholar and political activist who not only played an important role in the 1979 revolution but also was popular in liberal and progressive circles for his analytical writings in the 1950s and 1960s, which promoted the idea of Islam as a religion that was relevant and "in tune with the exigencies of the time."[13] Thus, at a time when Marxism and the Tudeh party seemed to dominate much of the intellectual discourse in Iran, Taleqani argued for a revolutionary reading of the Qur'an that could present more effective solutions to the concerns of the day. The passage below is an excerpt from Islam and Ownership, *one of Taleqani's most celebrated works, where he discusses the concept of ownership and justice from the perspective of Islam and the Qur'an.*

1. Excerpts from *Islam and Ownership*[14]

". . . Wealth, which is a means, should not be mistaken for a goal and replaced by it. It is difficult for people who have opened their eyes in the economic environment of the century of industrial development to imagine societies based on faith and human feelings. These people are alienated and astonished, living under governments which have usurped the means of production and material elements. They have forgotten human values and real human desires and they perceive all aspects of life through economic considerations and class conflicts. They have elevated the value of wealth

---

13. Hamid Dabashi, *The Theology of Discontent: The Ideological Foundation of the Islamic Revolution in Iran.* New York: New York University Press, 1993, p. 219.

14. The excerpt here is reproduced from Seyyed Mahmood Taleqani, *Islam and Ownership.* Translated from the Persian by Ahmad Jabbari and Farhang Rajaee. Lexington, KY: Mazda Publishers, 1983, pp. 75-77. (Reprinted with permission of Mazda Publishers.)

so high that, compared to it, they consider man a powerless instrument and make him prostrate before the means and the machinery of production. Since it is hard for such a people to imagine a society based on faith or something resembling it, the realization of such a society is all the more difficult. In fact, in such corners of the modern world where agitators and power seekers are not operating and their growls are not heard, there exists relative peace, cooperation and sincerity. Did not cooperation and kindness govern small communities before the nation-state was born in modern history? Do not kindness and affection govern in the small environment of a healthy family? Is it not possible to restore peace and prosperity between man, his spouse, and his children, even when the instinct of amassing wealth—which results in lying, disloyalty, and taking advantage of one another—takes the place of kindness and affection? Is human community not a macrocosm of the family unit? Small and large communities, established under the guardianship and care of exalted prophets and just and righteous men, are models which herald the possibility of realizing spiritual and healthy communities. The early community of Islam—during the time when the flame of faith enlightened the thoughts and the Islamic *khelafat* (caliphate) had not changed to absolute monarchy (*saltanat-e motlaq*)—is the most notable example of such a community. Even later, tyranny and the violation of laws and limits centered only around the absolute and autocratic powers that used Islam as a camouflage for their objectives and atrocities. If we move away from the centers of power and their agents and compare the Muslim masses with other communities, we see that there existed less infringement, injustice, and violation of rights among Muslims than in other societies. During many centuries from the dawn of Islam until the birth of colonialism and *gharbzadegi* (weststruckness), neither landownership nor capitalism in the Islamic world resembled that of other countries. Unlike the feudal lords of Western lands and other countries, Muslim landowners did not have absolute ownership over land and the peasants. They would not massacre or expel them *en masse*. They were not lawmakers, guardians (*motavali*), judges, or executioners. They were, more or less, ruled by Islamic faith and legal injunctions. Muslim capitalists in accordance with Islamic principles and injunctions were restrained from openly engaging in usury and hoarding or taking away the rights of workers and peasants. On the contrary, most Muslim landowners and capitalists were sources of great charities and services. The following are among the normal and common activities of wealthy Muslims either while alive or posthumously after their death: establishing charitable institutions, hospitals, and endowments, constructing roads, bridges, and inns; and providing immense financial help and care for the poor.

Before the crusades, the emergence of the technology, and the all-embracing influence of Western colonialism, class conflict, as had been foreseen and which occurred in Europe, had not emerged in Muslim countries. Generally, the ruling class in Islamic countries did not emerge from large landowners or capitalists proper. It mostly consisted of invaders who established their power by arms and plundered the public treasury and spent it to keep themselves in power. . . .

As Islam attests to the reality of human potentials and talents, it considers man, with his special composition, as the founder of society, economy, and history. Human potentials and talents are so intertwined that the nature and effect of each one cannot be studied separately. In fact, individuals seek material desires while preserving spiritual values and vice versa. In this respect, Islamic theories and laws are based on scientific assumptions and are not divorced from human desires. Islam, whose call and theoretical and practical principles are to elevate man's stature in all realms, does not have a myopic view. If man is taken to be an instrument of production and distribution, and he exists solely to satisfy needs and attain food and shelter—totally preoccupied with satisfying these needs—only then can there exist, independent from man, a place for imaginary theories of economics and their application. Such a misconception and intellectual deception has led the intellectual leaders of the technological age to unrealistic and useless scientific hypotheses. Even if these hypotheses prove to have some use and outcome, because they are limited and relative, they cannot offer satisfactory solutions for man at a given time and place. Furthermore, they constantly add to human conflict and bewilderment. Theoretical and legal principles, independent of men's moral conscience and his other desires and ideals, can be understood and implemented only for a special group or class in a short span of time.

Before presenting its plan and establishing its foundation, Islam considers and prepares the intellectual grounds. By purging the mind of *sherk* [polytheism] and the soul from wickedness, Islam embellishes human beings with faith and righteousness. Then it puts into practice its comprehensive plan (principles and laws) and shows its practice and execution with the cooperation of qualified and willing men (guardians and reformers). A cynic either does not pay attention to the aim of the landlord, (i.e. God) or is not familiar with his intentions and ideas. He considers only one corner of the structure of Islam from within and does not see the general features of this grand design. (This is similar to well-intentioned comments made by common people with limited view about a building, without considering the position of the lot, the needs of its inhabitants, or the general environment. Their comments either do not conform to the views of the owner or do not cover all aspects of the building.)"

Third-Worldism and Cultural Authenticity

As a result of the restrictions imposed by the Pahlavi regime on political activity and freedom of expression, as well as the inspiration that third world movements had provided in challenging western powers, secular leftist intellectuals in the Iran of the late 1960s and 1970s increasingly engaged in a discourse that could perhaps best be described as one of nativism or cultural authenticity. Below are two different examples of this trend: the first is an excerpt from an essay by Manuchehr Hezarkhani (b. 1934), an essayist and translator who translated and wrote about the works of Frantz Fanon and Aimé Césaire; the second is an excerpt from the self-defense of Khosrow Golesorkhi (1944-1974), a poet, journalist, and communist activist, at his trial[15] (on charges of having plotted to kidnap the crown prince in 1974), which ended in his execution in the same year. While the first passage is an illustration of how the topic of "authentic culture" gained ground as part of a third-worldist discourse that came to dominate intellectual discourse in Iran from the late 1960s onwards, the second is of interest both for its use of religious imagery and for what it reveals of the understanding of Islam among leftist intellectuals like Golesorkhi in the Iran of the 1970s. It was seen as a system of belief that was praised for its egalitarian and revolutionary qualities, and was thus celebrated for its potential to serve as a catalyst for change.

---

15. Golesorkhi's defiant self-defense at a show trial that was broadcast live on national television, during which he denounced the Pahlavi regime, captured the public imagination.

1. Manuchehr Hezarkhani on the Question of Culture in the Anti-Imperialist Struggle[16]

Does the "cultural question" exist in the anti-imperialist struggle?

. . . Even though imperialism is not such a novel concern, and the political and economic aspects of the imperialist domination have been described and analyzed carefully numerous times before, attention to its cultural component is relatively new. . . . Like any social system, imperialism consists of a particular economic base and a corresponding politico-ideological superstructure. . . . The imperialist culture is the manifestation of the ideological domination of imperialism in colonized societies. Therefore, there can be no anti-imperialist struggle that does not include a discussion of the cultural component.

For many years, western imperialism has dominated the world because of its technological advantage. For the adventurous pioneers and swordsmen of imperialism who conquered countries by force of the sword and the gun, one after the other, this same technological advantage was enough justification for imperialist action. However, ever since imperialism began to consider itself as also representing "civilization," it became necessary to fit the plunder of the dominated people into a philosophical framework. Bits and pieces of the scientific and cultural aspects of this philosophy were put together fast in the bourgeois workshops of Europe, and thus was born the ideology of imperialism: that is, the dissemination of civilization in the world!

. . . Even though the imperialist ideology based on the absolute superiority of western civilization was constructed . . . in order to trick the colonized, it also led to terrible wounds in the culture of the imperialists like a double-edged sword. For little by little, imperialists came to believe that if they had a better life and civilization, it was because they came from a superior race. Racism in its different shapes and forms entered western culture and civilization and gradually turned into one of its pillars. . . .

There is not a big gap between the humiliation of the "depraved race" and the humiliation of mankind and the negation of human dignity and

---

16. This excerpt is part of the introductory essay written by Manuchehr Hezarkhani for his translation of four speeches by Alioune Diop, Jacques Rabemananjara, Frantz Fanon, and Aimé Césaire, published in a volume entitled *Nezhadparasti va farhang* (Racism and Culture). Tehran: Ketab-e Zaman, 1348/ 1969. This introductory essay was also published in the monthly *Ferdawsi*, August 5, 1968, p. 11.

character. How quickly those advocating "liberty, equality, and fraternity" took this step! The native cultures and civilizations were first negated and then decimated. . . . Wasn't it that the blind laws of capitalism and its "superior civilization" would not tolerate any kind of opponent or intruder? Wasn't it that "the obvious truth" of the absolute superiority of the West had to be exported along with its capital to the colonies? So in order for the populations of native societies to be turned into laboring arms, it was necessary that they no longer be human. In order for them to be no longer human, what was necessary was a complete cultural destruction, an annihilation of the moral and spiritual values in all colonized societies. . . .

All the roots that link the native to a society, a tradition, an ethnicity and a history must be cut one after the other, and this is only possible by means of a thorough and systematic brainwashing. So imperialism monopolizes not only the commentary on native history but also the writing of it. It was the imperialists who wrote the histories of their colonies; they invented a history and force-fed the native with this bogus history. The result of all these so-called histories, in whatever shape or form, was the complete and absolute denial of the actual and authentic history of the native. Fragments of this authentic history which have been accumulated in the museums of the "civilized" countries for the satisfaction of the curiosity of those interested in antique artefacts, cannot be considered to have any cultural value. Rather, they are called the peculiarities, the specifics, or if they are very generous, the mysteries of an ancient society.

For the imperialist ideology has decreed that before the emergence of "civilization," that is capitalist society, it was all darkness and ignorance, whereas after the appearance of "civilization," it was light and science. . . . The result of this forgery of history and this brainwashing in colonized society is the emergence of the colonized; that is rootless and lifeless people without any memory of the past and any vision for the future. . . .

However, in order to protect and preserve this system of lies and deceit, it is necessary to have guardians. Just as in order to preserve its economic domination in the colonies, imperialism needed a new social base in the form of a false native bourgeoisie . . . dependent on imperialist capital. . . Similarly, in order to preserve its cultural and ideological domination, imperialism continues to be in need of a cultural base. The raison d'être of the class of title-holders and parasites is a result of this hidden need of imperialism. This social base and class of title-holders consist of those same imperialist elites and selected few. It is not that they have consciously wanted to form such a class, but that it is the need to create such a class that leads to the creation and growth of such a social class. . . . The elite, too, as a social class and at the base of an imperialist society, are put in a special situation, which gives them a special social role. This role is the preservation of the domination of imperialist ideology.

When the native culture has been strangulated and destroyed, the void that it leaves behind has to be filled. That culture that is disseminated by the elite to fill this void is a tormented and submissive pseudo-culture, which is at most a ridiculous caricature of the culture of imperialists. . . . That which is imported into the colonies are the most negative, destructive and depraved forms of western culture. The importers and wholesalers, selling this cultural trash, by virtue of their social role, try to bring about the "progress" of society by means of creating seeming similarities between the manifestations of the spiritual lives of the classes of title-holders of native societies and the culture of western societies. The problem that they have however, is that the native society, despite its lifelessness, continues to reject this "modern cultural link." This imported pseudo-culture is all ignorant imitation. . . . It is from this perspective that the anti-imperialist struggle takes on very broad dimensions, and it is for this reason that the question of the cultural-ideological struggle with capitalist imperialism has become part of the global anti-imperialist movement for some time. . . .

2. Excerpts from Khosrow Golesorkhi's Self-Defense at His Trial, January 1974[17]

Life is belief and jihad. I will begin my statement with a saying from *Mawla* Husayn,[18] the great martyr of the peoples of the Middle East. I who am a Marxist-Leninist found social justice for the first time in the School of Islam and then reached socialism.

In this court, I do not bargain for my life. . . . I am but an insignificant drop in the greatness and hardship of the resilient peoples of Iran. . . . Yes, I do not bargain for my life since I am the child of a defiant and courageous people.

17. "Matn-e kamel-e defa`iyat-e Khosrow Golesorkhi" (The full text of the defense proceedings of Khosrow Golesorkhi), http://ghiasabadi.com/golesorkhi.html.
18. Husayn was Prophet Mohammad's grandson and the third imam of the Shi'is. He is considered the great martyr because he was killed at the battle of Karbala by the Umayyad army in 680 C.E.

I began my words with Islam. True Islam in Iran has always paid its dues to the liberation movements of Iran. . . . Today, too, true Islam pays its dues to the national liberation movements of Iran. When Marx says, "in a class-based society, wealth is accumulated on one side, and poverty, hunger, and misery on another, while it is the dispossessed classes that produce wealth," and *Mawla*[19] `Ali says, "a palace is only erected when thousands of people are impoverished," one sees that there are many similarities [between the two]. It is thus that in history, one can refer to *Mawla* `Ali as the first socialist in the world. . . . The life of *Mawla* Husayn is an example of our present days when risking our life for the dispossessed of our country, we are tried in this court. He [Husayn] was in a minority whereas Yazid[20] had a court, an army, sovereignty and power. He [Husayn] stood his ground and was martyred. Yazid may have occupied a corner of history, but that which has been repeated throughout history was the way of *Mawla* Husayn and his resistance, not the rule of Yazid. That which nations have followed and continue to follow is the way of *Mawla* Husayn. It is in this way that in a Marxist society, true Islam can be justified as a superstructure, and we, too, approve of such an Islam, the Islam of Husayn and the *Mawla* `Ali.

19. *Mawla* is a religious title meaning Master or Lord.
20. Yazid I (r. 680-683) was the second caliph of the Umayyad caliphate.

PART THREE

THE IRANIAN REVOLUTION: 1978–1979

7

The Months Leading to the 1979 Revolution

"Iran, and the Colonialism of the Red and the Black," Ettela`at, January 7, 1978[1]

The Iranian revolution of 1978-1979 is usually divided into three distinct phases: the first stage, that of open letters in 1977; the second, that of street demonstrations between January and September 1978; and the third, that of strikes carried out by public employees, ranging from schoolteachers to electrical and oil workers, that paralyzed much of the country. The article below, which was published in the afternoon daily Ettela`at *on January 7, 1978, is generally considered to have been what led to the first demonstrations in 1978, and thus to have set off the series of events that ultimately led to the overthrow of the monarchy. Although ostensibly written by a certain Ahmad Rashidi-Motlaq, this was a pseudonym, and the identity of the actual author has never been confirmed.*

These days, on the occasion of the month of Muharram and the mourning of Husayn,[2] thoughts have turned once again to the colonialism of the black

---

1. Originally published in the daily newspaper *Ettela`at* on 17 Day 1356/ 7 January 1978, this article has been reprinted in Houshang Asadi, "Chera Kayhan an maqaleh ra montasher nakard" (Why did Kayhan not publish that article), *roozonline*, 15 Bahman 1392/ 4 February 2014.

2. The month of Muharram is the first month of the Islamic calendar, and Husayn, the third imam of the Shi'is, is believed to have been martyred at the battle of Karbala on the tenth of Muharram in 680 C.E.

and the red, that is to say, the alliance of old and new colonialism.[3] The colonialism of the red and the black, of the old and new variety, has a spirit of violation, domination, and plunder. Even though they share a similar inherent characteristic, rarely have these two recognized kinds of colonialism colluded with each other, except in specific cases. One such instance is the close and intimate collusion of these two colonialisms against the Iranian revolution, especially the progressive program of land reforms in Iran. The beginning of the revolution of the Shah and the people[4] on 6 Bahman 2521/ [26 January 1963][5] united the colonialism of the red and the black, each of which seemed to have its own specific plan for our country. [This unity] manifested itself in the riots of the 15-16 Khordad 1342/ 5-6 June 1963.

Following the sinister disturbances of 15 Khordad/ 5 June [1963] which had been planned to stop and thwart the brilliant revolution of the Shah and the People, those who studied these events became disconcerted by the fact that they could clearly detect the footprints of black colonialism in one place, and that of the red colonialism in another. On the one hand, [there were] elements of the Tudeh party[6] who saw all their hopes for deceiving the peasants and establishing peasant associations dashed by the implementation of the land reforms, and who took part in the riots. On the other, [there were] large landowners who had robbed millions of Iranian peasants for years and who in the hope of defeating this program and returning to the previous situation, put money into the hands of agents of the Tudeh and other political bankrupts. It is interesting that this group of people, who believed that they could stop the wheels of the [White] Revolution and remove the land that had been turned over to the peasants from the ownership of the latter, appealed to the 'ulama, thinking that the opposition of the 'ulama, who enjoyed a certain amount of respect in Iranian society, could not only cause trouble for the program of the Revolution but also, as one of the large landowners had imagined, [get] "the peasants to return the lands

3. According to Charles Kurzman, "the collusion of the black and the red was a standard phrase in the Pahlavi lexicon to refer to a putative alliance between feudal (black) and leftist (red) opponents of the monarchy's modernization project." See Charles Kurzman, *The Unthinkable Revolution in Iran*. Cambridge, MA: Harvard University Press, 2004, p. 33.

4. The "Revolution of the Shah and the People" was a reference to the "White Revolution." See "Perspectives on the White Revolution" in chapter 5.

5. The Iranian dates mentioned in this article are according to the Imperial calendar, which was in effect only for a short period between March 1976 and September 1978.

6. The Tudeh party was the name of the communist party in Iran. See "The 1940s and the Tudeh Party" in chapter 5.

alleging that they had been lands that had been taken by force." However, the *'ulama* were more intelligent than to rise up against the Revolution of the Shah and the People, which had been designed by the leader of the Iranian Revolution according to the principles and teachings of Islam, and for the purpose of creating justice and putting an end to the exploitation of one individual by another.

In order to persist in their domination [of society], the landowners continued to maintain control over a range of people, from gendarmes to ministers; from preachers to thugs. [However], when they encountered a lack of attention on the part of the *'ulama*, they had to face the question of how to create havoc against the Revolution. When the distinguished *'ulama* were not ready to assist them, they decided to find a cleric who was adventurous, had no faith, was loyal and supported by imperialist centers, and was particularly opportunistic and able to fulfil their aim. They found such a man with ease: a man whose past was unknown, and who was associated with the most extreme and reactionary elements of imperialism. [Furthermore], since he had not found a footing among the distinguished *'ulama* of the country . . . he was in search of an opportunity to insert himself into the political currents at any cost, and earn a name and some fame for himself.

Ruhollah Khomeini was a suitable agent for this purpose. The Red and Black Reaction found him to be the most appropriate person to confront the Iranian Revolution. He was the person who was identified as the agent of the shameful event of 15 Khordad/ 5 June [1963].

Ruhollah Khomeini was known as "Seyyed Hendi" (the Indian Seyyed). Even his closest relatives continue to have no explanation about his designation to India. According to one account, he has spent some time in India and while there, has had links with centers of British imperialism, and for this reason has come to be known as "the Indian Seyyed." According to another, in his youth, he used to write love poetry and would use the pen name "hendi" (the Indian) and for this reason has come to be known as "hendi." Others believe that since his studies took place in India, he chose the last name "hendi" because he was taught by one teacher since his childhood. What is certain, however, is that everyone remembers him as the trouble-maker of 15 Khordad/ [5 June, 1963]; as one who set out against the Iranian Revolution and who shed the blood of innocents in order to carry out the plan of the Red and Black Colonialism and . . . fought against the redistribution of land, women's emancipation, and the nationalization of forests. He showed that there are still people who are ready to put themselves truly in the hands of conspirators and anti-democratic agents.

In order to find the root-causes of the 15 Khordad/ 5 June [1963] and the role played by its central character, attention to the contents of a report, an announcement, and an interview will be much help.

A few weeks before the trouble of 15 Khordad/ 5 June [1963], a report was published by OPEC which stated that the "income of the British government from Iranian oil was several times the total of the money that was earned by Iran at the time." [Furthermore], several days before the trouble [of 5 June], an announcement came into the open in Tehran saying that an Arab adventurer called Mohammad Tawfiq al-Qaysi had been arrested at Mehrabad airport with a baggage full of ten million rials in cash. This money was to be given to certain people. Several days after the trouble, the Prime Minister of the time revealed in an interview, "It is clear to us that money arrived from overseas, reached individuals and was distributed among different groups in order to implement evil plans."

Fortunately, the Iranian [White] Revolution succeeded. The last resistance of large landowners and Tudeh agents was defeated, and the way to progress, advancement, and the implementation of the principles of social justice was paved. In Iranian history, 15 Khordad/ 5 June [1963] will remain a painful memory about the enemies of the Iranian people. Millions of Iranian Muslims will remember how the enemies [of the country] will join hands whenever it suits their interests, even if they be wearing the sacred and revered clothing of the clergy.

"I, Too, Have Heard the Voice of Your Revolution": The Text of Mohammad Reza Pahlavi's Address to the Nation, November 5, 1978[7]

By November 1978, Iran had suffered months of protests and clashes. In October, another phase in the unrest had begun in the form of national strikes by public employees. These had in effect brought about the paralysis of the Iranian economy. In an attempt to appease the protestors, the Shah

---

7. The Persian text of the address is available at www.parsine.com/fa/news/62526/ 1357.

had changed his prime ministers twice, but to no avail. Perhaps his most surprising decision was to address the nation on national television on November 5, during which he referred to the unrest that had enveloped the country as a "revolution of the Iranian people." Observers came to regard this address as what in effect "crystallized for the first time the idea that this was, or could be, a revolution,"[8] and thus considered it a sign of weakness on the part of the Shah.

Dear Iranian people! In the open political atmosphere that gradually came about in the last two years, you, the Iranian people, rose up against oppression and corruption. I, as the king of Iran and as an Iranian individual, cannot disapprove of the revolution of the Iranian nation!

Unfortunately, alongside this revolution, others had intrigues and took advantage of your emotions and anger, leading to disturbances, chaos, and rebellion. The wave of strikes, many of which were just [at the outset], have also taken on a [different] character and direction in recent times, stopping the wheels of the country's economy, wasting away the everyday life of the people, and even bringing an end to the flow of oil on which the life of the country depends. This is such that the everyday movement of the people and the safeguarding of the needs of the people have shut down too. The insecurity, mayhem, uprisings and killings have reached such a level in many parts of our country that the independence of our country has been put in peril. The regrettable events that set fire to the capital yesterday[9] can no longer continue or be tolerated by the people and the country. Following the resignation of the government, and in order to prevent the disintegration of the country and the breaking down of national unity, and in order to stop the decline, chaos, anarchy and killings, and to establish the rule of law, and bring about peace and order, I gave my all to establish a coalition government. However, only once it became clear that there was no possibility of such a coalition, I had no choice but to appoint a provisional government.

---

8. Michael Axworthy, *Revolutionary Iran: A History of the Islamic Republic.* Oxford: Oxford University Press, 2013, p. 117.

9. On November 4, 1978, in the midst of angry demonstrations in Tehran, protestors set fire to 400 banks, both private and public, reducing many to ashes. See Baqer ʿAqeli, *Ruzshomar-e tarikh-e Iran az mashruteh ta enqelab-e Eslami* (The chronology of Iranian history: From the constitution to the Islamic revolution). Tehran: Nashr-e goftar, 1370/ 1991, p. 373.

I am aware that in the name of stopping the chaos and anarchy, past mistakes and the weight of repression might be repeated. I am aware that it is possible for some people to think that in the name of the interests and progress of the country, and by creating pressure, there is the danger of a repeat of an unholy compromise between financial and political corruption. However, I, as your king who has taken the oath to protect the integrity of the territory of the country as well as the Twelver Shi'i religion, repeat my oath once again before the Iranian people, and swear that [henceforth] past mistakes will never be repeated, but that [instead] amends will be made for the [past] mistakes in every way. I undertake that after establishing peace and order, a national government will be appointed to fulfil basic freedoms and carry out free elections as soon as possible, so that the constitution, which is the reason for the sacrifices of the Constitutional Revolution, can be put into effect completely. I, too, have heard the message of your revolution!

I am the protector of constitutional monarchy which is a divine gift that has been entrusted to the king by the nation, as well as that which you have sacrificed for. I guarantee that in the future, the government of Iran will be on the basis of the constitution, social justice, national will, and [that it will keep] away from oppression, injustice, and corruption. In the current situation, in order to prevent the fall and disintegration of Iran, the establishment of peace and order is the main duty of the royal armed forces, which, in preserving their own national integrity, have always been dependent on the Iranian people and loyal to their own pledges. With your cooperation, my dear compatriots, this peace and order must be established as soon as possible so that the next national government which will be responsible for the institution of freedoms, the implementation of reforms, especially the establishment of free elections, can begin its work as soon as possible. In these thirty-odd years, you and I have seen many sensitive events, and we have put behind us many dangers—I hope that in these delicate, dangerous and fateful moments, God Almighty will include us in his grace, so that we, alongside each other, can reach our main goals, namely peace, prosperity, freedom, and the dignity of Iran and Iranians.

I hereby request the Grand Ayatollahs and the distinguished `ulama who are the spiritual and religious leaders of society, and the protectors of Islam especially of the Shi'i religion, to strive for the protection of the only Shi'i country in the world by means of their guidance, and to appeal to the people for peace and order. I want the intellectual leaders of the youth to smooth the way for a methodical struggle for the establishment of a real democracy by inviting the youth to peace and order. I ask you, Iranian fathers and mothers, who like me are worried about the future of Iran and that of your children, to guide them and stop them from participating in the disturbances and chaos through passion and zeal, bringing harm to themselves and their country.

I ask you, young people, who embody the future of Iran, not to bring about the destruction of our country, and damage the present and future of Iran.

I ask you, the political leaders of society, to make use of your forces for the sake of the salvation of the country, free from ideological differences and mindful of the historically sensitive and exceptional situation that our country finds itself in.

I ask you, laborers, workers, and peasants who have [always] enabled the turning of the wheels of the country's economy, to strive further for the economic preservation and revival of the country.

I ask all of you, my dear compatriots to think of Iran. I ask you that we all think of Iran. In these historic moments, let us all think of Iran together. Know that I stand with you on the path to the revolution of the Iranian people against imperialism, oppression and corruption. I will be with you to protect the integrity of the territory [of Iran], and the national unity, and to preserve the Islamic rites and to establish the basic freedoms, and the victory and fulfilment of the aspirations and ideals of the Iranian people.

In the dangerous days that we have before us, I hope that God Almighty will extend his favor and grace over us. May He always help and preserve the country and people of Iran. God Willing!

The Proceedings of the Council of the Commanders of the Royal Armed Forces, January 29, 1979

In addition to the departure of the Shah on January 16, 1979, and the return of Ayatollah Khomeini on February 1, 1979, an important factor that enabled the revolutionaries to claim victory on February 11, 1979, was the decision by the Commanders of the Armed Forces to declare neutrality. Below are excerpts from the transcript of a meeting held by the Command-

ers of the Armed Forces on January 29, 1979, two days before the return of Ayatollah Khomeini. What is interesting about these discussions is the fact that the Commanders clearly had no contingency plan; in fact, they seem to have been as taken aback by the situation that they found themselves in as had the Shah, and they were equally at a loss as to what to do with regard to the eventuality of both the resignation of the then Prime Minister Shahpour Bakhtiar and the return from exile of Ayatollah Khomeini.

Text: *We Will Melt Like Snow*[10]

[`Abbas] Qarabaghi:[11] Let's suppose that His Excellency the Prime Minister has resigned. . . . After all, we should think about this—that for example, this afternoon or tomorrow, or next week, or I don't know, ten days from now, he has resigned for some reason. The Regency Council does not succeed to choose someone. There is no one, or suppose that no one accepts the responsibility [to become Prime Minister], just like when His Majesty himself was still in the country, and no one accepted [to become Prime Minister.] . . . Suppose that we have no Prime Minister and at the same time, people march onto the airport, in order to occupy and open it so that His Excellency the Ayatollah can return. In such conditions, what is the duty of the armed forces? What is our task? What are we to do? I would like that the gentlemen present express their views, whatever they may be. Then I will say a few words myself. The point of the meeting is that we discuss things so as not to let ourselves continue to be surprised by the events.

[Mehdi] Rahimi:[12] . . . If God forbid, he [Bakhtiar] resigns, this will be the last stage and I think that then we would need to have a military man as Prime Minister together with a military cabinet. That will be the last thing that we can do to preserve the country. I think that we have no options other than this, unless there is someone else besides Bakhtiar who can replace him. It is very unlikely that in such a situation, someone would have

10. *Mesl-e barf ab khahim shod: mozakerat-e shawra-ye farmandehan-e Artesh.* Tehran: Nashr-e Ney, 1365/ 1987, pp. 206-223. This publication consists of the transcripts of the discussions held by the Council of the Royal Armed Forces in the course of three meetings in January-February 1979.

11. General `Abbas Qarabaghi (1918-2000) was the last Chief of Staff of the Iranian Armed Forces.

12. Lieutenant-General Mehdi Rahimi (1921-1979) was the last military governor of Tehran, and among the first people to be executed by a firing squad in the early days of the revolution in February 1979.

this kind of courage to come and replace him. . . . If there is another way, what is it? It means that we have lost the country.

[`Abdollah] Khajehnouri:[13] What Lieutenant-General Rahimi just said, has a practical problem. Who is to choose the military Prime Minster? If we were to choose him ourselves, that would be a coup d'état.

Rahimi: No, it will be the task of Regency Council or the *majles*. . . .

Khajehnouri: But what if the members of the Regency Council don't find anyone?

Rahimi: They should carry out their political tasks. Perhaps we will reach the stage that a coup d'état would become necessary. I don't know!

[`Abdol `Ali] Badreh'i:[14] I think it very unlikely that he [the Prime Minister] will resign. Of course, well, there is a big possibility that if he does not resign, that God forbid, he will be killed. . . . Because I think that if he [the Prime Minister] wanted to resign, he would have gone to Paris. They would have either reached an agreement with him or not. In the event of reaching an agreement, then as it is the view of Mr. Khomeini that he [Bakhtiar] first resign, he would have gone there [to Paris] and resigned. Then he would have discussed it. . . . Since he didn't go [to Paris] and since he is a very decisive man, I don't think, and if there is a possibility, it is a very small one, that he will resign. His own view is that he will stand and work until his last breath. . . . But what I think is that whether he resigns or not, our aim must be to protect the armed forces, and the only way we can do so is to abstain from these confrontations. Because as you say, whatever action is taken, it will be blamed on the army, regardless of whether it is the government or someone else who issues the orders, or if it is the protestors that bring about a situation where they force the soldiers to shoot to kill. In any case, it will all be blamed on the army. I think that the only way for us to save the army is to return the army to the barracks. . . . In any case, an army is there forever, for any occasion. However, in view of the situation that we are in now, with everyone being scattered in the cities and provinces . . . [it means that] in effect we have no army at hand; everyone is dispersed. With regard to the ground forces, I can say that they are not under the control of the commanders. . . . I think that in any case, if you

13. Lieutenant-General `Abdollah Khajehnouri was also among the members of the armed forces who were executed in March 1979.

14. Lieutenant-General `Abdol `Ali Badreh'i (1919-1979) was the Commander of the Ground Forces and the head of the Royal Guard.

agree, we should assemble the army, so that perhaps when those who are now distributing proclamations praising the army saying that you have nothing to do, see that there is no more army, they will stop shedding blood and setting things on fire. Perhaps the protests will then become peaceful, and the army will also be able to extract itself [from the situation].

[Ahmad `Ali] Mohaqqeqi:[15] Sir! My view has been consistent from the first day. . . . If the problem is something political that we don't know about, that is different. However, if our challenge is Khomeini alone, and we are trying to appease him, he will not be appeased. . . .Things are getting worse by the day. I have said it a thousand times; tomorrow will be [even] worse than today. Now, we can no longer recruit 600 soldiers for training. We have written letters; instead of 600 people who were supposed to go to Jahrom, we were able to send [only] 90 people. There is no way that things can get better. . . . Think that the worst situation is what we have before us now. . . . If this head of government wants to rule, he should get the agents to arrest both the former and the present subversives, imprison them, [or] hang them. We should proceed in a swift and revolutionary way and no one will be able to do anything. [In fact], everyone will return to our side. But if we want to proceed in this willy-nilly way, after this [Prime Minster] leaves, no one will come and dare become Prime Minister. . . . If we are to take decisive action, we should do so now. . . .

Khajehnouri: In general, it seems to me that there are two solutions, two ways to proceed regarding Ayatollah Khomeini whom we are concerned with now. These two ways consist of either letting him return in these conditions or not. . . . If we let him come, we can still think of two things: that he either comes and says or is made to say that he will set up a provisional government. Once the situation has calmed down, then public opinion should be consulted, and the people be asked their views regarding the regime. He will either say this or, when he returns, immediately declare that he will set up a revolutionary council, and that in fact a republic has to come into being now. . . . If we were not to allow him to return to Iran, then the current situation will continue in the way that it is now . . . and it will be to the disadvantage of the royal armed forces and this won't be acceptable. . . . In these conditions, if we were not to allow him to return, then the only thing that we could do, as General Rahimi has said, is to take

15. Lieutenant-General Ahmad `Ali Mohaqqeqi was the head of the Iranian gendarmerie in 1978-1979.

decisive action and have the army take full control of the country. This will risk serious loss of life and confrontation with people. . . . But this is the only solution. Trying to reach an agreement [with the protestors] and delaying making a decision will result in the destruction of the armed forces.

"Why Do I Oppose the Islamic Republic?"
Ayandegan, January 15, 1979[16]

Mostafa Rahimi (1926-2002) was a writer, essayist, and translator, most celebrated for his translations of works by Jean-Paul Sartre, Albert Camus, Simone de Beauvoir, and Berthold Brecht. This was the first open letter that was written to Ayatollah Khomeini, and published in the daily Ayandegan *on January 15, 1979, a day before the Shah left Iran for good and some two weeks before Ayatollah Khomeini was to return to Iran after having spent fifteen years in exile. It is interesting for our purposes not only because of its timing but also because it captures to some extent the mood of the revolutionary days. It expresses some of the sentiment of the secularists who admired Khomeini, and had supported the revolution, but at the same time felt uneasy when they first heard the term "Islamic Republic." There was no response to the letter; instead,* Ayandegan *was one of the first newspapers to be shut down by the revolutionary government, in August 1979, and Rahimi himself continued to be shunned by the regime until his death in 2002. Excerpts from the early part of the letter have been translated below.*

At the outset, I must say that the author of this letter not only is in complete agreement with the views and *fatwas*[17] of Your Excellency in the following matters [listed below] but also considers their dissemination and promotion to be his national, social and spiritual duty:

---

16. This was originally published in the left-leaning daily *Ayandegan* on January 15, 1979. The complete text of the article is available at http://www.iranrights.org/farsi/document-274.php.

17. A *fatwa* is a legal judgment or a ruling by a qualified jurist on a matter that is related to Islamic law.

1. All that you have said in opposition to the present illegitimate regime in Iran;

2. All that you have said in opposition to American imperialism and any other imperialist government;

3. All that you have said in opposition to the policies of the Soviet Union, China and any other communist government;

4. All that you have said in opposition to the Zionist Israeli government. I mention this last point because I have translated or written commentaries on some of the works of [Jean-Paul] Sartre. However, as I have said clearly before, I completely disagree with Sartre's views on Israel.[18]

It is redundant to say that the author of this letter is Shi'i and born to Shi'i parents. I have not only always respected the principles of the various religions in my writings, but as I will explain, I consider the continuation of society impossible without the pillar of spirituality and sanctity.[19]

That which has led me to write this letter to Your Excellency is my intense respect for you. It is an unadulterated respect, not on the basis of emotions and hero-worship, but on that of reflection. In circumstances that no one else could have done so, you became both the spokesperson for the oppressed people of Iran against the present and thoroughly corrupt regime, and also raised your voice against the big repressive powers.[20]

However, these are not the reasons that have led to this letter; rather there are points that, as far as I know, no one as yet has written about openly to you from inside the country.[21] The problem arose when some of your supporters put forth the issue of the Islamic Republic as the demand of all the people of this country. I, as a writer and lawyer . . . oppose the Islamic Republic, and I will state to you the reasons for my opposition in all sincerity because in a more or less similar case, I imagine that discussion with the person of Marx would be easier than discussion with Marxists. Also, you can be the only addressee of this letter for the reasons listed below:

18. Even though Sartre had been very outspoken in favor of third-worldist causes such as the Algerian War of Independence, in the Arab-Israeli conflict, he sided with Israel.

19. The Persian word that the author uses here is *ruhaniyat*, which means both "sanctity" and "the clergy." The author most probably chose this word to emphasize this double entendre.

20. What he means by the "big repressive powers" are the United States and the Soviet Union.

21. At this point, Khomeini was still in exile in Paris and had not yet returned to Iran.

a) For many years, I have reached the conclusion that the way to the liberation of mankind is the merging of two philosophies: democracy and socialism. Even though they both seem to have come from the West, in essence all nations and cultures have had a share in developing them. Today, that which has weakened democracy is capitalism, and that which has corrupted socialism is power which has been mixed with communism. So the bringing together of socialism and democracy is not an easy task and such an objective is the responsibility of all thinkers and nations.
. . .

I have also thought that if democracy and socialism don't come together in an environment full of morality and spirituality, their synthesis will never be humane. You know well that in the oppressive atmosphere of Iran, the clear expression of such matters was impossible. . . . Today, I want to get help from your spirituality and sanctity.

b) The terrifying oppression of the last twenty-five years put an end to all useful political associations and also broke all truth-telling pens. . . . The courageous exposure of these acts of oppression by you and your struggle in combatting them, have turned all eyes towards you, so that today the huge burden of both the political and spiritual leadership is on your shoulders. As much as this matter is worthy of honor, it also engenders responsibility.

c) For all these reasons, you are in a unique position to announce an absolute republic. That is, if instead of an Islamic republic, you were to announce a total republic; that is, instead of calling for government by a certain group of people, you were to accept the government and sovereignty of all the people, you would not only have created a huge spiritual revolution in Iran, but in the materialistic age that we live in, you would have given a great dimension to both the `ulama and spirituality. History would, furthermore, record your position as ranking with Gandhi or even higher. The main problem of our century, after all, is not the overthrow of a corrupt and puppet government. Despite the priority that this task has for us Iranians, it is not a global problem. The foremost problem of the world which will also become a foremost problem for us, immediately after the overthrow of the [shah's] regime, is that following the assassination of Gandhi, the twentieth-century lost its humanized spirituality. If you continue to support the slogan of the Islamic republic, you would have given life to that famous materialist thesis which claims that recorded history is the history of struggles between social classes. Furthermore, if it is said that Ayatollah Khomeini wants to put the class of clergy in government as successor to another class or group, what will you say? And in that case, where is the spirituality and ethics that our century has been in search of?

d) If, however, you were to accept the sovereignty of the nation, the Iranian people who, until now, have almost ultimately been defeated in all their uprisings, will be able to breathe a sigh of relief and celebrate on the morrow of victory.

e) The westerners have been saying for several centuries . . . that the nations of the East do not deserve unconditional freedom and democracy, and that they must always beat their chests for the banner of some despot. Such nonsense must be answered through action. The Indians proved such claims wrong; has the turn of Iran not come?

. . . It is for all these reasons, and following the valuable traditions of Islam that I, now, lay open my heart before you and say why I oppose the Islamic Republic.

1. The revolution that has come about, and about the greatness of which both friend and foe are in agreement, concerns all the people of Iran. . . . All revolutions have two pillars, neither of which can be without the other. First, there has to be a people to carry out the revolution; second, there has to be a leader or leaders who must recognize the appropriate moment, and guide the revolution by means of appropriate slogans and guidance. By and large, the second pillar belongs to you but what is one to say about the first pillar? And why is it that in building the Iran of the future, the forthright views of the people should not be solicited? Can one claim that all the martyrs who have watered the tree of revolution with their own blood in the course of the black years, all sup-

ported the Islamic Republic? Can one claim that all the political prisoners who provided the preliminary grounds for the freedom of Iran with their lives and their sense of honor were supporters of such a view?

2. To the extent that I understand, the Islamic Republic means that sovereignty belongs to the clergy. This is against the rights that have been gained by the Iranian people in the Constitutional Revolution, when at the cost of their many sacrifices, they accomplished this big privilege, namely, that "the strength of the country comes from the people." From the political, social, and legal perspectives, this path is irreversible. Of course the people always have the right to rise up to write a better and more progressive constitution, but it is not logical that they should pass on their sovereign rights to any other person or persons. . . .

3. For the reasons mentioned-above, the Islamic republic is in opposition to democratic values. Democracy in the sense of the government of all the people is absolute, and whatever imposes conditions on this, harms the basis of the democracy or the republic. In this way, the term Islamic republic is contradictory, much like terms such as the "dictatorship of peace," or "bourgeois democracy." If a country is a republic, according to definition, sovereignty has to be in the hands of all the people. Any [added] attribute harms this characteristic. If a country is Islamic, it can no longer be a republic, since this would imply that the rules of government have been determined in advance, and that no one has the right to question those rules and regulations. . . .

4. Please forgive me for teaching philosophy to Loqman.[22] However, on many occasions in the course of history, have great men learnt points from the criticisms of ordinary folk. So allow me to say that calling for an Islamic Republic in our age is in contradiction to the democratic spirit of the time of the Prophet Muhammad and the rightly guided caliphs. After all, as a result of the politics of the world, the issues relating to livelihood and subsistence are in a state of constant flux. I, therefore, ask, according to which rules and regulations will an Islamic Republic resolve the complex economic and legal issues or those regarding political freedom? No doubt, you will answer that it will [do so] according to the changes of time, but what if after your life of 120

22. This is an expression that is used when a person gives advice to someone who is of higher rank or is obviously more knowledgeable and has greater wisdom.

years, your successor says that he wants to resolve these issues solely according to the rules and regulations of centuries ago (just as even now, most of the naïve individuals and a number of the well-known supporters of the Islamic Republic argue). What is to be done then, and on the basis of which principles can one give them an answer?!

5. If we set up rules and regulations in advance for the sovereignty of the people, with regard to that which concerns the people, we would have, willy-nilly, marginalized the people themselves. In religious matters, the relations between man and God are the work of the grand ayatollahs, and others have no business in it. . . . However, the setting up of rules and regulations regarding matters dealing with people's livelihood is the business of the people themselves. . . . Which issue of livelihood is there that is free of a political aspect? In order to solve such matters, who is more qualified than the people? Why should a people who created the greatest epic in the history of Iran with their own blood be marginalized when it comes to determining their own fate?

6. It is deserving of the rank of the clergy that it not tarnish itself with political positions.

. . . If there were not the hopeful kernels of freedom and free-mindedness in your statements, I would never have written this letter to you. My fear is from those who until yesterday would say, "Come, let's move the people against the common enemy with the help of religion, and tomorrow each group will be free in expressing its views." However today, instead of listening to what I and people like me have to say, they are thinking about becoming parliamentarians and ministers.

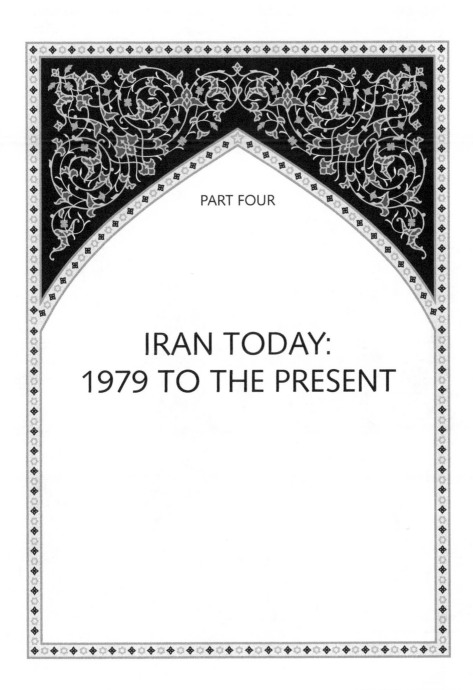

PART FOUR

IRAN TODAY:
1979 TO THE PRESENT

8

Defining the Islamic Republic

The Constitution of the Islamic Republic

The constitution of the Islamic Republic was first ratified by means of a referendum held on December 2 and 3, 1979, and consisted of 175 articles. It was revised in 1989 and approved by means of another referendum on July 28 of that year. The amended version consisted of 177 articles and included changes in "forty-nine areas,"[1] the most important of which concerned the definition of the Leader and the strengthening of the office of the President while eliminating that of the Prime Minister. The passages below consist of two sections of the 1979 Constitution, namely, the "General Principles" (Chapter 1) and "The Rights of the People" (Chapter 3). These sections have been chosen to bring attention to the dual nature of the constitution. In addition, articles from the 1989 Amendment to the Constitution that relate to the authority of the Leadership, the Council of Guardians, and the Office of the Presidency are also included.

---

1. Mohsen Milani, "Shi'ism and the State in the Constitution of the Islamic Republic of Iran," in Samih K. Farsoun and Mehrdad Mashayekhi, eds., *Iran: Political Culture in the Islamic Republic.* London and New York: Routledge, 1992, p. 150.

1. The 1979 Constitution of the Islamic Republic²

Chapter I: General Principles

Art. 1. "The form of government of Iran is that of an Islamic Republic, which received an affirmative vote from the Iranian people on the basis of their longstanding belief in the Qur'anic government of truth and justice, after their victorious Islamic Revolution led by the eminent *marja`-i taqlid*, Ayatullah al-Uzma Imam Khomeini, in the referendum of Farvardin 9 and 10 in the year 1358 of the solar Islamic calendar, corresponding to Jummadi al-Ula 1 and 2 in the year 1399 of the lunar Islamic calendar [March 29 and 30, 1979].

Art. 2. The Islamic Republic is a system of government based on belief in:

a. the One God (as stated in the Islamic creed 'There is no god but God'), His exclusive possession of sovereignty and the right to legislate, and the necessity of submission to His commands;

b. divine revelation and its fundamental role in the expounding of laws;

c. the return to God in the hereafter, and the constructive role of this belief in man's ascending progress toward God;

d. the justice of God in creation and legislation;

e. continuous leadership and guidance, and its fundamental role in assuring the continuity of the revolution of Islam;

f. the exalted dignity and value of man, and his freedom, joined to responsibilities, before God;

which secures equity, justice, political, economic, social, and cultural independence, and national solidarity, by recourse to:

a. continuous *ijtihad* of the *fuqaha* possessing the necessary qualifications, exercised on the basis of the Book of God and the Sunna of the *Ma'sumin*, upon all of whom be peace;

b. recourse to arts and sciences and the most advanced results of human experience, together with the effort to carry them still

2. *Constitution of the Islamic Republic of Iran.* Translated from the Persian by Hamid Algar. Berkeley, CA: Mizan Press, 1980, pp. 26-33, 36-42. (Reprinted with permission of Hamid Algar.) A more recent translation of the 1989 Constitution of the Islamic Republic has also been published by Firoozeh Papan-Matin, trans., "The Constitution of the Islamic Republic of Iran (1989 Edition), *Journal of the International Society for Iranian Studies*, vol. 47, no. 1, January 2014, pp. 159-200.

farther forward;

c. rejection of all forms of oppression, both the infliction and the endurance of it, and of dominance, both its imposition and its acceptance.

Art. 3. In order to attain the objectives specified in Article 2, the government of the Islamic Republic of Iran has the duty of directing all its resources to the following goals:

a. the creation of a favorable environment for the growth of spiritual virtues based upon faith and piety and the struggle against all forms of vice and corruption;

b. raising the level of public awareness in all areas, through the correct use of the press, the mass media, and other means;

c. free education and physical training for everyone at all levels, and the facilitation and expansion of higher education;

d. strengthening the spirit of inquiry, investigation, and initiative in all areas of science, technology, and culture, as well as Islamic studies, by establishing research centers and encouraging researchers;

e. the complete expulsion of imperialism and the prevention of foreign influence;

f. the elimination of all forms of tyranny and autocracy and all attempts to monopolize power;

g. the securing of political and social freedoms within the limits of the law;

h. ensuring the participation of the entire people in the determination of their political, economic, social and cultural destiny;

i. the abolition of all forms of impermissible discrimination and the provision of just opportunities for all, in both material and non-material matters;

j. the creation of a proper administrative system and the elimination of unnecessary government organizations;

k. strengthening the defense of the nation to the utmost degree by means of universal military training for the sake of preserving the independence, territorial integrity and Islamic order of the country;

l. planning a correct and just economic system in accordance with Islamic criteria, in order to create prosperity, remove poverty,

and abolish all forms of deprivation with respect to food, housing, work, and health care, and the provision of universal insurance;

m. the attainment of self-sufficiency in industrial, agricultural, and
military science, and technology, and all related matters;

n. securing the comprehensive rights of all citizens, both women
and men, and the establishment of judicial security for all, as
well as the equality of all before the law;

o. the expansion and strengthening of Islamic brotherhood and
public cooperation among all the people;

p. the formulation of the foreign policy of the country on the basis
of Islamic criteria, brotherly commitment to all Muslims, and
the unstinting support of all oppressed and deprived people
throughout the world.

Art. 4. All civil, penal, financial, economic, administrative, cultural, military, political, and other laws and regulations must be based on Islamic
criteria. This principle applies absolutely and generally to all articles of the
Constitution as well as to all laws and regulations, and the *fuqaha* on the
Council of Guardians have the duty of supervising its implementation.

Art. 5. During the Occultation of the Lord of the Age (may God hasten
his renewed manifestation!), the governance and leadership of the nation
will devolve upon the just and pious *faqih* who is acquainted with the circumstances of his age; courageous, resourceful, and possessed of administrative ability; and recognized and accepted as leader by the majority of
the people. In the event that no *faqih* should be so recognized by the majority, the leader, or the Leadership Council, composed of *fuqaha* possessing the aforementioned qualifications, will assume these responsibilities in
accordance with Article 107.

Art. 6. In the Islamic Republic of Iran, the affairs of the country must
be administered on the basis of public opinion expressed by means of elections, including the election of the President of the Republic, the representatives of the National Consultative Assembly, and the members of
councils, or by means of referenda in matters specified in other articles of
this Constitution.

Art. 7. In accordance with the command of the Qur'an contained in the
verses 'Their affairs are by consultation among them' (42:38) and 'Consult
them on affairs' (3:159), councils and consultative bodies—such as the

National Consultative Assembly, the Provincial Councils and the Municipal Councils, and the City, Neighborhood Division, and Village Councils—belong to the decision-making and administrative organs of the country.

The nature of these councils, together with the manner of their formation and the limits of their powers and functions, is determined by the Constitution and laws arising from it.

Art. 8. In the Islamic Republic of Iran, summoning men to good by enjoining good and forbidding evil is a universal and mutual duty that must be fulfilled by the people with respect to each other, by the government with respect to the people, and by the people with respect to the government. The conditions, limits and nature of this duty will be specified by law. This is in accordance with the Qur'anic verse 'The believers, men and women, are the protectors of each other; they enjoin the good and forbid the evil' (9:71).

Art. 9. In the Islamic Republic of Iran, the freedom, independence, unity, and territorial integrity of the country are inseparable from each other, and their preservation is the duty of the government and of all individual citizens. No individual, group, or authority has the right to infringe in the slightest way upon the political, cultural, economic, and military independence or the territorial integrity of Iran under the pretext of exercising freedom. Similarly, no authority has the right to withdraw legitimate freedoms, even by establishing laws and regulations for that purpose, under the pretext of preserving the independence and territorial integrity of the country.

Art. 10. In accordance with the verse 'This your nation is a single nation, and I am your Lord, so worship Me,' all Muslims form a single nation, and the government of the Islamic Republic of Iran has the duty of formulating its general policies with a view to the merging and union of all Muslim peoples, and it must constantly strive to bring about the political, economic, and cultural unity of the Islamic world.

Art. 11. Since the family is the fundamental unit of Islamic society, all pertinent laws, regulations, and programs must tend to facilitate the foundation of a family and to protect the sanctity and stability of family relations on the basis of the law and ethics of Islam.

Art. 12. The official religion of Iran is Islam and the Twelver Ja`fari school of thought, and this principle shall remain eternally immutable. Other Islamic schools of thought, including the Hanafi, Shafi'i, Maliki, Hanbali, and Zaydi schools, are to be accorded full respect, and their followers are free to act in accordance with their own jurisprudence in performing their religious devotions. These schools enjoy official status for the purposes of religious education and matters of personal status (marriage, divorce, inheritance, and bequests), being accepted in the courts for cases relating to such matters. In areas of the country where Muslims following one of these schools of thought constitute the majority, local regulations, within the bounds of the jurisdiction of local councils, are to be in accordance with the respective school of thought, without infringing upon the rights of the followers of other schools.

Art. 13. Zoroastrian, Jewish, and Christian Iranians are the only recognized minorities, with the right freely to perform their religious ceremonies within the limits of the law and to act according to their own customs in matters of personal status and religious education.

Art. 14. In accordance with the verse 'God does not forbid you to deal kindly and justly with those who have not fought against you because of your religion and who have not expelled you from your homes' (60:8), the government of the Islamic Republic of Iran and all Muslims are duty-bound to treat non-Muslims in an ethical fashion and in accordance with Islamic justice and equity and to respect their human rights. This principle applies to all who refrain from engaging in conspiracy or activity against Islam and the Islamic Republic of Iran.

Chapter III: The Rights of the People

Art. 19. Whatever the ethnic group or tribe to which they belong, all people of Iran enjoy equal rights, and factors such as color, race, and language do not bestow any privilege.

Art. 20. All citizens of the nation, both women and men, equally enjoy the protection of the law and enjoy all human, political, economic, social, and cultural rights, in conformity with Islamic criteria.

Art. 21. The government must assure the rights of women in all respects, in conformity with Islamic criteria, and accomplish the following goals:

  a. create a favorable environment for the growth of woman's personality and the restoration of her rights, tangible, and intangible;

  b. the protection of mothers, particularly during pregnancy and childrearing, and the protection of children without guardians;

c. the creation of a competent court to protect and preserve the family;

d. the provision of special insurance for widows and aged and destitute women;

e. the granting of guardianship of children to their mothers whenever suitable in order to protect the interests of the children, in the absence of a legal guardian.

Art. 22. The dignity, life, property, rights, dwelling, and occupation of the individual are inviolate, except in cases sanctioned by the law.

Art. 23. The interrogation of persons concerning their opinions is forbidden, and no one may be molested or taken to task simply for holding a certain opinion.

Art. 24. Publications and the press are free to present all matters except those that are detrimental to the fundamental principles of Islam or the rights of the public. The details of this exception will be specified by the law.

Art. 25. The inspection of letters and the failure to deliver them, the recording and disclosure of telephone conversations, the disclosure of telegraphic and telex communications or the willful failure to transmit them, wiretapping, and all forms of covert investigation are forbidden, except as provided by law.

Art. 26. The formation of political and professional parties, associations, and societies, as well as religious societies, whether they be Islamic or pertain to one of the recognized religious minorities, is freely permitted on condition that they do not violate the principles of independence, freedom, national unity, the criteria of Islam, or the basis of the Islamic Republic. No one may be prevented from participating in the aforementioned groups, or be compelled to participate in them.

Art. 27. Public gatherings and marches may freely be held, on condition that arms are not carried and that they are not detrimental to the fundamental principles of Islam.

Art. 28. Everyone has the right to choose any employment he wishes, if it is not opposed to Islam, the public interest, or the rights of others. The government has the duty, while bearing in mind the needs of society for different kinds of work, to provide every citizen with the opportunity to work, and to create equal conditions for obtaining it.

Art. 29. The right to benefit from social security with respect to retirement, unemployment, old age, disability, and destitution benefits, as well as benefits relating to being stranded and emergencies, health services, medicine, and medical care, provided through insurance or other means is a universal right.

The government must assure the foregoing rights and financial protection by drawing on the national income, in accordance with the law, and on income derived from the participation of the people.

Art. 30. The government must provide all citizens with free education to the end of middle school, and must expand higher education to the level required by the country for self-sufficiency.

Art. 31. To own a dwelling commensurate with one's needs is the right of every individual and family in Iran. The government must make land available for the implementation of this principle, according priority to those whose need is greatest, in particular the rural population and the workers.

Art. 32. No one can be arrested except in accordance with judgment and the procedure established by law. In the case of arrest, charges and supporting evidence must be communicated immediately in writing to the prisoner and be elucidated to him, and a provisional dossier must be forwarded to the competent judicial authorities within a maximum of twenty-four hours so that the preliminaries to the trial can be completed as swiftly as possible. Punishments for the infringement of these principles will be determined by law.

Art. 33. No one can be banished from his place of residence, prevented from residing in his preferred location, or compelled to reside in a given locality, except as provided in law.

Art. 34. It is the indisputable right of every citizen to seek justice, and everyone must have access to the competent courts in order to present his case. All members of the nation have the right of access to such courts, and no one can be barred from courts to which they have a legal right of recourse.

Art. 35. Both parties to a dispute have the right in all courts of law to select a lawyer, and if they are unable to do so, arrangements must be made to provide them with legal counsel.

Art. 36. The passing and execution of sentence must be performed only by the appropriate court and in accordance with the law.

Art. 37. Innocence is to be presumed, and no one is to be regarded as guilty unless his guilt has been established by the competent court.

Art. 38. Any form of torture for the purpose of extracting confessions or gaining information is forbidden. It is not permissible to compel individuals to give testimony, make confessions, or swear oaths, and any testimony, confession, or oath obtained in this fashion is worthless and invalid. Punishments for the infringement of these principles will be determined by law.

Art. 39. All affronts to the dignity and honor of persons arrested, detained, imprisoned, or banished in accordance with the law, whatever form they may take, are forbidden and punishable.

Art. 40. No one can make the exercise of his rights a pretext for harming others or encroaching on the public interest.

Art. 41. Iranian nationality is the indisputable right of every Iranian, and the government cannot withdraw nationality from any Iranian unless he himself requests it or acquires the nationality of another country.

Art. 42. Foreign nationals may acquire Iranian nationality within the framework of the relevant laws. Nationality may be withdrawn from such persons if another state accepts them as its nationals or if they request it."

2. The 1989 Amendment to the Constitution of the Islamic Republic[3]

Art. 5. During the occultation of his holiness, the Lord of the Age (may God Almighty hasten his appearance), the governance and religious leadership of the nation in the Islamic Republic of Iran is the responsibility of the just and pious faqih who is acquainted with his age, courageous and possessed of administrative ability, in accordance with Article 107.

Art. 57. The powers of government in the Islamic Republic of Iran consist of the legislative, the executive, and the judiciary. They operate under the supervision of the absolute authority of the governance and the religious leadership of the nation and according to the forthcoming articles of this law. These powers are independent of one another.

Art. 60. The exercise of the executive power is by means of the President of the Republic and the ministers except for matters that are directly assigned to the Leadership by this Constitution.

---

3. The Persian text "Qanun-e asasi-ye Jomhuri-ye Eslami-ye Iran" (The Constitution of the Islamic Republic of Iran) is available at rc.majlis.ir/fa/content/iran_constitution. The translation, for the most part, is my own.

Art. 70. The President of the Republic, his deputies, and his ministers have the right to participate in the open sessions of Parliament[4] either individually or as a group. They can be accompanied by their advisers. If the members of Parliament deem it necessary, the ministers are obliged to attend. Conversely if they request it, their demands will be heard. The invitation to the President by the Parliament must be approved by a majority.

Art. 87. The President of the Republic must obtain a vote of confidence from Parliament for the Council of Ministers, after it is formed and before any undertakings. During his term, the President can also request a vote of confidence from Parliament for the Council of Ministers on matters that are important and are subject to dispute.

Art. 88. Whenever at least one quarter of the total members of the Islamic Consultative Assembly asks a question from the President, or whenever any member of the Assembly asks a question from a responsible minister about his duties, the President or the minister [in question] are required to appear in the Assembly. The response of the President should not be delayed by more than a month and that of the minister by more than ten days; except with a valid excuse so recognized by the Islamic Consultative Assembly.

Art. 89.

i. Members of the Islamic Consultative Assembly can censure the Council of Ministers, or any individual minister on matters they deem necessary. The censure can be presented to the Assembly if it is signed by at least ten members. The Council of Ministers or the minister subject to censure must be present in the Assembly within ten days of the submission of the censure, in order to respond and ask for a vote of confidence from the Assembly. If the Council of Ministers or the minister in question fails to appear in the Assembly, the members of the Assembly who submitted the censure shall provide the necessary explanation. If the assembly deems it necessary, it will declare a vote of no confidence. If the Assembly does not give a vote of confidence, the Council of Ministers or the minister in question will be removed. In both cases, the ministers in question cannot become members in the cabinet that is subsequently formed.

---

4. In this translation, Parliament and Islamic Consultative Assembly are used interchangeably.

ii. In the event that at least one third of the members of the Islamic Consultative Assembly censure the President in his capacity as head of the executive power and administration of the country, the President must be present in the Assembly within a month of the submission of the censure and give adequate explanations in response to the issues in question. Following the statements of the members of the Assembly, both in favor and against, and the response of the President, if a two-thirds majority of the members vote for the lack of competence of the President, the details will be communicated to the Leader for purposes of applying paragraph 10 of Article 110.

Art. 91. In order to protect the ordinances of Islam and the Constitution by assuring that legislation passed by the Islamic Consultative Assembly does not conflict with them, a council called the Guardian Council is established with the following composition:

i. Six just *fuqaha* [Islamic jurists] who are acquainted with the needs of the time and the issues of the day. These are selected by the Leader.

ii. Six [lay] jurists, specializing in different fields of law, from among Muslim jurists who are presented by the head of the judiciary to the Islamic Consultative Assembly and are selected by the vote of the Assembly.

Art. 99. The Guardian Council is responsible for supervising the elections of the Assembly of experts, the President of the Republic, the Islamic Consultative Assembly, and referrals to public opinion and referenda.

Art. 107. After the honorable source of emulation, the great Leader of the global Islamic Revolution, and the founder of the Islamic Republic of Iran, the venerated Ayatollah, Imam Khomeini, may his noble character be sanctified, who was recognized and accepted by the undisputed majority of the people as the *marja'* and the Leader, the responsibility for designating the Leader shall be with the [Assembly of] Experts who are voted by the people. The Experts consider all the qualified jurists as discussed in Articles 5 and 109, and consult with one another about them. If they find one of them to be the most knowledgeable about the rules and subjects of jurisprudence, or political and social issues, or acceptability to the public, or significance in any one of the qualifications indicated in Article 109, that person shall be selected as the Leader; otherwise, one of the Experts is chosen and declared as the Leader. The Leader who is appointed by the [Assembly of] Experts will have responsibility over the governance and all the tasks that derive from it. The Leader is equal before the law with all other people in the country.

Art. 108. The law regarding the number and qualifications of the Experts, the manner of their election, and the internal guidelines regulating the meetings in their first term must be drawn up by the *fuqaha* [jurists] of the first Guardian Council, and be approved by a majority among them and submitted to the Leader for the final approval. After that, any [subsequent] change or review of this law and approval of the regulations related to the responsibilities of the Experts fall within the authority of the [Assembly of] Experts themselves.

Art. 109. The qualifications and attributes of the Leader:

i.   Suitability with respect to learning as required to give *fatwa*s in various domains of *fiqh* [jurisprudence].

ii. Required justice and piety necessary for leading the Muslim nation.

iii. Sound political and social perspicacity, prudence, courage, and the necessary administrative ability and strength for leadership.

In case there are a number of candidates who satisfy these qualifications, the person with a more effective political and jurisprudential insight will have priority.

Art. 110. The powers and tasks of the Leader:

i.   Determining the overall politics of the Islamic Republic of Iran after consultation with the Expediency Council.

ii. Supervising the proper implementation of the general policies of the Islamic Republic of Iran.

iii. Issuing referenda.

iv. Commanding the armed forces.

v.   Declaring war, peace, and mobilizing forces.

vi. Issuing appointments, dismissals, and accepting the resignation of:

    a. the jurists of the Guardian Council

    b. the highest position of the judiciary

    c. the president of the radio and television of the Islamic Republic of Iran

    d. the chief of the general staff

    e. the commander-in-chief of the Corps of the Guards of the Islamic Revolution

    f. the supreme commanders-in-chief of the security and armed forces

vii. Regulating the ties between the three branches of government and resolving any conflict among them.

viii. Resolving issues in the Islamic Republic that cannot be settled by ordinary means through the Expediency Council.

ix. Ratifying the appointment of the President of the Republic following his election by the public. The qualification of the candidates for presidency, with respect to the conditions set forth by the constitution, must be confirmed by the Guardian Council prior to the general elections and approved by the Leader for the first term.

x. Dismissing the President of the Republic, with due regard for the interests of the country, after the issue of a ruling by the Supreme Court convicting him of deviation from his legal duties, or a vote by the Islamic Consultative Assembly testifying to his competence, on the basis of Article 89.

xi. Pardoning or reducing the sentences of convicts, within the bounds of Islamic criteria, following the recommendation of the head of the judiciary to that effect. The Leader can transfer some of his duties and powers to another person.

Art. 111. Whenever the Leader becomes incapable of fulfilling his legal duties or loses one of the qualifications mentioned in Articles 5 and 109; or it becomes clear that he has been lacking in some of the qualification from the outset, he will be dismissed. The determination of this issue will fall to the Assembly of Experts, as mentioned in Article 108.

In the event of the death, resignation, or dismissal of the Leader, the Experts are responsible for appointing a new Leader as soon as possible. Until the [new] Leader is introduced, a council consisting of the President of the Republic, the head of the judiciary, and one of the jurists of the Guardian Council, selected by the Expediency Council, will temporarily assume all the responsibilities of the Leadership. In the event that during this time, one of the aforementioned, for any reason, cannot fulfill his duties, another individual will be assigned in his place, in accordance with the vote of the Assembly and with respect to maintaining the majority of the jurists in the Council.

With regard to the responsibilities outlined in Article 110, sections 1, 3, 5, and 10, and segments "d," "e," and "f" of section 6, the Council can take action after having obtained three-fourths approval of the members of the Expediency Council.

Whenever the Leader, due to illness or other incidents, becomes temporarily unable to fulfill the duties of Leadership, the Council mentioned in this Article will assume his responsibilities.

Art. 112. The Expediency Council will convene on the order of the Leader to determine what is best in cases where the Guardian Council finds legislation made by the Islamic Consultative Assembly to be in violation of the *Shari`a* or the Constitution; and the Assembly does not sustain the opinion of the Guardian Council with regard to the interests of the system; or for consulting on affairs that the Leadership will refer to the Expediency Council; or other duties that are mentioned in the constitution.

The Leadership appoints both the permanent and the transitional members of this Council.

Regulations regarding the Council will be prepared and approved by its members themselves and approved by the Leadership.

Art. 113. After the Leadership, the President of the Republic is the highest official position of the country. He is responsible for implementing the constitution and heading the executive power, except in matters that directly pertain to the Leadership.

Art. 121. The President of the Republic must take the following oath and sign it at a session held at the Islamic Consultative Assembly in the presence of the head of the judiciary and the members of the Guardian Council:

In the name of God, the Compassionate, the Merciful,

As President of the Republic, I take an oath, before the Noble Qur'an and the Iranian nation, on God the Powerful and Almighty, that I will guard the official religion of the country, the order of the Islamic Republic, and the constitution of the country; that I will devote all my capabilities and competence toward fulfilling the responsibilities that I have undertaken, and devote myself to the service of the people and the advancement of the country, dissemination of religion and morality, and the support of truth and justice. I will protect the freedom and dignity of the individuals and the rights that the constitution has granted the nation. I will not withdraw from any endeavor toward safeguarding the borders and the political, economic, and cultural independence of the country. By seeking help from God and following the Prophet of Islam, and the Immaculate Imams, peace be upon them, I will guard the power that the nation has bestowed upon me as a sacred trust, and surrender it to whomever the people elect after me.

Art. 124. In order to fulfill his legal duties, the President of the Republic can have deputies.

The first deputy of the President of the Republic, with his consent, will have the responsibility of administering the Council of Ministers and co-ordinating the other deputies.

Art. 126. The President of the Republic is directly responsible for matters pertaining to the budget and planning, and the administrative and employment affairs of the country; he can transfer their administration to another person.

Art. 127. In special instances, as dictated by necessity and with the approval of the Council of Ministers, the President of the Republic can assign one or more special representatives with specific powers. In these instances, the decisions made by the aforementioned representative or representatives are considered tantamount to the decisions of the President of the Republic and the Council of Ministers.

Art. 128. Ambassadors to foreign countries are selected upon the recommendation of the Minister of Foreign Affairs and the approval of the President of the Republic. The President of the Republic signs the credentials of the ambassadors and accepts the credentials of ambassadors from other countries.

Art. 130. The President of the Republic submits his resignation to the Leader; until such time that it is accepted, he continues with his duties.

Art. 131. In case of the death, dismissal, resignation, absence or sickness, lasting more than two months, of the President of the Republic, or in case the term of presidency is over but as a result of obstacles, the new President of the Republic is still not elected or other circumstances of this kind, the first deputy of the President of the Republic, with the consent of the Leadership, assumes the powers and responsibilities of the President. A council consisting of the Speaker of Parliament, the Head of the Judiciary, and the first deputy of the President of the Republic is obliged to make arrangements so that within a maximum of fifty days, the new President of the Republic is elected. In case the first deputy dies or other circumstances prevent him from fulfilling his duties, or in case the President of the Republic does not have a first deputy, the Leader assigns another person in his stead.

Art. 132. During the period when the powers and responsibilities of the President of the Republic are assigned to the first deputy or another person, in accordance with Article 131, it is not possible to impeach ministers or to give them a vote of no-confidence; or to undertake steps to review the constitution or have a referendum.

Art. 133. The ministers are appointed by the President of the Republic and presented to Parliament for a vote of confidence. A change in the Parliament does not necessitate a new vote of confidence for the ministers. The law determines the number of ministers and the limits of their power.

Art. 134. The President of the Republic is the head of the Council of Ministers. He supervises the work of the ministers and takes all necessary measures to coordinate the decisions made by the ministers and the cabinet. With the cooperation of the ministers, he determines the programs and policies of the government and implements the law. If there are disagreements or if there is intervention in the legal duties of government institutions, and if such matters do not necessitate an interpretation or legal changes, then the decisions of the Council of Ministers, adopted on the basis of the recommendation of the President of the Republic, are binding. The President of the Republic is responsible to Parliament for the actions of the Council of Ministers.

Art. 135. The ministers remain in their posts as long as they are not dismissed or issued a vote of no-confidence by Parliament as a result of impeachment or asking for a vote of confidence.

The resignation of any individual minister or the Council of Ministers is submitted to the President of the Republic. Until the appointment of a new government, the Council of Ministers continues with its duties. The President of the Republic can appoint a supervisor for the ministries that do not have a minister for a maximum of three months.

Art. 136. The President of the Republic can dismiss ministers. In such a case, he must obtain a vote of confidence for the new minister/s from Parliament. If half the members of the Council of Ministers change after the Parliament has given its vote of confidence to the government, the President must again solicit a vote of confidence from the Islamic Consultative Assembly.

Art. 137. Each of the ministers is responsible for his own specific duties to the President of the Republic and the Parliament. He is also responsible for the actions of others in matters that have been approved by the Council of Ministers.

Art. 140. Accusations against the President of the Republic, his deputies, and the ministers, in cases of common crimes, are investigated with the knowledge of the Islamic Consultative Assembly in common courts of justice.

Art. 141. The President of the Republic, his deputies, ministers, and the government employees cannot hold more than one governmental position. They are prohibited from holding any other post in institutions whose capital, in part or in entirety, belongs to the government or public institutions. Nor can they be a representative at the Islamic Consultative Assembly, or an attorney of court, a legal advisor or the president, executive manager, or member of the board of directors of any kind of private company; except for cooperative companies affiliated with government offices and institutions. Educational positions at universities and research institutes are exempt from this rule.

Art. 142. The financial holdings of the Leader, the President of the Republic, his deputies, the ministers, and their spouses and children, will be examined by the head of the judiciary before and after their term of office, in order to determine that they have not increased illegitimately.

Art. 175. Freedom of expression and dissemination of ideas must be assured through the mass media [radio and television] of the Islamic Republic of Iran, with due observance of the Islamic criteria and the welfare of the country. The Leader appoints and dismisses the head of the radio and television of the Islamic Republic of Iran. A council consisting of representatives of the President of the Republic, the head of the judiciary, and the Islamic Consultative Assembly (two persons from each), will supervise this organization. The law determines the course, the administration, and supervision of this organization.

Art. 176. To secure national interests and to safeguard the Islamic Revolution, territorial integrity, and national sovereignty, the Supreme National Security Council will be established under the chairmanship of the President of the Republic, and will have the following tasks:

i.   Determining the defense and national security policies within the framework of the general policies determined by the Leader.

ii. Coordinating political, intelligence, social, cultural and economic activities in relation to general measures in the domains of defense and security.

    iii. Making use of the material and spiritual resources of the country to counter internal and external threats.

The members of the Council are as follows: the Head of the three Powers; the Commander-in-Chief of the Armed Forces; the Head of Planning and Budget; two representatives selected by the Leader; the Ministers of Foreign Affairs, State and Intelligence; the relevant minister according to the case [under review], and the holder of the highest office in the Army and the Guardians of the Revolution [*Pasdaran*].

Commensurate with its duties, the Supreme National Security Council will convene sub-councils such as the Defense Council and the National Security Council. The chairmanship of each of the sub-councils is the responsibility of the President of the Republic or one of the members of the Supreme Council appointed by the President of the Republic.

The scope of the authority and the tasks of the sub-councils are determined by the Law, and the Supreme Council will ratify their formation.

The decisions made by the Supreme National Security Council will be effective after they have been approved by the Leader.

Art. 177. Revisions to the Constitution of the Islamic Republic of Iran, should the need arise, will take place as follows:

In a statement addressed to the President of the Republic, the Leader, after consultation with the Expediency Council, will propose amendments or improvements to the Constitution [to be made by] the Council for the Revision of the Constitution, which [in turn] consists of:

1. Members of the Guardian Council
2. Heads of the Three Powers
3. Permanent members of the Expediency Council
4. Five members of the Assembly of Experts
5. Ten individuals selected by the Leader
6. Three members of the Council of Ministers
7. Three members of the Judiciary
8. Ten members of the Islamic Consultative Assembly
9. Three University Professors

The Law will determine the method of working, the manner of selection, and the terms and conditions of the Council. The decisions of the Council, after the approval and signature of the Leader, will have to be approved by an absolute majority vote in a national referendum. The provision of Article 59 of the Constitution with regard to the referendum for "the revision of the Constitution" does not apply. The contents of the Articles of the Constitution related to the Islamic character of the political system, the basis of all the rules and regulations according to the Islamic criteria, the religious footing, the objectives of the Islamic Republic of Iran, the republican aspect of the government, the *vilayat-e amr*, the imamate of the *umma*, as well as the administration of the affairs of the country based on the will of the people, the official religion of Iran [Islam], and the school [Twelver Ja`fari], cannot be changed.

"Accepting the UN Resolution Is More Deadly to Me than Drinking a Cup of Poison!": Ayatollah Khomeini's Statement on Accepting a Ceasefire with Iraq According to UN Resolution 598, July 20, 1988[5]

On July 20, 1988, on the occasion of the first anniversary of the clashes that had taken place between Iranian pilgrims and Saudi Arabian security forces in July 1987, and which had claimed over 400 lives,[6] Ayatollah Khomeini addressed the nation. It was as part of this statement that Khomeini declared his new position with regard to accepting United Nations Resolution 598.[7] Below, only excerpts from that part of the statement relating to the acceptance of the UN resolution have been translated.

5. "Imam Khomeini: qabul-e qat`-nameh az nushidan-e jam-e zahr bara-ye man koshandeh-tar ast," *Jamaran* website.

6. On July 31, 1987, clashes took place between Iranian pilgrims in Mecca and Saudi Arabian Police and National Guards. There is controversy over the details of the incident with each side blaming the other, but what there is agreement about is that the clashes resulted in the death of 402 people (275 Iranians, 85 Saudis, and 42 other pilgrims) and over 640 injured.

7. United Nations Resolution 598 called for an immediate ceasefire between Iran and Iraq, the repatriation of the prisoners of war, and the withdrawal of the two sides to the international border. Both Iran and Iraq accepted the ceasefire on July 20, 1988, and it was put into effect on August 8, 1988.

As for the acceptance of the [UN] resolution which was truly a very bitter and unpleasant issue for everyone, especially for me: it is that until a few days ago, I believed in the same stated methods of defense and [past] positions in the war, and I saw the interest of the system [the Islamic Republic], the country, and the revolution in putting them into effect. However, as a result of the events and factors that I won't discuss for the time being, and which God willing, will become clear in the future, and considering the advice of all high-ranking political and military experts of the country, whose commitment and sympathy and honesty I trust, I agreed to accept the resolution and the ceasefire. At this juncture, I consider it [the resolution] to be in the interest of the revolution and the system. God knows that if it were not that all our honor and prestige should be sacrificed for Islam, I would never have consented to this, and death and martyrdom would have been more pleasant for me. But what choice is there since we all have to submit to the satisfaction of God Almighty. . . .

Here, I thank and appreciate all my dear children at the fronts of fire and blood who from the beginning have struggled and strived in one way or another in respect to the war. And I invite all the people of Iran to be vigilant, patient and resistant. It is possible that in the future, some people, either consciously or unconsciously, might ask the question what was the point of all the blood [shed], the martyrdoms, and the sacrifices? These people surely know nothing of the spiritual world and the philosophy of martyrdom. They don't know that for someone who has gone on a jihad only to please God, and has surrendered to a life of sincerity and service, the events of the day will do no harm to his ever-lasting and eternal exalted position. We have to cover much ground to be able to fully understand the value and the path of our martyrs; we have to continue to seek it over time through the course of the revolution and that of the future generations. Certainly, the blood of the martyrs has insured the revolution and Islam. The blood of the martyrs has given a lesson in resistance to the world for all eternity. And God knows that the way of martyrdom cannot be ignored and it is the nations and the future generations who will follow the way of the martyrs. . . . Happy are those who died through martyrdom! Happy are those who died in this convoy of light! Happy are those who brought up such jewels in their laps!

Dear God! Continue to keep this book of martyrdom open to the enthusiasts, and don't deprive us from reaching it either! Dear God! Our country and people are still at the beginning of their struggle, and they are in need of the flame of martyrdom. May you, yourself, preserve and guard this bright light! Happy are you, the Iranian people! Happy are you, women and men! Happy are those who risk their lives, the prisoners [of war], the missing [in war] and the exalted families of the martyrs! Woe unto me for still living and having to drink down the poisoned cup of the acceptance of the resolution! I feel ashamed before the greatness and sacrifice of this great nation!

Woe onto those who were not part of this convoy of travelers! Woe onto those who have passed by this big arena of war and martyrdom and great divine test in silence and indifference, or with disparagement and censure!

. . . Whether I be present in or absent from your midst, I command and instruct you not to allow the revolution to fall into the hands of the unworthy and the outsiders. Don't let the pioneers of martyrdom and blood be forgotten in the twists and turns of everyday life. I absolutely enjoin the dear Iranian nation to be vigilant and alert. Accepting the resolution by the Islamic Republic does not mean that the issue of the war has been resolved. By announcing this decision, the propaganda weapon of the bullies against us has been stamped out; but one cannot predict the outlook of events absolutely and seriously. The enemy has not yet given up on his evil acts. It could be that he finds excuses to continue with his aggressive ways. We must be ready and prepared to ward off potential enemy aggression.

And our nation should not consider the problem resolved for now. Of course, we officially announce that our aim is not a new tactic in the continuation of the war. It could be that the enemies want to continue with their attacks using these same excuses. Our armed forces should never be unaware of the deceit and duplicity of the enemy. [Rather] in all circumstances, the defense potential of the country must be in the best situation. Our people who in the long years of war and struggle have felt the many dimensions of hostility, animosity and enmity of the enemies of God and themselves, should consider more seriously the danger of the attack of bullies in different shapes and forms. For the time being, like in the past, all the armed forces, whether the army, the revolutionary guards (*sepah*), or the *basij* on the fronts, should continue with their missions to defend against the mischief of World Arrogance[8] and Iraq. . . .

---

8. "World Arrogance" is a reference to the United States.

In these days, it is possible that many people, because of their emotions and feelings, talk about the whys and wherefores [of this decision]. Even though, this issue in itself consists of a very beautiful value, now is not the time to discuss it. How many were those who until yesterday would hold a front against the system, and only spoke of peace and peace-making in order to bring about the fall of the system and the rule of the Islamic Republic of Iran. Today, too, they put forth deceitful talk with that same aim, and the mercenaries of World Arrogance, those same ones who until yesterday, under the false veil of peace, had stabbed the hearts of the nation in the back, today have [suddenly] become the supporters of the war. And the philistine nationalists, who for the sake of doing away with the blood of the dear martyrs and the destruction of the dignity and honor of the people, have started their poisonous propaganda. God willing, our dear Iranian people will answer all the[se] acts of sedition with vigilance and insight.

I repeat that accepting this issue [ceasefire] is more deadly to me than taking poison, but I am pleased to please God and it is for His satisfaction that I have drunk this [cup of poison]. The point that should be made is that in accepting this resolution, those responsible for the country have made the decision independently; no other party or country has interfered in this matter.

Esteemed and noble people of Iran, I know each one of you like my own children, and you know that I love you dearly, and that I know you. You, too, know me. In the present conditions, that which caused this [development] was my divine duty. You know that I had made a promise to you to fight until the very last drop of blood and the very last breath, but today's decision was only for the sake of expediency; it was only in the hope of His forgiveness and satisfaction that I turned my back on what I had said. If I ever had any sense of honor, I traded it with God. My dear ones, you know that I have tried not to put my own comfort before your own, or the satisfaction of God. Dear God, you know that we have no desire to compromise with unbelief. . . .

Dear God! You know that World Arrogance and the world-dominating America have scattered the flowers of your garden of prophethood! Dear God! In the world full of oppression, cruelty and injustice, you are our only support! We are all on our own, and know no one other than you, and have not wanted to know anyone other than you! Help us, since you are the best helper. . . .

The Open Letter of the Commanders of the Revolutionary Guards to Mohammad Khatami, July 1999[9]

Following the weeklong student unrest in July 1999, which was seen at the time as the first major public protest in Iran since the early days of the 1979 revolution,[10] twenty-four commanders of the Revolutionary Guards wrote and signed an open letter to President Mohammad Khatami, who had won the Presidential election in May 1997 and advocated a reformist approach to government. This letter, which was considered to be a clear ultimatum to the President, was published in a number of the hardline and conservative dailies in Tehran. The full text of the letter has been translated below. Other than its reproachful tone, what is of interest here is that it exhibits clear differences in approach and world view between certain hardline elements and the reformist President at the time.

To the Honorable President of the Republic, His Excellency Hojjat al-Islam Mr. Seyyed Mohammad Khatami,

Greetings! We are writing to inform you that following the recent events, in our capacity as a group of people who have served in the sacred defense of the noble nation of Iran,[11] we considered it our duty to bring some matters to the attention of Your Excellency, a respected scholar. In view of your generosity and the valuable slogan . . . that you advocate—that one should hear all statements and ideas even if they be disapproving—we hope that you see to this matter which may be the grievance of thousands of tormented revolutionaries who observe the events of the revolution with trepidation and are in disbelief and amazement at the silence, naiveté, and nonchalance of the authorities who owe their positions of power to the blood [and sacrifice] of the thousands of martyrs.

Mr. Khatami! There is no doubt that we all consider Your Excellency a humble, revolutionary, and pious man with deep religious roots in the sem-

---

9. The Persian text of this letter is available on a number of different websites, including http://teribun.ir/archives/114391.

10. The student unrest had begun on the eve of July 9, 1999, originally in protest at the closure of a reformist newspaper, *Salam*. However, it was exacerbated by an attack the following night on the student dormitories at Tehran University by unidentified plainclothes men, resulting in the death and injury of a number of students.

11. "Sacred defense" is a reference to the Iran-Iraq War between 1980 and 1988.

inary, and sympathy and compassion towards the revolution. However, the approach to certain events that we have all witnessed the enemies [of the revolution] celebrate with glee, prioritizing the pursuit of certain mistakes and transgressions and exaggerating them, while neglecting or belittling others that were similar in terms of the breaking of the law and vilification, have caused certain anti-revolutionary currents to become more brazen. On the other side, and by the same token, the supporters of the revolution have suffered humiliation every day by means of a combination of repulsion and repugnance, and continue to observe the results of all this blood that has been shed, in despair, sorrow and disbelief.

Mr. President—as the great and virtuous Leader of this revolution has said, the attack on Tehran University[12] was a distasteful, bad, and disgraceful act. Despite the fact that the strongest and toughest measures were taken to tackle this problem, all the people accepted and endorsed these tough measures because the original act was so indecent. However, the important and uncertain question is, was this all that there was to the catastrophe?

Is this matter alone worthy of pursuit, attention, objection and protest? Is this matter alone deserving of the resignation of a number of ministers, the convening of the National Security Council, and the setting up of an investigative committee? Does dishonoring and insulting the fundamentals of this system [of the Islamic Republic] not merit regret and following up? Is the *velayat-e faqih*[13] any less precious than Tehran University? Is the protection of the person of the Imam, that unparalleled human being, any less prized than disrespect to a student? Is causing interruption to the security of the country for several days, attacking and setting fire to every believer and pious person not a calamity? Is questioning the Islamic Republic, this legacy of tens of thousands of martyrs, and chanting slogans against it not a catastrophe?

Mr. Khatami, several nights ago when it was reported that a number of people who were chanting slogans against the Exalted Leader of the Revolution were moving towards the Shahid Motahhari Compound,[14] our

---

12. This is a reference to the raid on the student dormitories at Tehran University referred to in footnote 10, above.

13. *Velayat-e faqih,* or rule of the jurist, is the theory of government that was put in place in the aftermath of the 1979 revolution, and constitutes the basis of the constitution of the Islamic Republic of Iran.

14. Shahid Motahhari Compound is the location of one of the branches of the judiciary in Tehran.

young children looked into our eyes as if they were asking us, where has your manly zeal gone?

Mr. President! Today when we saw the face of the Exalted Leader of the revolution, we asked God for our own deaths since our hands are bound, and with our eyes wounded and our throats blocked, we have to witness the withering of a tree which has been the result of fourteen centuries of suffering of Shi'is and Islam.

Mr. Khatami! You know well that while we are strong, we are helpless only because of the prudence of friends. For every one knows that today, the hypocrites and enemies [of the system] have joined the ranks of this battle, under the guise of students, and that vengeful, opportunistic, and short-sighted insiders are fanning the flames and do not hesitate to say or write anything just to further provoke the situation.

Mr. Khatami! Until when should we watch with tears in our eyes, and suffer? Until when should we practice democracy through chaos and insults, and exercise revolutionary patience at the cost of losing the system?

Mr. President! Thousands of the families of martyrs and war veterans voted for you. . . . They expect you to tackle these problems honestly. Today we clearly see the footprints of the enemy in these incidents, and we hear their loud and drunken laughter. Take the opportunity today, for tomorrow will be too late, and the regret that you'll have tomorrow will be irrevocable.

Great Seyyed! Consider the speeches of the so-called friends in the gathering of students: is all their talk not mere encouragement and provocation to chaos and the breaking of the law?

Is this the meaning of the year of the Imam? Is this the way to safeguard his valuable legacy? Is the carelessness of a small number of people who call themselves Hezbollah, a license to break the head of every pious person and bring about dishonor?

Mr. Khatami, look at the media of the world; don't you hear the sound of their [celebratory] drums and tambourines?

Mr. President, if you don't make a revolutionary decision today, and do not act upon your national and Islamic mandate, tomorrow will be so late and irretrievable that it is unimaginable.

Finally, with the utmost respect and affection that we have for you, we hereby announce that our patience has reached a tipping point. Should you not attend to this matter, we will no longer consider it acceptable to remain patient.

[Signed:] The Commanders [of the Revolutionary Guards] and Servants of the Noble Nation of Iran during the [Period of the] Sacred Defense.

"The Danger That Threatens [Both] the 'Islamic' and 'Republican' Components of the Islamic Republic," March 31, 2014[15]

Mohammad Reza `Aref, a reformist politician, served in a number of capacities in Mohammad Khatami's cabinet, including that of the First Vice-President between 2001 and 2005. Below is the text of a short article that he published on his personal website on the occasion of April 1, also known as the "Day of the Islamic Republic," that is, when the people voted overwhelmingly for an Islamic Republic in a referendum in 1979. This article is of interest on two levels: first, even though it is written from a conciliatory and reformist perspective, it is an indirect albeit mild rebuke of the conservative hardliners who advocate that an Islamic Republic has to be first and foremost Islamic, and then a republic. Second, it shows that thirty-five years after the establishment of the Islamic Republic, the question of defining it, that is, how "Islamic" or how "republican" the Islamic Republic should be, has not yet been resolved, and that there continue to be different approaches to and interpretations of what an Islamic Republic means.

On April 1, the People of Iran said "yes" to the Islamic Republic with decisiveness. [Both] before and after this epic day, different discussions have been put forth regarding the meaning of the "Islamic Republic." These discussions continue to this day and the scholars together with the social and political activists continue to talk about this subject-matter to greater or lesser degrees. In my opinion, such discussions are both useful and necessary, and can help us better understand the essence of the system of rule in place in our country.

From the very beginning, the main question has been the relationship between the "Islamic" and the "Republican" natures of the Islamic Repub-

---

15. The Persian text is available at http://www.entekhab.ir/fa/news/15421, 11 Farvardin 1393/ 31 March 2014.

lic. The "republican" nature of the system means that priority is given to the wishes of the people, and the "Islamic" nature means that Islamic values take priority over everything else. The question then is, when we say the "Islamic Republic," which component do we consider taking precedence over the other? Are the votes and wishes of the people the final arbiter, or is the aim, the establishment of Islamic values even if the people have no liking for them?

I believe that the meaning of the "Islamic Republic" that people have voted for is that the majority of the people voted for Islam. Thus, there is no contradiction between the "Islamic" and the "republican" components. The combination of the "Islamic Republic" is based on an external reality in Iran; it is not merely a conceptual combination. Of course, there is this view that in a society, [it is possible that] the wish of the majority of the people be something other than Islam. However, the reality of the Iranian society shows that the people of Iran generally believe in Islamic values, even though there may be differences in the extent of these values.

In other words, neither is the "republican" component of the Islamic republic a threat to its "Islamic" component, nor is its Islamic component a threat to its "republican" component. Those who are concerned about the Islamic aspect of the system have to rest assured that we will consult the nation regarding all matters. The majority of the people will not choose anything other than Islam. As for those who are uneasy about the "republican" aspect of the Islamic republic, they should know that the Islam that has been established in our country is the result of the vote of the people.

The issue of the "republican" and "Islamic" components goes further back than what happened on 1 April 1979. That day was a confirmation of what had existed in our country for centuries. It is centuries that the Iranian people have chosen Islam as a pure truth. Therefore, our system has its roots in the choice of the people.

Those who in the four corners of the country, patronizingly, interpret Islam themselves, and based on this same interpretation, close the door to the possibility of people playing a role in determining the fate of the country, on the pretext that the participation of the people will threaten the Islamic component of the Islamic republic, should know that it is these same people who have embraced Islam for centuries. Similarly, this same system of rule [of the Islamic Republic] which has plaintiffs today is the result of the choice of the people.

Those who fear religion and on this pretext, worry about democracy, should know that the choice of the Iranian people, at least in the last several centuries, has never been outside of Islam. Therefore, on the pretext of threatening the Islamic component, the way to different views within the system of rule should not be banned.

Islam has determined the intellectual framework, and the Iranian people, for the most part, have accepted it. But within this framework, there are different dispositions, and those who on the pretext of [safeguarding] the Islamic component consider any tendency other than their own as unislamic will strike a blow to both the "Islamic" and "republican" aspects of the system of rule. A patronizing look at the Iranian nation—which has chosen Islam for hundreds of years—a lack of trust in the choices made by the people, and attempting to deviate [from those choices]—[all three of these] will endanger both the "Islamic" and "republican" aspects of the system simultaneously.

The Islamic Republic accepts religious minorities warmly. The peaceful co-existence of the people of Iran, who are Muslim, with religious minorities, has a past that is as long, if not longer than when Iran accepted Islam. Therefore, even though our system of rule is a republic, this republic does not refute the rights of minorities. Iran is among the countries where ethnic conflict is almost non-existent. . . . Iranians have been experiencing peaceful co-existence for centuries. On the other hand, the Islamic nature of the system of rule, also, does not repudiate the rights of religious minorities. If our standard in the "Islamic" component is the behavior of the messenger of God, the Imams, and Koranic teachings, these three main sources of religion, have accepted the rights of the minorities with fairness and sympathy. . . .

Any kind of violation of the rights of religious minorities which have been stipulated in the constitution of our country, is rooted neither in the "republican" nor "Islamic" component of the system of rule, but [rather] in the erroneous and narrow-minded understanding of these two factors.

It is hoped that with a better and more accurate understanding of what constitutes the Islamic Republic . . . and by putting aside the patronizing and narrow-minded attitude, we [can] bring about the means to consolidate increasingly the bases of the Islamic Republic. We should know that our misunderstanding of what the Islamic Republic means will make us vulnerable in both the areas of the "republican" and "Islamic" aspects, and this is a big danger for our society.

9

Voices of Reform and Societal Transformations

Voices of Reform

By the mid to late 1990s, in the pages of a growing number of reformist newspapers and journals, an alternative reformist discourse began to take shape whose purpose in part was to critique and challenge from within the official ideology of the theocracy in place. Below are three very different examples of challenges and arguments put forth in favor of reform.

1. "The Official Reading of Religion: Crises, Challenges, Solutions: An Interview with Mohammad Mojtahed Shabestari," *Rah-e no*, August 1998[1]

This is an excerpt of an interview with Mohammad Mojtahed Shabestari (b. 1936), a theologian, philosopher, and one of the well-known advocates of religious reform. What makes this interview, published in 1997, interesting is Mojtahed Shabestari's argument regarding the limited nature of religious knowledge in general, and its unsuitability to manage modern life in particular.

. . . Today, there is a chronic crisis and failure in the official reading of religion in our society. This crisis and failure is a result of numerous factors,

---

1. "Qera'at-e rasmi az din: bohranha, chaleshha, rah-e halha: dar goftogu ba Mohammad Mojtahed Shabestar.i." *Rah-e no,* vol. 1, no. 19, 7 Shahrivar 1377/ August 1998, pp. 18-24.

and I will just talk about the most important ones. The major reason for this situation is an irrational claim which is inconsistent with the reality about Islam as a religion. The claim is that Islam as a religion consists of such political, economic, and legal systems, emanating from jurisprudence, that one can live with them throughout the ages, and that God, too, has willed that humans do so. This claim and its consequences have resulted in a deep crisis in the official reading of religion in our society. Throughout history, Islam has not manifested itself to consist of systems that can be compatible with all ages. In fact, no religion can have such systems. Furthermore, this is not a logical claim, and the absence of such systems in any religion including Islam is not a deficiency. Since this claim has no basis in the reality of the life of Muslims today, the fact that those in charge of the official reading insist upon it, has led to the crisis.

This analysis will become clear when we pay attention to two issues: the first is to consider the way and structure of the life of Muslims between the emergence and expansion of Islam until the emergence of modernity in Islamic countries; and second, to consider the kind of modern lives that Muslims have led from about one hundred and fifty years ago, following the advent of modernity. These two ways of life must be clarified first. In the past, the way of life of Muslims was in keeping with the innate circumstances of their setting on the one hand, and the customs and traditions of the time, on the other. In such a context, in addition to playing a spiritual role, the juristic and religious decrees made a certain contribution to the social aspects of life. This consisted of monitoring the actions taken by Muslims through free will in their social life, in order to protect the social order and remove the differences between people by way of acting according to these decrees. Acting on these rulings was considered to be both acting on God's commands, and implementing justice and ethics, as well as securing the social order on the basis of removing the differences and conflicts. In fact . . . religious life also served the purpose of social life. Jurists would determine what was lawful and what was not based on the deductions that they had made from the Qur'an and *Sunna*, and people would apply them to their daily lives. . . . In those aspects of life where no rulings or verdicts were made, they would say that this was the domain of the permissible (*mobahat*). . . . In this way, with a ruling of what was considered juridically lawful and what, unlawful, both, daily life would pass and God's command would be obeyed. Life, at this time, was agricultural, pastoral, half-feudal, and at times, based on trade. As I said, this kind of life was in keeping with the innate circumstances on the one hand, and customs and traditions, on the other. In such a context, the science of jurisprudence . . . dominated the basis upon which people acted on these decrees, and thus secured the social order. Whenever the ruler wanted to introduce a new custom or decision into the social life of Muslims, he would have had to evaluate it in relation to what was juridically considered to be lawful and what was not, in order to ensure that it would not be in opposition to God's command. . . . This is a summary of the way of life in the past and the role that juridical rules played in it. . . . Throughout history, certain political, commercial, legal, economic, cultural and social systems came about among Muslims, each of which had its own historical reasons and causes. . . . [In short], these systems had emerged from certain historical conditions of the time; they were not eternal systems; [a claim] that makes no sense. . . .

However, from about one hundred and fifty years ago, Muslims have accepted a new way of life which is completely different from their lives in the past. This modern way of life which some refer to as "progress" and "development," consists of consciously and methodically taking control of the innate circumstances of their setting on the one hand, and the realities and social and human relations on the other, in order to develop human life in all its aspects, when its span, requirements and even identity are not known in advance. Today, the issues of this life are explained under the headings: economic, cultural, political, and social development. . . . This way of modern living takes place with the help of the natural sciences and industry on the one hand, and that of the philosophy of law, ethics, politics, social and human sciences on the other. . The engine of this way of life consists of the strong will of contemporary human beings to discover new horizons in human life without these horizons having been determined or predicted with any clarity or certainty in advance. . . . In life, new horizons will be discovered gradually on the basis of development and progress; they will not be clear in advance, and no one knows what requirements they will have and what they will do to humans. Even if some have said that the ultimate aim of this development and progress is to find release from ignorance, poverty, sickness and so on, these interpretations are very unclear and inadequate for they do not explain all the issues related to development and progress.

Today, all the nations of the world have chosen this modern way of life, including Muslims. This is the reality of what in the past used to be called the adoption of modernity, and today is called development. . . . The planning and execution of the first, second, and third development plans which started in all Muslim countries many decades ago, have all been on this basis and that of choosing this way of life. . . . In short, today, Muslims, too, have chosen development and progress, and they have no choice but this. The forerunners of this way of life are the western countries for it is they who have created certain realities which all nations including Muslim ones have no choice but to accept, and to choose a life that is compatible with that. In Iran, too, the first, second and third development plans which were put forth following the victory of the Islamic Revolution, together with the development plans that had existed before [in the pre-revolutionary days], have all come about in order to make the life of the Iranian people in keeping with these same realities and way of life in the world today. There is no doubt that if the life of Muslims does not adapt to the life of the modern world, these nations will lose the ability to continue to engage in civilized life in the modern world. . . .

Today, our problem is that despite the fundamental change that has occurred in the way of life of Muslims, the official reading of Islam has continued to have the same content and shape as before. It wants to continue to judge this way of modern life with the language that determines what is lawful and what is not from a juristic perspective, and determine what the state should do and what it should not whereas the management of this modern way of life is beyond the scope of juristic decrees. Rather, the management of this modern way of life, namely, government in the developing Muslim societies, requires scientific and technical know-how. The most that one can expect in terms of compatibility with juristic decrees from this kind of management is that in particular cases, it can ensure that it is not in contradiction with what is absolutely unlawful in Islam. However, how to plan, regulate, and administer development and progress, [all of] which constitute the main tasks of governments today, is a scientific and technical issue, and cannot be determined by juristic decrees. In other words, today, the science of jurisprudence and that which determines what is juridically lawful and what is not, cannot determine the government plan whereas in the past it had been possible.

Q: You talked about the modern way of life which you said Muslims too follow. What are the characteristics of this way of life? How has this modern life taken shape that it cannot be managed with determining what is lawful and unlawful?

A: I will mention some main characteristics of this modern way of life:

First, this life originates from the will of humans to become empowered and live better lives;

Second, all of its existence depends on the progress of modern natural and social sciences;

Third, it is a hundred percent industrial;

Fourth, it is fulfilled through planning;

Fifth, accepting the views of the majority, mutual respect, the political participation of all with collective wisdom, and democratic rule constitute necessary conditions of modern life;

Sixth, in this modern way of life, law has taken on a very broad meaning and concept. Most of the laws and regulations that are implemented in these developing or developed nations, are laws and regulations that standardize the process of development and progress, not laws [whose purpose is to] remove personal differences and to settle on bringing about order . . . ;

Seventh, the most important task of governments in countries today is the scientific management of this broad process of progress and development which [in turn] has created new cultural, economic and welfare duties for government. The process of progress and development has created a thousand and one problems within the countries and on the international scene in the world today. The wars and periods of peace in the world are related to this same issue as are the economic, political, and cultural relations between nations, and the problems concerning colonialism and neo-colonialism, anti-imperialist struggles, even the Islamic revolution . . . ;

Eighth, this modern life does not mean that religiosity has to be put aside; an advocate of development can be both God-loving and God-knowing. . . . The religious can critique the general process of development together with the ensuing human and social upheavals, by means of religious concepts, but they cannot present a plan for religious progress and development . . . ;

Ninth, the consequences of this way of life are entirely unpre-
dictable. In particular, many unanticipated cultural developments will
appear from this modern way life.

Q: So your view is that in fact, it is not possible to manage modern life
by means of turning to the Qur'an or the *Sunna* or juridical decrees whereas
the official reading of Islam still makes this claim. This incompatibility between the reality and the official claims for religious expression creates a
crisis. In your view, what are the assumptions that constitute the basis of
the official reading of religion?

A: As I said before, one cannot expect such a reading from any religion.
Such a notion is a distortion of reality and religion, and will create problems. As for the current official reading, it is based on several foundations
including the following presuppositions:

First: considering human knowledge as one-dimensional, and placing all other learning in the shadow of religious learning. In other
words, judging the truth and falsehood of all other knowledge on the
basis of religious criteria, and as a result, not giving serious value to
the social sciences and humanities, modern philosophical anthropology, sociology of religion, history and historiography, and so on, and
most important of all, insisting on the earlier epistemology of the
older generations about religion.

Second: imagining language to have a single structure, neglecting
the fact that the structures of all languages including Arabic have a
historical basis, and that no language has the capacity to express all
possible knowledge . . . such as expressing the righteous political and
economic systems for all time.

Third: this notion that there exists only one understanding or one
philosophy of history, and that history is logical and systematic.
Whereas there can be other concepts of history which have no notion
of logicality or systematization, disregarding the fact that it may not
be possible to philosophize about prophethood and its goals.

Fourth: this notion that the meaning of the texts, or at least of those
texts that the gentlemen call *nusus* (religious texts) comes to mind directly from the words and sentences, and that some texts have only
one understanding and interpretation. This is neglecting the complex
discussions that the science of hermeneutics has put forth nowadays,
and the fact that texts, without exception, allow different interpreta-

tions, and that the notion of "the sole possible and correct interpretation" has no meaning at all.

Fifth: the presumption that in the domain of learning, one can talk
about the proof of a truth or a reality, and pay no attention to the philosophical and logical discussions that have been mentioned against
such claims. . . .

2. "Revolution and Reform," *Neshat*, 1999[2]

*Following the election of Mohammad Khatami in 1997, there was a degree
of optimism about the possibility of change and reform. A new vibrant
press, which saw its task as furthering the project of reform, began to flour-
ish, thus providing an opportunity for the notion of reform to be discussed
and critiqued from a variety of perspectives. The passage below is an excerpt from a column by Morteza Mardiha (b. 1960), an essayist and con-
tributor to the reformist press at the time; it is of interest because it aims
to gain an understanding of the idea of reform by comparing and contrasting it with that of revolution, something that Iran has had much experience
of in its modern history.[3]*

In 1978, Iran began a process of revolution, and in 1997, it began one of
reform. There are differences between revolutions and reform and they can
be assessed by means of a comparison between the two phenomena. This
evaluation can help with understanding the first event, and making a more
correct prognosis of the most recent development.

. . . Revolutions, first, start off, and then choose their leaders and ideas
in an outright way. The relationship between their leaders, ideas, and the
people is impassioned and intense. [Revolutions] consider law and order
as their enemy, and set about tearing them down without hesitation. Reform, however, only emerges after it has found its leaders and ideas. The
relations between its leaders, ideas, and people are wise and cautious. Laws

---

2. Morteza Mardiha, "Enqelab va eslah," originally published in *Neshat* daily and reprinted in his
collection *Ba mas'uliyyat-e sardabir: moqaddameh-i bar projeh-ye eslah* (With the responsibility
of the editor: An introduction to the project of reform). Tehran: Jame'eh-ye iraniyan, 1378/ 1999, pp.
122-123.

3. For more, see Negin Nabavi, "From 'Reform' to 'Rights': Mapping a Changing Discourse in
Iran, 1997-2009," in Negin Nabavi, ed., *Iran: From Theocracy to the Green Movement*. New York:
Palgrave Macmillan, 2012, pp. 39-54.

are its main tools, and order, its requirement. Revolutions are the parent and offspring of tension. They cannot be called to account, nor do they think in terms of benefit and loss. . . . [Revolutions] act without reflection, and it is for this reason that they represent the open site for experimentation and mistakes. Reform, however, is only possible in times of calm and peace. It is concerned with accurate accounting, and takes note of the benefits and losses for every act. It is cautious in spending material and intellectual energy, and does not have the ability to tolerate the wasting of energy and resources. It is for this reason that it [reform] does not doubt [the usefulness of] constant verification of the choices [it has] made.

Revolutions are always in search of novelty. They don't accept ready-made prescriptions, but regard themselves as blueprints for others to follow. Since they basically have a disapproving stance in regard to the status quo, they have many options. Anyone from anywhere can act independently and all these disparate steps will result in one outcome. Reform [by contrast] tends to be less concerned with innovation. It seeks to learn from the experience of others, and therefore recognizes the need to study and examine. Since it is in search of reparation and regeneration, it has limited options, and the end towards which it works, has to be coordinated. Revolutions are proud and self-obsessed; they see things in simple terms and make big plans. From their perspective, all problems are external; it is enough for barriers to be removed and all will fall into place. Reform [however] is modest and open to criticism. When faced with problems, it [reform] thinks and looks for solutions. Understanding the complexities of reality slows the pace of reform and limits the parameters of its actions. It sees problems as essentially internal, intrinsic, and structural and considers the solution to them to require patience, hardship and long-term steps.

Revolutions are forthright, sincere, fast, hasty, hot-tempered, in search of eliminating enemies, ambitious and romantic whereas reform is suspicious, complex, cautious, kind, in search of a compromise, contented and realistic. People who show a reformist tendency in the process of revolution are accused of being right-wing and are eliminated from the course of the revolution, and those who adopt revolutionary methods in the process of reform get accused of being left-wing and take a distance from it. In the 1978 revolution, the reformist tendency was abandoned, and in the reform of 1997, being a revolutionary got a negative response.

3. "The Movement for Human Rights," *Jomhuriyat*, July 14, 2004[4]

Advocating for human rights was a discourse that grew out of the reform movement.[5] The passage below is an excerpt from an article written in 2004 by Emaddedin Baqi, a reformist journalist, essayist, and human rights activist, who since the early 2000s has become increasingly vocal about the importance of respecting human rights. What is interesting in the article below is not only Baqi's argument about the practical advantages of promoting human rights in a country like Iran, but also how in his capacity as a lay religious intellectual, he thinks that there is no contradiction between human rights and religion in general and Islam in particular.

These days, the topic of human rights has become one of the most consequential topics of the day in the cultural, political and journalistic domains of the country. Until now, the demands of the reformist movement had revolved around the principle of calling for democracy. [But] from now on, the level of the demands must be raised as it is already happening by itself. Today, we need to replace the movement for democracy with the movement for the promotion of human rights because democracy is only one among the thirty articles of the Universal Declaration of Human Rights. Of course, this same article carries much weight in the Universal Declaration to the point that a few years ago, UNESCO organized a conference called "the Conference of Human Rights and Democracy." Since the contents of human rights are much more accessible, if we follow the movement for human rights instead of the movement for democracy, democracy will inevitably come to the fore as a result of the rights that are written in the Universal Declaration. . . . If we do not want incidents like the serial murders[6] to occur in the country ever again, the way forward is that we institutionalize the movement for human rights in this country.

Today, the notion of human rights is put forth as a universal concept.

---

4. Emaddedin Baqi, "Jonbesh-e hoquq-e bashar," *Jomhuriyat*, July 14, 2004. The Persian text is also available at http://www.emadbaghi.com/archives/000176.php.

5. See Negin Nabavi, "From 'Reform' to 'Rights': Mapping a Changing Discourse in Iran, 1997-2009," in Negin Nabavi, ed., *Iran: From Theocracy to the Green Movement.* New York: Palgrave Macmillan, 2012, pp. 39-54.

6. The "serial murders" refer to a series of murders and disappearances of Iranian dissident intellectuals that took place between 1988 and 1998. Following a public outcry, in 1999, the authorities claimed that these serial murders had been the work of "rogue elements" within the Ministry of Intelligence.

It is an international norm which imposes itself on the political trends of all countries. Perhaps one can say that the universalization of human rights started from the time when the Universal Declaration of Human Rights was ratified in the General Assembly of the United Nations and the covenants entered it into force. Perhaps this is the first international law that the governments of all member states are obliged to adapt their own constitutions and laws to. The universalization of human rights does not mean that subsequently, human rights will not be violated anywhere, especially since today the violations of human rights, torture, and killings continue even though more than two hundred years have passed since [the idea of human rights] was put forth, and more than fifty years have passed since it became an international norm. However surely, these rights can act as a preventive factor. Furthermore, respecting human rights at the international level, and being successful at it, would require that human rights also be respected at the national level. In other words, it is not possible to defend human rights at the level of slogans on the international stage, and violate it in the national domain at [one and] the same time. . . .

In our country, the issue of human rights is faced with serious challenges, which are in part political, and in part theoretical. We live in a society where the dominant culture is religious. Of course, the human rights paradigm has had contradictions with aspects of traditional culture in all countries, even in France itself. These challenges have existed in any society that has wanted to establish human rights. In some western societies, there is a dispute over some of the issues of human rights among Orthodox Christians and Catholics. In our society, too, like other countries, this theoretical challenge exists, since [human rights] are considered in opposition to religious teachings. This opposition is from two [different] standpoints: Some [take this view] from the position of defending human rights and dismissing religion, whereas others do so from the position of defending religion and dismissing human rights.

It seems that this challenge will be very short-lived in Iran since there are characteristics in Islamic teachings, such as the practice of jurisprudence, that is, the return to religious texts and reinterpreting them, which can provide a solution to this challenge. One of the points that should be paid attention to in all this is the discussion of the contradiction between religion and human rights. This is a discussion that is at present talked about more or less in some circles, but three important points should be remembered on this subject:

1. One view is that essentially human rights have religious roots, and in any case, human rights have arisen from developments that happened in Europe after the Renaissance. The standard-bearers of the Renaissance were the Protestants who laid the grounds for the reformation, which in turn provided the backing for the new concept of human rights. . . .

2. Those who say that religion and human rights are incompatible, or even those who criticize the defenders of the compatibility of religion and human rights by saying "why do they want to revive religion in another way by putting forth this kind of discussion, and that an invigorated religion can one day emerge as a problem in the way of human rights," do not realize that this claim about the incompatibility of religion and human rights is itself against human rights, because it is not possible to belittle the opinions of millions of people in the name of human rights. In principle, from the sociological perspective, someone who is apprehensive about the progress of human rights cannot rally the feelings of millions of believers against this process of the progress of human right since when you talk about the contradiction between these two things, you are in effect telling believers that that which we are working towards and want to realize is in contradiction to your religion and belief, and we want to undermine it. Well, this has no result other than you placing a large population in the way of this process, and creating one of the reasons for the lack of success and the very slow progress of human rights.

3. The third point is that from the theoretical perspective, I think that there is in fact no contradiction. You may be able to extract elements from Islamic culture which are in contradiction to the notion of human rights. Islamic jurisprudence, too, is part of Islamic culture; however, the subject of human rights has no difference with the essence of religions. A metaphor that I always use, is the famous one used by Ayatollah Khomeini in his commentary on the chapter *Hamd*,[7] where he says that three people had differences with each other. At lunch, one said that we should eat `*inab* (Arabic for grapes), another said, no, we should eat *üzüm* (Turkish for grapes), and the third said that we should eat *angur* (Persian for grapes). They fell out with each other over this, so

7. This is the first chapter of the Qur'an, also known as *Surat al-Fatiha*.

a fourth person who realized what their difference was went and brought a bunch of grapes, and all three said that this is what we want. So it became clear that they [all] wanted the same thing, but in three different languages, and their difference had arisen because the languages that they had used [to refer to the same thing] were different. I think that that which is mentioned in the Universal Declaration of Human rights has no difference with that which the prophets came for. In any case, the philosophy behind the sending of prophets, and the revelation was also the respect for the rights and dignity of human beings. . . .

About "One Million Signatures Demanding Changes to Discriminatory Laws"[8]

Officially launched in summer 2006, following two demonstrations in 2005 and 2006 that had been broken up by security forces, the "One Million Signatures Campaign" represented a new approach to women's rights in Iran. Basing itself on the model of the 1992 "One Million Signatures Campaign" in Morocco, this was a grassroots movement whose aim was both to collect one million signatures in support of changing discriminatory laws against women and to get as many people from as many walks of life as possible interested and involved in the movement through face-to-face interviews on the streets. The passage below is an excerpt from the campaign's website.

"Iranian women's rights activists are initiating a wide campaign demanding an end to legal discrimination against women in Iranian law. The Campaign, 'One Million Signatures Demanding Changes to Discriminatory Laws,' which aims to collect one million signatures to demand changes to discriminatory laws against women, is a follow-up effort to the peaceful protest of the same aim, which took place on June 12, 2006 in Haft-e Tir Square in Tehran. Preparation activities in support of this campaign will be officially launched on August 27, during a seminar entitled 'The Impact of Laws on Women's Lives.'

8. This excerpt is reprinted from the website of the campaign, "Change for Equality," we-change.org/site/English/spip.php?article18.

The collection of a million signatures in support of changes to the law is only one of several aims of this campaign. The campaign will also aim to achieve the following:

1. Promotion of Collaboration and Cooperation for Social Change: This campaign intends to serve as catalyst in promoting cooperation between a wide spectrum of social activists in creating and advocating for positive social change.

2. Identification of Women's Needs and Priorities: This collaborative campaign aims to develop connections and linkages with a broad base of women's groups from different backgrounds. Direct contact between equal rights defenders and other women's and citizens' groups will allow those involved in the campaign to identify the everyday concerns of women, especially their legal needs and problems. On the other hand, this direct contact will increase awareness among the general population about the inequities that exist within the law.

3. Amplifying Women's Voices: Through this campaign, the organizers hope to be able to connect with groups whose demands are left unheard. The campaign, relying on the needs identified by women themselves, aims to amplify the voices of women whose needs are often not addressed at the national policy level.

4. Increasing Knowledge, Promoting Democratic Action: This campaign is committed to increasing and improving knowledge through dialogue, collaboration and democratic action. The campaign steadfastly adheres to the notion that real and sustainable change can be achieved only if it is community and needs driven, and reflective of the desires and demands of society at large. Changes to women's status in society need to be based on the belief that legal problems faced by women are not a private matter, but rather symptomatic of larger social problems faced broadly by women. In other words, this campaign is committed to carrying out bottom-up reform and to creating change through grassroots and civil society initiatives, and seeks to strengthen public action and empower women.

5. Paying our Dues: The initiators of this campaign recognize that social change and the elimination of injustice are not easily achieved. It is through commitment to collaboration and hard work that we will be able to build the solidarity necessary to create change. Surely this sol-

idarity and collaboration in pushing forth the objectives of the campaign will have a positive impact on the future of our country. The experiences of women's democratic movements around the globe, and particularly, in countries within the region, have demonstrated that solidarity and commitment to the goals of collective action are key components to successful elimination of discrimination. The struggle for equal rights in Iran will indeed be a lengthy, difficult, and arduous process. The true path to achievement of equality will not be paved through existing power structures or a dialogue with men and women in positions of power. Rather, achieving the goals of this campaign will be based largely on a strategy which seeks to raise awareness among individual women and citizens about their identity and their status within society.

6. The Power of Numbers: The successful implementation of this campaign will prove once and for all that the demand for changes to discriminatory laws is not limited to a few thousand women, who have supported these types of efforts in the past. In fact, the successful implementation of this campaign will demonstrate that support for legal changes are broad-based and that a large majority of men and women are suffering from inequities that are promoted by Iranian law. The Campaign will strive to demonstrate that women are, and have consistently employed a variety of means and venues to voice their objections to the laws, such as the writing of books, articles, production of films and other forms of artistic expression, and through social activism. Those women with fewer and more limited resources have demonstrated their objection through more difficult channels, such as recourse in the courts, running away from home, or more destructive means such as suicide, or self-immolation. In an effort to demonstrate the widespread dissatisfaction with the status quo, the Campaign will aim to highlight the many strategies used by women to challenge discrimination in the law.

7. Power in Plurality: The successful implementation of this campaign will also shed light on the fact that the demand for changes in the law is not only voiced by a specific group of women. In an effort to silence the voices of women calling for change, critics claim that demands for legal change are expressed by a particular group of women, who are out of touch with the realities of ordinary Iranian women. These critics

wrongly claim that only elite and socially and economically advantaged women seek changes to laws, in direct opposition to the real needs and sensitivities of the masses of Iranian women. These claims are indeed incorrect, as discriminatory and unjust laws negatively impact the lives of all women, whether they are educated or not, live in upper class neighborhoods or poor communities, are married or single, live in rural areas or in cities, and so on. The Campaign will work to address some of these issues.

. . . The Demands of the Campaign are not in contradiction to Islamic principles: The demand to reform and change discriminatory laws is not in contradiction to Islamic principles and is in line with Iran's international commitments. Iran is a signatory to the UN Convention on Civil and Political Rights and as such, is required to eliminate all forms of discrimination. Based on these commitments, the government of Iran needs to take specific action in reforming laws that promote discrimination.

On the other hand, these demands are in no way contradictory to the foundations of Islam. In fact, the changes being demanded by this campaign have been a point of contention and debate among Islamic jurists and scholars for some time. Ayatollah Sane`i and Ayatollah Bojnurdi, to name a few, have for years called for a revision and reform of laws which are discriminatory against women, and have explicitly stated that such reforms are indeed not contradictory to the basic beliefs of Islam. A million signatures supporting changes to discriminatory laws, will demonstrate to decision-makers and the public at large that a large segment of the Iranian population is in support of revising discriminatory laws against women and that these demands are not limited to a small segment of society. This campaign will also demonstrate to lawmakers that Iranian women are serious in their demands to change current laws."

Women and Cinema

Since the 1990s, women have appeared in increasing numbers in leading roles both in front of and behind the camera. The passages below are excerpts from two interviews with two well-known women filmmakers, Rakhshan Bani-E`temad and Pouran Derakhshandeh. What is of interest

*here is how in their capacity as filmmakers, they try to question and chal-
lenge patriarchal attitudes towards women and gender.*

1. An Interview with Rakhshan Bani-E`temad

*Rakhshan Bani-E`temad (b. 1954) is a celebrated woman filmmaker and
screenwriter whose feature films have gained recognition for depicting the
everyday lives of ordinary people, and for highlighting the resilience of
Iranian women. In 2009, she made a documentary called* We Are Half the
Population, *which presented the demands that Iranian women activists
were making of the then presidential candidates. The passage below is an
interview with Rakhshan Bani-E`temad about this documentary.*

Text: "Rakhshan Bani-E`temad: My Film Is a Presentation of the Organ-
ized Nature of the Demands of Iranian Women"[9]

Q: Ms. Bani-E`temad, in view of the fact that you usually make feature
films about the social issues that you are interested in, how was it that this
time you decided to make a documentary on the subject of the social demands of Iranian women?

A: I had begun doing research on the subject of women's demands from
a year before. Naturally, the topic in question was not unfamiliar to me.
However, when we reached the time of the [2009 Presidential] election and
the events that followed, women's rights activists came together despite
having different and at times even contradictory viewpoints, and put forth
these demands in terms of their commonalities in the electoral atmosphere.
They tried to prevent such serious issues from being sidelined and dimin-
ished by other concerns in society. It was for this reason that I thought that
the moment was right to make a film which I had been thinking about for
more than a year.

From the outset, my aim had been to make and distribute this film before
the [2009 Presidential] election. It was as a result of rigorous planning and
a small exceptional working group that could not have worked harder that
we were able to finish and distribute this film. In my capacity as the director

---

9. "Rakhshan Bani-E`temad: Film-e man era'eh-ye sazman yafteh-ye motalebat-e zanan-e Iran
ast." The text of this interview is available at www.radiofarda.com/content/f35_BaniEtemad_IV
/1963434.html.

and producer of the film, I announced the distribution and dissemination of the film to be without [any] prohibitions so that each person who received a copy of the film could duplicate and disseminate it. Thankfully, this film was disseminated in Tehran, the provinces, and other gatherings in an astonishing way. It was screened in private groups as well as at several universities. I think that were I to have had sufficient time to distribute this film through professional channels, the film would still not have had the chance to circulate to the extent that it has today.

Q: In effect you could have used many ways to make this documentary. For example, you could have taken your camera among the women and their problems in the streets, alleyways, factories and farms, and make your point in that way. Yet, you preferred to focus the greatest part of your documentary on the fact that women's rights activists exist in Iran and that they have things to say. You had them sit in front of the camera. You chose to talk to your audience about women's issues through the words of this particular group. Why did you prefer to do things in this way?

A: Exactly, I deliberately decided to discuss women's demands in this way. The main problem is that putting forth women's demands from the perspective of women's rights activists has always been sidelined and considered taboo, for it has been characterized as westoxication, and as being separate from the core of the society, or as being exclusivist and elitist. For this reason, such arguments could never get a proper, public response. Women activists have therefore always had great difficulty in finding a venue to put forth such topics for discussion.

What I wanted to show in this film was that aside from the extremist views that exist in any context, such demands are shared by both religious and non-religious women. These commonalities show that these demands come from the core of society and it is for this reason that I wanted to provide proof from the heart of society itself. Thus in this film, I wanted to draw attention to the organized nature of these demands which from now on can also be followed through the movement of women's rights activists.

2. An Interview with Pouran Derakhshandeh

Pouran Derakhshandeh (b. 1951) is another female filmmaker and screenwriter, whose films, whether feature films or documentaries, are considered by critics to serve primarily as "educational means" to bring attention to social ills. The passage below consists of excerpts from an interview with Derakhshandeh published in Zanan *monthly in 2007. It concerns her film* Eternal Children, *which focused on disabled children and their treatment in Iranian society.*

Text: "An Interview with Pouran Derakshandeh: I Am Not on Good Terms with Depicting Poverty"[10]

. . . Disability knows no social class. It is like addiction. Rich people, too, have disabled children. I hate to show only the appearance of poverty and to link a series of problems to it. My previous films, too, are in this way. I have not tried to include poverty as a way to emphasize the main issues of my films. In the film "Lost Time," the woman physician is an obstetrician but she, herself, cannot have children, so she is considered as socially disabled. Even though she is well-off, has benefited from higher education and has a nice husband, she is preoccupied with another problem. In this film, I have tried to depict creativity as the equal of physical birth. What is the difference between an artist, a composer, a writer, and a woman who has the ability to bear children? Anyway, the work of the former is more long-lasting too! I think that this was the first feminist film in Iran [in 1989] but it was given a C grade. . . .[11]

Q: I think that the women in your films are on the whole very practical.

A: Yes. It would be more accurate to say that these are women who are gaining awareness and have something to say. Have you seen my film "Candle in the Wind"? The woman character there falls in love with her professor, but at some point, decides to have independence and give up this way of life. In "Eternal Children," the fiancé of Ali's brother decides to go against the wishes of her family and to start a life with a family that has a child with Down syndrome. . . . [The two women characters] are important characters in the film. They are after gaining awareness; they want to enhance their understanding. This trait essentially defines the women in my films.

10. Fereshteh Habibi, "Goftogu ba Pouran Derakhshandeh: Ba faqrnama'i miyaneh-ye khubi nadaram," *Zanan*, vol. 16, no. 152, Dey 1386/ January-February 2007, pp. 40-43.
11. Until 2001, films in Iran were categorized and graded. Whereas the higher-graded ones were screened in better cinemas and for longer periods, the lower-graded ones were not.

Q: And by contrast, how do you depict men characters?

A: I have known women more. When women gain awareness, society becomes alert. Women, themselves, constitute half the population, and they nurture the other half. For centuries, women have been under pressure from a patriarchal society. Now they want to be released from this pressure. This is not the same as confronting men; rather, it is a quiet protest. In fact, I think that taking sides and confronting men will only exacerbate the pressure. The roots of patriarchy are very strong and women must pull themselves up gradually to stand next to men. I have this approach regarding women in my films. I am not one to depict accommodating, poor, miserable, or, for that matter, brazen women. Instead, I have depicted a woman who is independent and stands on her own feet. I, myself, have lived and made it in this way. I did not become a filmmaker by making a fuss.

10

The Tenth Presidential Election and Its Aftermath

"Goodbye the World Cup; Hello Mr. Ahmadinejad!" *E`temad-e melli*, June 20, 2009[1]

The tenth presidential election took place on June 12, 2009, and resulted in the reelection of Mahmoud Ahmadinejad for a second term. However, this election proved both controversial and consequential in that a large number of people thought the results fraudulent, leading to widespread protests that took eight months to put down, as well as fissures within the Islamic Republic establishment. The passage below is an article that was published within a week of the election in the reformist daily E`temad-e melli, *which was later shut down. Although at face value it is a commentary on Iran's failure to qualify for the 2010 soccer World Cup, and is written by Siamak Rahmani, a sports commentator, it is of interest because it conveys the mood of the country in the aftermath of the election in an indirect manner—by juxtaposing the results of the mismanagement of the soccer team with the results of the tenth presidential election.*

We failed to qualify, Mr. Ahmadinejad. It is 12:24 a.m., and the referee of the game between North Korea and Saudi Arabia has blown the whistle. The game has ended in a draw and we have failed to qualify for the 2010

---

1. Siamak Rahmani, "Khoda-hafez jam-e jahani; salam aqa-ye Ahmadinejad!" *E`temad-e melli*, June 20, 2009, p. 1.

World Cup, Mr. Ahmadinejad. The television is broadcasting epic songs and is congratulating your victory [in the presidential election], right after our failure to qualify for the World Cup. We did not get to the World Cup, Mr. Ahmadinejad!

To tell you the truth, I did not know whom to address this piece to. I decided to address it to you since I thought that you were a big soccer fan. We have seen your pictures; that time when you were playing in the team of the University of Science and Technology[2] and later, when you were kind enough to go to the training camp of the Iranian soccer team in your capacity as the President, that same team that went to the World Cup and lost. You must remember, Mr. Ahmadinejad; we remember you dressed in your sports gear. We remember the scene when you were standing and, with your famous smile, scored a penalty.

. . . But your happiness which was so clear in that memento was of no use to the national team, Mr. Ahmadinejad. We finished the 2006 World cup catastrophically. You cannot have forgotten, Mr. Ahmadinejad. After that catastrophic defeat, the managers [appointed by you] in the sports organization stood in front of the television cameras as if they were the saviors of soccer, and talked of changing the head of the soccer federation, Mr. Ahmadinejad. Perhaps it was in those very days that it became clear that we were going to lose the 2010 World Cup, Mr. Ahmadinejad. That same time when your friends in the Tehran municipality, having then become in charge of sports, decided to take everything into their own competent hands, Mr. Ahmadinejad. You may not remember, but we remember, Mr. Ahmadinejad. We spent many months fighting with FIFA, Mr. Ahmadinejad. Instead of accepting their recommendations, we tried to chant slogans . . . and we fell out with the whole world, Mr. Ahmadinejad.

How good it feels![3] But soccer is different, Mr. Ahmadinejad. It is not like the economy regarding which one can hold a few charts in front of people and say nothing about the cost of housing and the salary of government employees,[4] Mr. Ahmadinejad. Here it is the soccer field and everything is determined by the ball going into the goal, by the numbers that are

---

2. Mahmoud Ahmadinejad was a student at the University of Science and Technology in Tehran.

3. This is most probably a reference to the feeling of Mahmoud Ahmadinejad at having won the election.

4. This is a reference to one of the televised debates between Mahmoud Ahmadinejad and another of the candidates for the presidency in 2009, Mehdi Karroubi, during which Ahmadinejad showed colorful charts to argue that the Iranian economy had grown during his first term as President.

displayed on the score board and by whether one is or is not qualified for the World Cup, Mr. Ahmadinejad, and we failed to qualify, Mr. Ahmadinejad. This failure to qualify did not happen only when the referee of the game with South Korea blew the whistle announcing the draw. We had failed to qualify long before that, Mr. Ahmadinejad. We failed to qualify on the day when Afshin Qotbi was to become the manager of the National Team, but suddenly they announced the name of Ali Da'i. Everyone was surprised, Mr. Ahmadinejad. But in this land, it is not very strange to be surprised, Mr. Ahmadinejad. This is the land of wonders, is it not?! But then, perhaps it was not even then [that we failed to qualify.] Perhaps we failed to qualify for the World cup when some beautiful mind decided to ban a foreign manager from sitting on the benches of the National Team. Announcing such a stand was very nationalistic and populist, and probably it made you happy too, Mr. Ahmadinejad. But you should have thought of today, Mr. Ahmadinejad. Today when North Korea has reached the World Cup after forty-four years, and Iran, for all its size and development, has not. The Koreans, like us, are a nuclear power, and probably you are aware of the little that its miserable people have on their tables, Mr. Ahmadinejad. But then now they can [at least] be proud of the fact that they will be going to the World Cup in South Africa, where they can even chant their slogans. Not like us, Mr. Ahmadinejad.

I know that you don't like reading such things, Mr. Ahmadinejad—just as you don't like to see the people [demonstrating] in the streets—just as you don't want to think about the votes [cast] on Friday June 12. But then not much can be done, Mr. Ahmadinejad. Most probably, you have seen the green wristbands that were worn by `Ali Karimi, Nekunam, Mahdavi-Kia and the others in the game with South Korea.[5] Most probably, you were not too pleased at seeing those wristbands, but not much can be done, Mr. Ahmadinejad. This is the reality. The failure of the National team to qualify for the World Cup is a reality just as you and all your managers are a reality.

In all honesty, I thought a lot about whom I should address this piece to and in the end, I thought of you, Mr. Ahmadinejad. We are very sad that we did not qualify for the World Cup. But in view of the fact that you and your managers are there, expecting more than this would have been little

---

5. Members of the Iranian National Team wore green wristbands in the soccer game against South Korea. Green had come to be the color of the supporters of Ahmadinejad's main presidential rival, Mir-Hossein Mousavi, and thus that of the protestors who questioned the results of the election.

more than wishful thinking, Mr. Ahmadinejad. Like everything else, in sports too, we must experience bitterness. The difference is that in politics, economy and other domains, it is possible to tell the story as if things were otherwise, Mr. Ahmadinejad, but the results of soccer games, the failure to qualify for the Soccer World Cup cannot be told in a different way, Mr. Ahmadinejad. Here, it is the bare truth that speaks; it cannot be blocked like satellite waves by sending out jamming signals, Mr. Ahmadinejad; it cannot be disrupted like cellphone lines or text messaging,[6] Mr. Ahmadinejad. Even if you blame us journalists or the economic mafia or the pessimists, no one will be surprised. We have been surprised so many times that we cannot be any more, Mr. Ahmadinejad. I wrote this piece to you since I could not think of another person to address it to, Mr. Ahmadinejad, even though I know that not having qualified for the World Cup and all our other problems are not your fault. I know that you have not quite fully grasped the situation. Where is this nation to take its tears, Mr. Ahmadinejad? . . . We are in a dark place; good morning Mr. Ahmadinejad!

The Open Letter of Akbar Hashemi Rafsanjani to Seyyed Ali Khamene'i Regarding the Tenth Presidential Election, June 2009[7]

In the ten days that preceded the 2009 presidential elections, a series of six debates between the four presidential contenders was broadcast live on national Iranian television. The second of the debates was between Mahmoud Ahmadinejad, the incumbent President, and Mir-Hossein Mousavi, his primary rival. It proved quite sensational, because it both revealed the disdain that these two figures had for each other and provided an opportunity for Ahmadinejad to attack icons of the revolutionary establishment like Akbar Hashemi Rafsanjani—the two-time President of Iran between 1989 and 1997, who was then also the Head of the Assembly of Experts (2007-2011)—for being the "main puppet-master" and "corrupt." The

---

6. This is a reference to the blocking of satellite television, as well as the disruption of cellphones and text messaging, in the aftermath of the election as a means of preventing people from communicating with each other and thus organizing demonstrations in protest.

7. The full text of this open letter is available at www.bbc.co.uk/persian/iran/2009/06/090609 _op_ir88_hashemi_khamenei_letter.shtml.

passage below is an excerpt from an open letter by Rafsanjani to the Leader of the Islamic Republic in response to the accusations made by Ahmadinejad against him. Written three days before the June 12 election, it is of interest because it not only rejects the accusations made against him, but it also shows the extent of the political rift among members of the political elite at this time.

In the Name of God, the Compassionate, the Merciful

To His Eminence, the Supreme Leader, Ayatollah Khamene'i (may his dignity increase),

. . . I think that your Eminence knows well that I together with many of the influential dignitaries of the revolution as well as even yourself, have been the subject of attacks by reckless and anti-revolutionary individuals since the early years of our struggle [against the ancien régime] and the first years of the revolution. . . . We have always put the accusations and insults behind us patiently. In this new phase of accusations and attacks which started from about five years ago, too, I have been patient, and for the sake of God, the interests of the revolution, and the country, I have concealed my distress. As a result, I have received complaints from my relatives as well as many of those sympathetic to the cause of the revolution and Islam. However, what is important is that this time these accusations have been put forth by the President of the Republic on national television. Of course, at its appropriate time, the unspoken distortions and injustices of the election and the actions of the ninth government[8] will be laid open for the people and history.

History attests to the fact that the majority of the committed and revolutionary people of our country are less likely to be influenced by lies. The evidence consists of the honorable votes cast by the people for me in the last election for the Assembly of Experts. You know well that in view of my official responsibilities, I have said nothing on the media in favor or against the parties involved in the election. At certain necessary moments, I have limited myself to stating generalities regarding the importance of having a majority of people present at the ballot boxes and ensuring fair elections; I have [also] said officially that I have no intention of partaking in the election.

---

8. This is a reference to the first term of Mahmoud Ahmadinejad's presidency between 2005 and 2009.

Being aware of my views and politics, the four [presidential] candidates did not seek my opinion in order to run. Similarly, after having announced their candidacy, they did not ask me for support. Even if we did come across each other in certain gatherings, they did not hear anything from me other than the generalities that have been mentioned above. If a political party or association did ask for my opinion in terms of taking a stance in the election, I have said that they should act according to their own bylaws. Truly they are running and taking action on the basis of their own decision and that of their colleagues. Accusing them of being puppets[9] is an unjustifiable injustice and an affront.

It is also fit to pay attention to this truth that probably government agents are aware of my view that I do not consider the continuation of the current situation to be in the interest of the system and the country. Your Eminence, yourself, are also aware of my view and know my reasons. However, I have not publicized my view; rather it is the government agents that have exaggerated this matter. The aim of this exaggeration became clear in that debate.[10]

In view of this, supposing that I continue to keep quiet patiently as I have done in the past, undoubtedly a group of people, political parties and currents will no longer tolerate this situation, and volcanoes which are nourished within burning hearts, will take shape in society. We witness such examples in the electoral rallies in the squares, streets and universities.[11]

If the system does not want or is not able to tackle such ugly and sinful phenomena like the accusations, lies, and falsehoods that have been mentioned in that debate, and if those responsible of implementing the law do not want or are not able to verify the clear violations of the law, in announcing individuals to be corrupt, allegations that can only be made after the violation has been proven in court, and if an individual in his capacity as the President of the republic, allows himself to commit such major and unethical sins, without observing the dignity of his sacred position and despite his oath to observe the *shari`a* and the law, how can we consider ourselves among the followers of the sacred Islamic system?

9. In the televised debate between Ahmadinejad and Mousavi, the former referred to Rafsanjani as "the main puppet-master."

10. This is a reference to the debate described above, which was broadcast live on national Iranian television on June 3, 2009.

11. Here Rafsanjani refers to the increasing number and size of rallies that were taking place in the two weeks that preceded the election—rallies that were attended by supporters of the different candidates.

The Honorable Leader of the Revolution: Now that the Imam,[12] . . . Ayatollah Dr. Beheshti[13] and many of our old companions in arms who either attained the lofty station of martyrdom or hastened to the afterlife, are no longer with us, you, I, and a few of our old companions and people of like-mind are left behind. In view of your position, responsibility, and rank, it is expected that your Eminence take effective measures as you see fit, to resolve this problem and remove the dangerous plots, put out the fire whose smoke can already be seen, and prevent the further blazing of this fire during the election and beyond.

Therefore, in the time that is left, it seems necessary to fulfil the rightful demand of your Eminence as well as that of the people in carrying out a fair and dignified election where the will of the majority will be respected. This is what can save the country from danger and bring about the consolidation of national unity and general trust, and prevent the troublemakers from . . . pouring fuel onto the fire by ignoring the law. . . .

Your friend, companion and comrade-in-arms of yesterday, today, and tomorrow,

Akbar Hashemi Rafsanjani

Letters from Prison

Following the disputed 2009 election, many human rights activists, journalists, and lawyers were arrested and sentenced to long jail terms. What was novel about these arrests was the spate of letters that were written from prison by activists, both men and women. These letters are remarkable not only because they represent defiance in the face of adversity, but also because they contain a sense of intimacy and informality, as well as a conviction that things cannot stay the way they are. These letters were often written to and from husbands and wives, one in jail and the other on the outside or both in jail at the same time. Sometimes they were addressed to young children, as is the case in the first letter below. Although personal, these letters were made public and available on a number of Persian web-

---

12. This is a reference to Ayatollah Ruhollah Khomeini, the leader of the 1979 revolution, who died in June 1989.

13. Ayatollah Mohammad Hosseini Beheshti (1929-1981) was one of the founders of the Islamic Republican Party. He later became its Secretary-General, as well as the head of Iran's judiciary.

sites. Below are two examples of such letters. The first is written by Nasrin Sotoudeh (b. 1963), a female lawyer and human rights activist who was arrested in September 2010 and convicted of "spreading propaganda against the state" and "conspiracy to undermine state security." She was released in September 2013. The second is by Masoud Bastani (b. 1978), a reformist journalist who was arrested in July 2009 for his blog postings. He was sentenced to six years in prison on charges of "spreading propaganda against the state."

1. Nasrin Sotoudeh to Her Three-Year-Old Son, Nima, March 2010[14]

My Dear Nima, hello!

It is difficult to write a letter to you; you who are so innocent that I cannot tell you where I am writing the letter from; you who have no conception of notions of prison, arrests, sentences, courts, oppression, censorship, repression or liberation, freedom, justice, equality. . . .

What should I talk to you about so that I can talk to you "now" as opposed to you in the future? How should I explain that my coming home to you is not in my hands? You who had told your father, "tell mummy to finish her work and come home!" How should I tell you that no "work" can keep me away from you for so long? In fact, no "work" has the right to keep me away from you for so long. No "work" has the right to disregard the rights of my children in the way that in the course of six months detention, I have been allowed to see you [only] for one hour.

What should I tell you when you asked me last week, "mummy, will you come home with us?" And I told you in front of the eyes of the guards, "My work will take a while. I will come later." Then, by nodding your head, you said ok, pulled my hand and with your little lips, gave a peck on my hands.

My dear Nima!

During these past six months, I have cried hard twice: the first time was in grieving for my father since I was banned from mourning him, and the second time was that same day when I couldn't go home with you. When I returned to my prison-cell, I cried uncontrollably.

---

14. The Persian text of this letter is available at www.Feministschool.com/spip.php?article6792.

Darling Nima!

Many times in cases relating to child custody, the courts have issued verdicts about how they cannot give visitation of three year-old children to fathers for twenty-four consecutive hours. In such verdicts, the most important reasoning of the court is the age of the children who cannot stay away from their mothers for more than twenty-four hours because that leads to psychological harm for the child.

However, this same judiciary can disregard the rights of a child because it imagines his mother to be seeking to undermine its security. Of course I don't want to talk to you about the fact that I was not seeking to do anything against their security, and that I was only objecting to the judicial verdicts that had been issued against my clients in my capacity as their attorney.

Of course, I have no desire to prove this to you and to say, for example, that the texts of all my interviews are plain and clear. Yet now, I have been sentenced to eleven years in prison because of my objections to the judicial verdicts which is the main job of any lawyer.

What I do want to say, however, is that first, I am not the first person to have received such an unjust sentence. I hope that I will be the last although I think it very unlikely. Secondly, I am pleased to be alongside my clients in prison; the clients who had to go to prison because my line of defense did not prove effective for reasons that had nothing to do with the courts or the law. At least, I am at peace. Thirdly, I like to say that as a woman who has had the privilege of defending many of the civil society activists and protestors, I am proud of my heavy sentence. Now the determination of women has proved that they can no longer be disregarded by others, whether opponents or supporters.

I don't know how to tell you about that which I like most? How should I ask you to pray for the judge or my interrogator or the judiciary? Pray that they may reach a heartfelt sense of justice and peace of mind so that perhaps we too can live in peace, like many countries in the world.

My darling! That which is the ultimate winner in such cases, is neither a good or bad defense—in this regard, my lawyers did their utmost in their unparalleled defense—rather it is the innocence and goodness of people who get crushed under the wheels of such outlandish verdicts. That innocence is surely the ultimate winner. It is for this reason that I want your childlike goodness to pray for all the innocent prisoners, not only the political prisoners.

In the hope of better days,
Mummy Nasrin
March 2010

2. Masoud Bastani to His Wife, Mahsa Amrabadi, September 2013[15]

My dear wife,

How strange things turn out! I am talking about prison letters; when you take a pen in your hand to write a short letter, but you continue to be baffled and confused at what great meaning of life may be hidden behind this letter of congratulations, and how you are to put it into words. Sentences are short, and they have a telegraphic rhythm. Actually, prison letters should be short, so that perhaps the words will be able to cross these tall barriers more easily.

How strange things turn out! I am talking about prison letters again! It seems as if in the last few years, these texts have become a genre of writing, or perhaps they have turned into a literary style. But as I have written to you before, I believe that these letters are testament to the changes that we have gone through; the changes that we have experienced during our time in prison and the time after prison!

I believe that these letters are our identity cards; an identity card that has hidden at its heart, our identity as well as that of the Green Movement. Here, when everyone is asleep, and silence prevails, I sit in a corner to write something on a blank piece of paper, but often times, here, it is I who am being written. So in prison, I write less, and instead, I am written more!

. . . By the way, congratulations on your freedom! For me, here, this word "freedom" takes on a greater weight. Perhaps from my standpoint, freedom for you does not only mean release from prison bars. The meaning of freedom will change to the point that you will feel the heaviness of a new burden on your shoulders. This will be to the point that I prefer to re-place it with a new sentence, and instead of congratulations, I want to write, "Freedom will put a heavy burden on your shoulders."

. . . You have been released from prison to tell the hidden and unseen

15. Masoud Bastani wrote the following letter on the release of his wife, also a journalist and activist, while he himself remained in jail. The Persian text of this letter is available at www.kaleme.com/1392/07/13/klm_160839.

truths of prison and your fellow-prisoners. You have been released from prison so as to be able to see prison in a tangible way, this time in a different atmosphere, and to try your best for the release of those who are still prisoners, for despite this freedom, a part of your being has remained in between the bars of this cage.

Once upon a time, the intellectuals in this land used to have many disputes over both the use of the word "commitment" as a prefix or a suffix for themselves, as well as over what it meant. But now I want to write to you about "committed freedom." This is a commitment that is born inevitably and gradually at happy and sad moments of prison, and it seems that it will be with you for good. Even your perspective will change, and now after having had the experience of prison, you will know that human rights have a much deeper and more profound meaning than any commonplace words. Now you know that behind any news that reaches you from prisoners, there is a hidden suffering.

It may be that such news no longer has any attraction for the media, or it may be contrary to their policies. However, now, protecting the rights of minorities, supporting freedom of expression, and pursuing the demands and rights of citizens are no longer political issues; rather they constitute a way to free yourself, and to bring about the release of your friends. In these past few years, you and I have experienced roles that perhaps would not happen in the life of any other individual. Once upon a time, you would come to see me, and sometimes I would come to Evin[16] to see you. Now you have had a taste of the waiting of the families of political prisoners when they stand in the visitors' line, and you understand the loneliness of the prisoner.

For you, now, being denied visits and furloughs, solitary confinement, life imprisonment, a prisoner without the right to have visitors, and lack of the implementation of the legal purport of political prisoners' rights, are no longer terms that you would come across in the news or the press. These are words that describe moments in the life of an individual. Now you know that you must try to change the perspective of Iranian society towards the citizen rights of marginalized minorities and Baha'is.

When we were on furlough, I remember well that you missed . . . all the Baha'i citizens who continued to be in Evin. . . . I believe that the commit-

16. Evin prison, in north Tehran, is notable in particular for its ward where political prisoners are held.

ment to this freedom lies in these very feelings . . . that continue to be with you even at the happiest of moments. . . .

I know! I know! You always used to say that after being freed, you wanted to return to [your job in] the newspaper but now you are uncertain how to go about it. There are always moments in life when one is lost, that is, when one loses one's own sense of being; one doesn't know who one is, and where one must stand, or how one should begin. I imagine that the days after being released from prison must be very much like such moments. . . . But I honestly recommend that the journalist in you must return to her newspaper. There are still many stories that you have not told . . . !"

Masoud Bastani, Sept. 2013

The Nuclear Deal between Iran and the P5+1 Group

On July 14, 2015, after years of talks, Iran and six world powers, namely the United States, the United Kingdom, France, China, Russia, and Germany, reached an agreement in Vienna limiting Iranian nuclear activity in exchange for lifting economic sanctions on Iran. Below are two perspectives published in the Iranian press in the first days that followed the announcement of this agreement. The first is in support, and broadly representative, of a reformist viewpoint, and the second is skeptical and broadly representative of a hardline conservative standpoint.

1. "An Agreement beyond a Single Issue," *Sharq*, July 15, 2015[17]

The agreement between Iran and the member states of the P5+1 group[18] is more than a nuclear agreement. This important fact was clear in the words of the Iranian and American presidents. Both countries are trying to take steps that are bigger and more significant than the nuclear agreement. The recent nuclear talks were one of the rare events and negotiations that took

17. Ebrahim Asgharzadeh, "Tavafoqi fara-tar az yek parvandeh," *Sharq*, 24 Tir 1394/ 15 July 2015, p. 6. It should be noted that the author of this article, Ebrahim Asgharzadeh, was one of the militant Iranian students who in November 1979 took over the U.S. Embassy in Tehran, seizing 52 U.S. diplomats hostage for 444 days. Since then, however, his politics and his views have changed; he has become a reformist, supporting not only the recent nuclear deal, but also a normalization of relations with the United States.

18. P5+1 refers to a group of six world powers consisting of the five permanent members of the United Nations Security Council plus Germany.

place before the eyes of the world and attracted the attention of world public opinion. These talks were not only between Iran and six other countries; an examination of the process that took place from the beginning [of the negotiations] until today gives the impression that apparently all the countries of the world had granted authority to these seven countries so that they could resolve this issue. It can be said that the negotiations and agreement between Iran and the P5+1 countries were even more important than the agreement between Carter and Brezhnev in 1979 which led to restrictions over weapons of mass destruction. [For] the recent agreement in Vienna prevented a deadly arms race in the troubled Middle East.

The Vienna agreement is a historic agreement. It is not important to know which side has had a bigger share. Today, everyone must help to protect this agreement. That which can seriously harm this important agreement is that the hardliners in both Iran and America try to use the contents of this agreement to confirm their own assumptions. Other than some expressions of opinion from both sides which have been intended solely for purposes of keeping control over the hardliners and for internal consumption, the leaders of both the American and Iranian governments must abstain from making any kind of assumptions about the agreement. The significance and success of the Vienna agreement is based on its durability. The signatory countries must do their best to ensure its continuity and durability. . . . The obligations and contents of this agreement must be respected.

This agreement is truly a win-win agreement. In fact, this point constitutes the very difference in the meaning between negotiation and war. In war, one side will inevitably have to lose for the opposing side to win in a unilateral way. However, negotiations can lead to the defeat or the victory of both sides. From now on, the Islamic Republic of Iran, along with benefiting from the blessing of the lifting of sanctions, will be able to have a share in the balance of power in the region, the world, and the international economic markets. On the other side, the United States, too, was saved from what it itself calls preemptive [military] intervention—and the many problems that it faced in Iraq and Afghanistan. Both [Iran and America] won and benefited from this agreement, while at the same time, this agreement safeguarded the national interests of both countries. Once the United Nations Security Council officially issues a new resolution, thus retracting its past resolutions against Iran, the Vienna agreement will in effect become official and have an international [body] guaranteeing its implementation.

Then, neither the Iranian Parliament nor the U.S. Congress will be able to cause a problem.

In the past, [both] at the end of the occupation of the U.S. embassy and with [the UN] resolution 598,[19] our national interests were not respected, and many of the legal rights of the Iranian people were ignored. However, in the recent negotiations, the Iranian team, through its learning and skill, was able to bring us a good agreement.

At the same time, just as the American hardliners will do everything they can to create hostility against the Vienna agreement, so too will homegrown hardliners try to instigate and reinforce fear of the agreement. However, that which is important is that commentaries be written about the agreement in its entirety, so that the reformist image that the world has been shown of Iranians today is not damaged. Perhaps talking today about Iran-U.S. relations and the common interests of the two countries is a little premature. However, these negotiations proved that it is possible to sit as an equal at the negotiating table with America on the basis of common interest, and succeed, too.

Besides the efforts of the Iranian negotiating team and the President, we should also acknowledge the astute choice made by the Iranian people in 2013, by means of which they showed a moderate and peaceful image to the world. The previous government and negotiating team took the country to the edge of the abyss through their weak performance based on sloganeering. They chanted slogans for years and called the United Nations resolutions "torn pieces of paper"—those same resolutions whose retraction we have been working for, for twenty-three months. They described the laws dominating the UN Security Council as the "law of the jungle" and removed Iran from any interaction with the world. We reformists should not get involved in the binary of a good versus a bad agreement; [instead], we believe in the binary of war and peace. Any agreement will have some difficulties in its implementation; we must get beyond the details. Those who believed in the binary of breakups and reconciliations besieged us from within, isolating us from the world for eight years. Of course, we won't forget that contrary to all the slogans that they chanted, in the last years of their government, they realized that the sanctions had to be lifted, and that we had to deal with America. If Hasan Rouhani had given us a

19. See chapter 8, footnote 7.

bad agreement, or had not reached an agreement at all, these same hardliners would have called him a traitor and would not have allowed him to take part in the next round of presidential elections.

2. "The Era of Sa`dabad Is Over," *Vatan-e Emrooz,* July 16, 2015[20]

The completion of the Joint Comprehensive Plan of Action (JCPOA) is a big step forward. As to how it will be judged, it seems that we have to wait until the exact translated text is made available and examined. After almost two years of nuclear negotiations . . . we know that an accurate examination of the talks and agreements must be made based on written evidence. Accordingly, even though the interpretations of Obama and John Kerry of the contents of the conclusion of the JCPOA are worrying and in contradiction to the statements made by Mr. Rouhani—and reminiscent of the fight over the factsheets issued after the agreements in Geneva and Lausanne—they cannot provide the basis for rejecting the JCPOA; nor do they correspond to the talk of the simple-minded who argue that these [assertions] are for internal consumption. Holding such positions requires discussion and examination.

Therefore it is important and logical that in the current circumstances, no hasty measures be taken whether in support or in opposition. . . . One should reach an honest judgment after reflection on the text. Of course, it is completely understandable that many in the country do not have a favorable view of the concluding text. The reasons are also clear.

The process that took place in the past two weeks in Vienna could not have led to a conclusion, at least on the surface. Six days before the JCPOA was finalized, the foundations of the negotiations were severely shaken because of the statements made by the two sides! Last Friday, the Iranian Foreign Minister talked of the "change of position" and greed of the Americans! And his American counterpart also threatened to leave the negotiating table!

These differences between the two sides, together with the tone adopted by each, were significant because they occurred two years into the negoti-

---

20. Seyyed `Abedin Nur al-Dini, "Dawran-e Sa`dabad gozashteh ast," *Vatan-e Emrooz,* 25 Tir 1394/ 16 July 2015, pp. 1, 6.

ations and in the last stages of the talks. Therefore, they could not have been related to preliminary matters. Nevertheless, from Friday afternoon on, the atmosphere of the talks gradually returned to the previous course and ultimately resulted in the JCPOA. Despite the questions raised in the media, so far no explanation has been given regarding the content of the difference [in views]. In other words, it is still not clear in what domains the American position has changed, and, now that the JCPOA has been completed, whether America has, once agaiFrom another side, has the behavior of the [Iranian] government in the aftermath of the Geneva agreement, the Lausanne statement, and now the JCPOA succeeded in gaining the public trust? Sadly, and in this same vein, the threats issued by the President to the critics of the JCPOA are not commensurate with the circumstances of a country that has gained victory in a dispute with a foreign country! In any case, the record of the behavior that took place in the aftermath of Geneva and Lausanne, as well as threatening the critics and advocating that they be silent, has resulted in a valuable experience in regard to public opinion, especially that of the revolutionaries. . . . Now, after almost two years of negotiations, public opinion has gained a realistic understanding of the developments, and the people prefer to assess the negotiations in practice, away from factional rivalries. This is a wise approach. Even if the text of the JCPOA is acceptable—it is too early to judge—that which is important is the implementation of this text and the obligations that it brings with it. That which is on paper must be seen in action. If certain promises have been made to the [Iranian] people, proof of their fulfilment is not what is on paper but rather in terms of people's wallets and food on their table. The gentlemen should remember that surely the tolerance that was allowed in the manner of the implementation of the Geneva agreement will have no place here in the JCPOA agreement. If in Geneva they were able to get away with excuses like "this agreement is a preliminary step," mitigating the violations of the Americans, now is the time for implementing every single obligation of the agreement. Surely, the slightest violation from the opposing side will mean the termination of this international agreement. Tolerance will no longer mean anything here.

Besides their paying attention to such issues, a special recommendation to our revolutionary brothers is that they preserve their religious and revolutionary zeal for the moment, and not forget an evident principle, namely, that the days of the give and takes of Sa`dabad and Paris[21] are over. The most important reason is the change in the expectations of the public regarding the preservation of their rights to a nuclear program; another is the constant presence and vigilance of the revolutionaries concerning the nuclear talks. . . . The revolutionaries no doubt know that the Islamic Republic will not accept an agreement that violates its red lines. We must trust the decisions of the Islamic Republic and accept them. In the end, however, I am not optimistic! This feeling is based on a broad revolutionary outlook that has been the result of centuries of experience. That "I am not optimistic" is, in fact, a foreshadowing of the lack of good will of [the United States as the leading symbol of] World Arrogance. This lack of good will is seen not so much in the text [of the agreement] but in its implementation, just as many such instances were seen in the past two years.

---

21. In October 2003, as a result of a series of talks between Iran and the foreign ministers of Britain, France, and Germany, Iran issued a statement (known as the Sa`dabad Statement), according to which it agreed to suspend its uranium enrichment and to cooperate with the IAEA in authorizing intrusive inspections of its nuclear sites during the course of the negotiations. A year later, on November 14, 2004, in another attempt at confidence-building, Iran signed an agreement in Paris with the same three EU countries undertaking to voluntarily freeze its uranium enrichment activities, and thus suspend the manufacture, assembly, installation, testing, and operation of its centrifuges. In some conservative circles in Iran, such agreements were considered tantamount to capitulation.

About the Author

Negin Nabavi is associate professor of history at Montclair State University. She has taught at Princeton University, New York University, and the University of Maryland. In addition to a number of articles, she is also the author of *Intellectuals and the State in Iran: Politics, Discourse, and the Dilemma of Authenticity* (2003) and has edited two volumes of collected essays, entitled, respectively, *Intellectual Trends in Twentieth-Century Iran: A Critical Survey* (2003) and *Iran: From Theocracy to the Green Movement* (2012).